TENURE,

DISCRIMINATION,
and the COURTS

TERRY L. LEAP

Second Edition

ILR Press
an imprint of
Cornell University Press
Ithaca and London

Library of Congress Cataloging-in-Publication Data

Leap, Terry L., 1948–
Tenure, discrimination, and the courts / Terry L. Leap.
p.   cm.
Includes bibliographical references and index.
ISBN 0-87564-348-7 (pbk)
1. College teachers—Legal status, laws, etc.—United States.
2. Discrimination in employment—Law and legislation—United States.
3. College teachers—Tenure—United States.   I. Title.
KF4240.L43   1995
344.73'078—dc20
[347.30478]   95-8943

To Margaret Elizabeth Lovett,
a lifelong friend

Printed on acid-free paper in the United States of America

5   4   3   2   1

CONTENTS

PREFACE

FACULTY MEMBERS WHOSE employment contracts are not renewed or who are denied a promotion or tenure usually find the event to be traumatic. Some move on to challenging positions at other institutions and vow to do better in their new jobs. Others are forced to accept less attractive positions at less prestigious colleges and universities. Still others leave the academic world entirely, disillusioned and bitter. Finally, some faculty, in ever-increasing numbers, resort to litigation.

More and more faculty are filing lawsuits against peer review committees, department heads, deans, and other administrators who, either rightly or wrongly, have denied them a promotion or tenure. In most cases, the litigation is unsuccessful. Colleges and universities are usually better equipped to endure civil suits than the typical middle-income faculty member. Some cases are settled out of court, but only after significant legal expenses have been incurred and hard feelings created. In a few instances, the faculty members prevail after years of administrative and court hearings that leave them emotionally exhausted and broke. Those who lose their cases may find solace in the fact that their lawsuits either created major disruptions for their employers or led to more equitable promotion and tenure processes at their institutions.

A difficult promotion or tenure decision can be fraught with legal problems, especially for unwary peer review committees and college administrators. Officials in the college or university must balance the interests of the faculty member and the institution. Their obligation to be fair affects not only the faculty member but also students, the faculty member's colleagues, and other constituents of the institution, such as alumni, taxpayers, and benefactors.

This book is based on a fifteen-year study of personnel/human resource management and employment law, especially equal employment opportunity legislation. I have also served as the head of a promotion and tenure committee in a large academic unit at a major state university. My study was motivated in part by a desire to learn more about how the courts react to faculty members who sue their institutions. It was also guided by the hope that my colleagues and I might avoid the mistakes of others.

Although an institution of higher learning is not in the business of dispensing justice, whether faculty are treated equitably at reappointment, promotion, and tenure time has important implications for its academic well-being. Several articles and books have been written on personnel decisions in academia. Some of these materials focus on the legal aspects of promotion and the denial of tenure. Many are written by attorneys who have an in-depth understanding of the relevant laws and court cases but lack the insider's view of the peer review process and the criteria used to make reappointment, promotion, and tenure decisions. Persons with a background in higher education have also written volumes about the criteria and means by which colleges and universities should assess a faculty member's research productivity and teaching effectiveness. Authors whose perspectives are purely educational, however, often have only a basic understanding of the legal developments and personnel practices affecting reappointment, promotion, and tenure decisions. Even the state and federal courts have found employment discrimination in academia to be imposing and difficult to analyze. In a number of instances, the courts have virtually thrown up their hands and allowed colleges and universities to do as they pleased. Although this legal posture works to the advantage of college administrators, it leaves faculty members much to be desired if they have been victimized by poor personnel decisions or invidious discrimination.

In writing this book I attempted to integrate legal, educational, and personnel/human resource management perspectives on reappointment, promotion, and tenure decisions. The cases, legal rulings, personnel practices, and ideas discussed here should be useful to faculty members and administrators in U.S. institutions of higher learning. The book should also serve as a source for legal counsel dealing with wrongful discharge or employment discrimination suits.

Topics discussed include (1) legislative background on the laws that protect faculty members from various forms of discrimination, (2) cases involving reappointment, promotion, or denial of tenure in academia, (3) the rationale used by the courts in adjudicating these cases, and (4) ways colleges and universities can reduce the likelihood of such suits.

I thank the following individuals for their helpful comments: Jennie Farley of the School of Industrial and Labor Relations, Cornell University; Judith P. Vladeck of the law firm Vladeck, Waldman, Elias, and Engelhard, PC; Roger Meiners of the University of Texas at Arlington; Susan C. Walker; and an anonymous reviewer. Thanks also go to promotion and marketing director Andrea Clardy, managing editor Faith Short, and copy editor Erica Fox. The comments and suggestions of the reviewers and editors greatly improved the quality of the manuscript. A special note of gratitude goes to Fran Benson of the ILR Press for her encouragement during the many months of research and writing. Finally, I would like to acknowledge the help of my graduate assistants, Ty Sukalski and Jennifer Elliott, and the administrative support of David W. Grigsby, head of the Department of Management, and Jerry Trapnell, dean of the College of Professional Studies at Clemson University.

1. Introduction

THE FORMAL VOTE took place twenty-four days later. The department had for their consideration Ted's bibliography (four articles, five reviews), his book on Sophocles (and the critiques of it, which ranged from "solid" to "monumental"), and various letters of recommendation, some from experts in the field whose names Ted would never know. But one certainly from the Regis Professor at Oxford.

Ted and Sara waited nervously in the Huron Avenue apartment. It was nail-biting time. They knew the meeting had begun at four, and yet by five-thirty there was still no word.

"What do you think?" Ted asked. "Is it a good sign or a bad sign?"

"For the last time, Lambros," Sara said firmly, "I don't know what the hell is going on. But you have my fervent conviction both as wife and classicist that you truly deserve tenure at Harvard."

"If the gods are just," he quickly added.

"Right." She nodded. "But remember, in academia *there are no gods*—just professors. Quirky, flawed, capricious human beings."

The phone rang.

Ted grabbed it.

It was Whitman. His voice betrayed nothing.

"Cedric, please, put me out of my misery. How did they vote?"

"I can't go into details, Ted, but I can tell you it was very, very close. I'm sorry, you didn't make it."

Ted Lambros lost the carefully polished Harvard veneer he had

1

worked a decade to acquire, and he repeated aloud what he had said ten years earlier when the college had denied him a full scholarship.

[Expletive]

Sara was immediately at her husband's side, her arms around him consolingly.

He would not hang up till he asked one final burning question.

"Cedric," he said as calmly as possible, "may I just know the pretext—uh—I mean the grounds—I mean, in general terms, what lost it for me?"

"It's hard to pinpoint, but there was some talk about 'waiting for the second Big Book.' "

"Oh," Ted responded, thinking bitterly, there are one or two tenured guys who still haven't written their *first* big book. But he said nothing more.[1]

Faculty Member's Perspective

College teaching ranks high on the list of the most prestigious occupations in the United States.[2] Persons outside academia often perceive the professor's job as one of quiet contemplation, far removed from the organizational politics, intense competition, and invidious discrimination faced by those who must work in the "real world." But the image of the quintessential professor who toils in seclusion on an idyllic campus surrounded by ivy-covered buildings and refined minds better describes a fantasy than reality. Although college teaching is a pleasant and rewarding occupation, the pressures facing an untenured professor—especially female and minority faculty—can be enormous. Professor Ted Lambros, a fictional character in the Eric Segal novel *The Class*, provides an accurate portrayal of the perils encountered in climbing the academic ladder at a prestigious university. His lifelong dream of becoming a tenured Harvard professor appears to be shattered. After serving as a faculty member elsewhere, however, he returns to his alma mater and eventually becomes a dean. Faculty who are denied reappointment or tenure usually do not have such happy fates.

Tenure and promotion through the academic ranks are the culmi-

---

[1]Eric Segal, *The Class* (New York: Bantam Books, 1985), pp. 296–97.
[2]See "Best-Rated Jobs in the U.S.," *San Francisco Chronicle*, May 19, 1988, p. A-5, col. 1, cited in Richard Delgado and Derrick Bell, "Minority Law Professors' Lives: The Bell-Delgado Survey," *Harvard Civil Rights–Civil Liberties Law Review* 24 (Spring 1989): 354.

nation of years of schooling and significant professional accomplish-ments. A person must first spend several years earning a Ph.D. or other terminal degree. He or she must then spend an additional five to seven years establishing the academic expertise, research and teaching competencies, and professional reputation to warrant a favorable promotion and tenure decision. In most cases, faculty are expected to conduct research that will generate publishable articles in refereed journals. They are also expected to perform well in the classroom, to serve on department and university committees, and to be active in professional and community organizations.

Few faculty make their way through graduate school and achieve tenure without some financial and personal hardship. The years leading up to a tenure decision are fraught with uncertainty, espe-cially for faculty in disciplines in which there is an oversupply of qualified academics. Some colleges and universities offer a working environment that is relaxed, cordial, and free from heavy work demands. At these institutions, faculty who demonstrate a reason-able level of competency can, in due time, expect to be promoted and achieve tenure. Other institutions have high expectations for their faculty with regard to publications, research funding, excellence in the classroom, and professional service. Such institutions often have rigorous tenure standards and offer permanent employment only to the most promising professors.

The pressures associated with achieving tenure are even more intense for faculty who must deal with discrimination linked to racial, sexist, or other prejudices. Senior faculty, department heads, deans, and upper-level college administrators, by virtue of their advanced education, are not normally thought to harbor prejudices that would lead to acts of illegal employment discrimination. Yet, as the cases discussed here illustrate, faculty and administrators at some of the most prestigious universities and colleges in the United States have violated equal employment opportunity laws and a number of others have been immersed in lengthy court battles because of questionable actions or personnel decisions involving female and minority faculty.

The process of reappointment, promotion, and tenure at many colleges and universities is shrouded in uncertainty, a condition that is conducive to surreptitious discrimination. The majority of academic personnel decisions are made in closed meetings, and the partici-pants are often sworn to secrecy. Those who cast votes concerning reappointments, promotions, and tenure are rarely required to provide a detailed account of their deliberations. Although the stated reason for nearly all adverse personnel decisions is that the faculty member's research was inadequate or teaching was ineffective, the criteria for promotion and tenure are often vaguely defined and subjectively applied. Standards of scholarship and teaching vary widely not only from one college or university to another, but also among departments within the same institution. Furthermore, the criteria for reappointment, promotion, and tenure have generally become more stringent over time. Performance standards for research, teaching, and service that spelled a favorable promotion or tenure decision for a faculty member only a few years ago may no longer guarantee the same result for a current faculty member. When promotion and tenure standards are raised, there may be accusations that senior faculty have "climbed aboard the ship and pulled the ladder up behind them." Junior faculty, like the fictional Ted Lambros, may believe that the faculty on their peer review committees have less impressive professional accomplishments than the faculty whom they are judging.

Denial of tenure usually means that a faculty member faces termination in the next academic year. The professor loses not only a long and often hard-fought battle, but he or she may also feel rejected and alienated from the academic community. Being terminated is especially traumatic to individuals whose life has been absorbed by graduate school, research and writing projects, teaching, professional service, and other creative endeavors. Many such faculty were excellent students and received terminal degrees from prestigious universities. In all likelihood, they received glowing recommendations from former professors who regarded them as rising stars with tremendous potential. Failure to achieve tenure represents the first major setback not only in their careers but in their lives.

Some terminated faculty "see the handwriting on the wall" and realize that a favorable reappointment, promotion, or tenure decision is unlikely, either because they have failed to complete the requirements for a terminal degree or because their teaching and scholarship are woefully inadequate. In a few cases, however, faculty have been led to believe that their performance was acceptable during the years leading up to the tenure or promotion decision; their annual performance evaluations may have included satisfactory (or higher) ratings, and they may have been routinely reappointed with no apparent reservations. Pay raises may have reinforced the faculty member's belief that he or she was advancing steadily toward a promotion or tenure.

Other terminated faculty face frustrating searches for reemployment because of unfavorable labor market conditions or because other institutions regard them as "tainted goods." Unable to find a suitable position elsewhere, an unemployed faculty member may be forced to make an oblique or even radical career change.[3] Although many terminated faculty quietly serve out the remainder of their contracts, an increasing number are bringing lawsuits against their institutions for wrongful discharge or employment discrimination.

COLLEGE AND UNIVERSITY ADMINISTRATOR'S PERSPECTIVE

College and university administrators generally believe that reappointment, promotion, and tenure decisions should be the prerogative of peer review committees, department heads, and deans. Intrusions by federal or state equal employment opportunity commissions or courts are often regarded as encroachments on institutional academic freedom. Furthermore, the courts have recognized that the criteria affecting reappointment, promotion, and tenure cannot be quantified and defined precisely; to do so creates inflexibilities and detracts from the ability of institutions of higher learning to make decisions that are in the best interests of their academic mission. University officials often note that the faculty member who was not promoted or tenured misunderstood department or college expectations, failed to follow performance guidelines, or ignored earlier warnings that his or her performance was unacceptable. For these and other reasons, the federal and state courts rarely second-guess reappointment, promotion, and tenure decisions in academia.

---

[3]Senior faculty often have strong professional ties with colleagues at other institutions. For this reason, it may be difficult for a junior faculty member who has been denied tenure to find work elsewhere within the same academic discipline, especially if collegiality or interpersonal problems played a role in the denial of tenure. As a result, a faculty member may claim that he or she was blacklisted by former colleagues. According to one court, blacklisting is not a form of illegal employment discrimination because it takes place after an employee's discharge and because it is not regarded as an "employment practice" under federal civil rights legislation. Federal law would likely provide protection, however, if unfavorable references were provided as a way of retaliating against a former employee who filed discrimination charges. See *Ferguson v. Mobil Oil Corp.*, 20 FEP Cases 1691 (1979); *Bilka v. Pepe's Inc.*, 38 FEP Cases 1655 (1985); and *Fisher v. Vassar College*, 64 FEP Cases 1380 (1994). In addition, a faculty member may bring defamation of character charges against former colleagues who provide reference information that is false (or substantially false) and injurious to his or her employment prospects.

There is no federal law that requires institutions of higher learning to make intelligent personnel decisions. Colleges and universities are free to make well-reasoned decisions that reward meritorious performance and reflect institutional needs. They are also free to make decisions that are based on trivial matters or that otherwise lack careful reasoning and refined judgment as long as such decisions are not affected by a faculty member's race, sex, religion, national origin, age, disability status, or other factors that are protected under federal or state law.[4] As one court noted:

> The Civil Rights Act of 1964, inter alia, prohibits discrimination in employment on the basis of race or national origin. It does not prohibit an employer from terminating an employee out of personal animosity, political or professional differences, differences of opinion on department administration and policy, or considerations of the employee's lack of requisite competence in one or more areas of his employment.[5]

It is equally true that colleges and universities can fail to reappoint, promote, or tenure a faculty member, regardless of his or her race, sex, or other protected classification, if the faculty member's levels of competence in research, teaching, and service do not measure up to institutional expectations. In *Sweeney v. Board of Trustees of Keene State College*, the judge noted:

> Factfinding biased in either direction can lead to socially harmful results: harm to the woman who is discriminated against without redress; harm, on the other hand, to a university and its students, and to more qualified applicants, if a lifetime job or promotion is conferred by the court upon a woman who would have been passed over had she been a male. . . . It behooves us to make clear that Title VII requires courts to be unflinching in upholding *both* the rights of the victims of sex discrimination *and* the right of universities and other employers to make sex blind discretionary decisions—even if a woman sometimes loses out.[6] (Emphasis in the original)

---

[4]See *Powell v. Syracuse University*, 17 FEP Cases 1321 (1978), and *Smith College v. Massachusetts Commission against Discrimination*, 20 FEP Cases 1659 (1978).

[5]*Chung v. Morehouse College*, 11 FEP Cases 1088 (1975).

[6]*Sweeney v. Board of Trustees of Keene State College*, 16 FEP Cases 378 (1978), quoted in *Smith College v. Massachusetts Commission against Discrimination*, 20 FEP Cases 1659 (1978).

A critical concern in tenure decisions is that they impose a financial obligation on a college or university for a number of years. Unlike employment decisions in most corporations, the decision to grant tenure cannot easily be reversed through a termination or layoff. As a vice president at the University of Connecticut stated:

> When in doubt, don't. Since the tenure decision is a commitment by the University to twenty or thirty years of support and several hundred thousand dollars of salary, from which there can be no turning back, we have felt that if we must err, we ought to err on the side of caution; we ought not to gamble widely.[7]

A university's decision to grant a promotion or tenure is, in part, a reward for past meritorious job performance as well as a vote of confidence regarding the person's potential to help the institution achieve its teaching, research, and service mission in the future. Peer review committees, department heads, deans, and other administrators are occasionally forced to give institutional needs precedence over an individual's career aspirations.[8] Demographic and economic factors, including an oversupply of qualified academicians in some disciplines, declining enrollments in institutions of higher learning, tighter budgets, and reduced federal funding have made tenure decisions even more critical for colleges and universities.[9] In a department with only a few faculty and limited resources, an inadequate professor can retard the development of an entire program.[10]

There are other reasons a college or university may be willing to endure a wrongful discharge or discrimination suit, even if it involves considerable legal expense and takes several years to work its way through the judicial system. First, the substantial autonomy enjoyed by those who make promotion and tenure decisions is a time-honored tradition in most institutions of higher learning. Administrators whose academic freedom and principles are challenged by a discrimination suit may be willing to fight it out in court rather than make a compromise settlement.

[7]Quoting Vice President Wilson of the University of Connecticut in *Lieberman v. Gant*, 23 FEP Cases 508 (1980).

[8]See *Smith v. University of North Carolina*, 23 FEP Cases 1742 (1980), and *White v. University of Massachusetts at Boston*, 59 FEP Cases 210 (1991).

[9]Frank M. Baglione, "Title VII and the Tenure Decision: The Need for a Qualified Academic Freedom Privilege Protecting Confidential Peer Review Materials in University Employment Discrimination Cases," *Suffolk Law Review* 21 (1987): 703.

[10]John H. Burton, Jr., "Tenured Faculty and the 'Uncapped' Age Discrimination in Employment Act," *Yale Law and Policy Review* 5 (Spring-Summer 1987): 454.

Second, the responsibility for major employment decisions in academia is diffused among a number of peer review committee members and administrators, and the risks associated with a negative promotion or tenure decision are spread among the members of the group. As long as peer review committee members and administrators adhere to university policies, make their decisions in good faith, and avoid actions such as sexual harassment or defamation of character that could lead to charges of personal injury, the threat of individual liability is reduced. Furthermore, the institution (or the institution's insurance company) will bear the costs of litigation. For these reasons, faculty and administrators who are involved in negative personnel actions are not likely to feel legally or financially threatened.

Third, some plaintiffs become causes célèbres. They seek widespread media exposure and sympathy among members of the academic community or publicly chastise college administrators for being racist, sexist, insensitive, or capricious. Such tactics may create good press, but they may reduce the chances of an informal settlement. They may also make it difficult for the plaintiff to return to the institution (if he or she wins the case) or find employment at another college or university.

FACTORS THAT PRECIPITATE LAWSUITS

Beginning in the 1970s, promotion and tenure became more difficult to achieve almost everywhere. The escalation of negative decisions, many of which involved female faculty members, led to an increased number of internal grievances and charges of illegal discrimination against colleges and universities.[11] The volume of federal litigation escalated rapidly following the extension of the antidiscrimination provisions of Title VII of the 1964 Civil Rights Act to academic institutions in 1972.[12] Several faculty have filed civil suits against both their employers and the administrators who played key roles in the decisions. Frequently, these cases have involved allegations of unfair treatment as well as claims of discrimination based on the faculty

---

[11]See George R. LaNoue, "The Federal Judiciary, Discrimination, and Academic Personnel Policy," *Policy Studies Journal* (Sept. 1981): 115.

[12]Charles J. Stevens, "Preventing Unnecessary Intrusions on University Autonomy: A Proposed Academic Freedom Privilege," *California Law Review* 69 (1981): 1538.

member's race, sex, or national origin. Some cases have been backed by solid evidence of illegal discrimination, whereas others have lacked convincing proof of unfair treatment. In many cases, the faculty member genuinely believed that an illegal motive played a role in the adverse decision and that he or she provided evidence to substantiate this claim. In other cases, the faculty member filed charges under a federal or state equal employment opportunity law either as a harassment tactic or with the slim hope that an administrative agency or court would rule that illegal discrimination was the impetus behind the unfavorable decision.

Published legal cases that deal with the denial of reappointment, promotion, or tenure of faculty members are diverse; however, they typically involve several accusations or issues.

A lack of institutional support and resources made it difficult for the faculty member to achieve an acceptable level of performance. In these cases, a faculty member claims that inadequate resources, low funding, or heavy teaching and service loads made it difficult or impossible to fulfill teaching, research, or service responsibilities. For example, Dr. Georgia Johnson, a physician at Michigan State University's Department of Medicine who was denied tenure, claimed that she was not provided adequate office space, telephone facilities, or secretarial support. In addition, she felt inconvenienced because her office was located away from the other offices in the department. Dr. Johnson also accused her department head of not liking her because he avoided sitting next to her at faculty meetings. The university claimed that Dr. Johnson's failure to pass medical board certification examinations, coupled with her abrasive personality and inability to perform her job satisfactorily, led to her dismissal. Dr. Johnson felt that the lack of resources, inadequate reviews of her performance, and the university's failure to provide training to improve her skills were racially motivated (she is black) and contributed to her inability to acquire the qualifications necessary for tenure. A U.S. district court ruled, however, that Dr. Johnson did not garner sufficient evidence to demonstrate either illegal race or sex discrimination on the part of Michigan State.[13]

Administrators respond to cases of this nature by stating that financial and political factors beyond their control created unforeseen problems. They may argue that faculty members must adapt to those problems rather than rationalize their subpar performance by blam-

---

[13]*Johnson v. Michigan State University*, 30 FEP Cases 260 (1982).

ing colleagues or administrators. College officials may also contend that the faculty member did not take full advantage of the resources that were available or that other faculty were able to remain productive despite the inadequate facilities and resources.

The institution failed to adhere to its promotion and tenure standards. A faculty member argues that administrators explained the criteria for reappointment, promotion, and tenure but failed to follow these guidelines. Thus, the faculty member labored for several years assuming one set of standards would be used, whereas the peer review committee, department head, or dean applied another set of criteria.

A female physical education instructor at Tufts University was denied tenure because of her lack of scholarly activity. In the past, the university had waived scholarship requirements for physical education faculty, but after restructuring of the program in the 1970s, faculty in physical education were required to engage in some form of scholarly activity. The plaintiff, Dawn Hooker, had no creative scholarship to her credit and was subsequently denied tenure. Hooker noted that the Tufts University football coach, Rocco Carzo, had received a promotion even though he apparently had engaged in no scholarly activities. Citing the university's right to change standards and that Hooker's qualifications for advancement could not be equitably compared with Carzo's credentials, a U.S. district court ruled in favor of Tufts University.[14]

Colleges and universities challenge accusations of unfair, changing standards by stating that the criteria for reappointment, promotion, and tenure must be reflective of the academic marketplace, the institution's mission, and the environment in higher education. In some cases, administrators claim that changes in performance expectations were published and disseminated but the faculty member either ignored or failed to abide by the new standards. College and university administrators may also argue that faculty members are professionals who should understand the expectations of an academic community without having them spelled out in detail.

Political rather than academic reasons led to the unfavorable promotion or tenure decision. A faculty member accuses the administration of favoring certain faculty over others and of applying differential performance standards in making personnel decisions. Thus, politics, rather than merit, allegedly influenced the decisions. A former professor at

[14]*Hooker v. Tufts University*, 37 FEP Cases (1983).

the Massachusetts Institute of Technology (MIT) and an expert on the development of science and technology in society, David Noble, initially received a favorable recommendation from an interdepartmental tenure review committee. But that decision was later reversed when it was discovered that Noble had criticized MIT in a book he had written. He left MIT and later achieved tenure at Drexel University in Philadelphia. Nonetheless, Noble filed a $1.5 million suit against MIT for firing him because of his left-wing views.[15] MIT and Noble later reached an out-of-court settlement, which involved no monetary restitution.

Administrators will usually claim that political views play no role in personnel decisions; they may label the faculty member a troublemaker who experienced interpersonal friction with colleagues. Peer review committees, department heads, or deans may bolster the administrator's arguments by saying that the faculty member's research did not meet quality standards or that he or she was not an effective teacher.

The institution failed to apply promotion and tenure standards in a consistent manner. A faculty member contends that a denial of reappointment, promotion, or tenure was unfair because other faculty with inferior credentials received more favorable treatment. Such contentions are usually accompanied by comparisons between the plaintiff's credentials and accomplishments and those of his or her colleagues in an attempt to show that either a mistake was made or that the adverse decision constituted illegal discrimination. There may also be allegations that higher-level college officials who make the final decisions on personnel matters are not qualified to evaluate the scholarship of faculty across the wide range of academic specialties that exist in large institutions.[16]

A number of cases have delved into the comparative qualifications of faculty members. One such case involved an Argentine-born

---

[15]David Goodman, "Professor Sues MIT over Tenure," *Progressive*, June 1987, p. 13. See also *Eichman v. Indiana State University Board of Trustees*, 597 F.2d 1104 (1979), 19 E.P.D. 9179 (7th Cir. 1979).

[16]See Aden Ross, "Tenure or the Great Chain of Being," *Change* 13 (July-Aug. 1987): 54, 55. "We Renaissance scholars vociferously defend our publications, blithely unaware that our college must somehow compute one social work article against two paintings against, perhaps, three bivouacs and one and a half architecture designs. . . . We then discover that our most distant evaluators are incapable of judging our work. I am a playwright; my provost is a physicist. How can I expect him to know what a theatrical production is worth? Or a newly developed brake lining, or diminutive crabapple tree research, or a harpsichord recital?"

biochemistry professor at Rutgers University who was repeatedly denied a promotion. The professor's record included peer review letters written by "internationally recognized leaders in the biochemistry field" who praised his work. The university claimed that the professor was not qualified for promotion, however, and cited the inadequacy of his research, which they regarded as "uncreative, moderate in quantity, and insufficiently recognized in his field." The professor sued Rutgers for national origin discrimination, and a U.S. district court held that he was reviewed for promotion under a harsher standard than other professors. The court pointed to the fact that the university promoted another chemistry professor based in large part on the quantity of her published work. Yet the foreign-born professor who was denied promotion had a more extensive list of publications than his colleague who was promoted. Because of Rutgers's own plainly stated criteria (research accomplishment, scholarly activity, and teaching effectiveness), the professor should have been promoted, according to the district court. Rutgers University was ordered to grant the professor a retroactive promotion and back pay.[17] The U.S. Court of Appeals (Third Circuit) upheld the district court's ruling and remedy.[18]

Administrators defend their actions in cases of this type by attempting to show that faculty members who benefited from a favorable personnel decision were superior to the faculty member who was denied reappointment, promotion, or tenure. In so doing, they usually attempt to demonstrate that the faculty member's qualifications failed to meet university standards or that his or her research, teaching, and service had serious deficiencies that made continued employment unacceptable. Colleges and universities also argue that administrators who are competent and thorough in their deliberations are capable of evaluating the professional accomplishments of faculty from a wide variety of disciplines.[19]

Peer review committees and college officials harbored racist, sexist, or other

---

[17]*Bennun v. Rutgers, the State University of New Jersey*, 56 FEP Cases 746 (1991). See Bureau of National Affairs (BNA), "National Origin Bias on Campus," *Fair Employment Practices*, June 21, 1990, p. 72. The U.S. Court of Appeals (Third Circuit) denied a rehearing of this case, 56 FEP Cases 1066 (1991), and the U.S. Supreme Court denied certiorari, 58 FEP Cases 64 (1992).

[18]*Bennun v. Rutgers*, 56 FEP Cases 746 (1991).

[19]Also see Joan Abramson, *The Invisible Woman: Discrimination in the Academic Profession* (San Francisco: Jossey-Bass, 1975), and Joan Abramson, *Old Boys and New Women: The Politics of Sex Discrimination* (New York: Praeger, 1979).

prejudices. A faculty member accuses the administration of applying irrelevant factors, such as race, sex, national origin, or lifestyle, to academic performance. Plaintiffs may bolster their cases by blaming administrators for creating a hostile working environment in which racist or sexist attitudes were condoned.

A Mexican-American instructor, Robert M. Briseno, who taught part time in a Nebraska community college, was replaced by a full-time instructor. Briseno was told that the person hired to replace him had superior qualifications. Briseno confronted the president of the college about the qualifications of his replacement and accused him of discriminating against Mexican-Americans. The president allegedly told Briseno that all Mexican-Americans hired by the college caused trouble. Although administrators almost always categorically deny allegations of race or sex bias, the president's comments along with other evidence resulted in a finding of illegal discrimination against the college by a U.S. district court. The U.S. Court of Appeals (Eighth Circuit) later affirmed the district court's ruling.[20]

[20]*Briseno v. Central Technical Community College Area*, 37 FEP Cases 57 (1984).

2. Potential Effects of Discrimination Litigation

R EGARDLESS OF WHETHER A CASE has merit, civil suits are time-consuming, costly, and traumatic for the parties involved.[1] The plaintiff must spend time and money seeking adequate legal counsel, whereas attorneys are often reluctant to accept wrongful discharge or employment discrimination cases involving academic institutions because such cases are difficult to win. An attorney may be willing to take a case on a contingency-fee basis if the probability of success and financial reward is high. He or she may take a case of questionable merit, however, only if the faculty member pays a retainer at the outset and understands that additional costs will be incurred as litigation progresses. Once counsel is obtained, legal costs may drain the plaintiff's often-meager financial resources. In a worst-case scenario, a faculty member may invest a considerable amount of money to obtain legal counsel and to procure evidence only to discover that his or her case is weak. Faculty members with limited funds and bleak employment prospects must decide whether to pursue litigation or use their savings for more pressing needs.[2]

The plaintiff may discover that the financial costs of litigation are exceeded only by the social and psychological costs. Faculty often

[1] For an excellent analysis of the costs and trauma associated with civil suits involving academic institutions, see George R. LaNoue and Barbara A. Lee, *Academics in Court: The Consequences of Faculty Discrimination* (Ann Arbor: University of Michigan Press, 1987). LaNoue and Lee provide an in-depth analysis of five major cases.

[2] At least one plaintiff, Marcia Lieberman, who filed sex discrimination charges against the University of Connecticut, was forced to file for bankruptcy because of extensive legal expenses. LaNoue and Lee, *Academics in Court*, p. 77.

find that lengthy legal proceedings consume a great deal of their time and energy. Some faculty become obsessed with the outcome of the litigation for financial reasons, because of a need for vindication, or because they hope to change the personnel practices that led to the grievance or lawsuit. They may become frustrated by delays, the seemingly endless proliferation and expense of court documentation, and the questionable and sometimes puzzling tactics of legal counsel. Some plaintiffs realize they made an ill-advised decision to pursue their case, especially when health or domestic problems result.[3] Others feel they have become stronger as the result of the litigation, perhaps because they have joined or formed support groups with persons who share or sympathize with their dilemma. Eleanor Swift, a professor of law at the University of California at Berkeley, made the following observations regarding her tenure denial and subsequent grievance against the university.

> A tenure victim is a woman professor who has spent long hard years learning how to teach, learning to publish, and learning how to find her own place within male-dominated law faculties. For the tenure victim, these years culminate in a tenure vote, or an administrative tenure review, or an executive action that both fires you from your job and tells you (probably for the first time in your life) that you don't meet certain standards of quality. Usually you're told that it's your scholarship that fails—it's "unsuccessful," "unpersuasive," "overly ambitious," or "makes no contribution." These are bitter words to hear about your work. And if you know the weak points of your articles better than anyone else does, and if you believe that academic judgments aspire to objectivity, then you take these words very seriously and very personally. To be a tenure victim is to suffer a terrible blow to your self-esteem. . . .
>
> The personal costs of pursuing a formal grievance are incalculable. All of the articles by discrimination plaintiffs tell the same story at this point—if you decide to file a complaint and proceed to a hearing, your case takes over your life. You become single-minded. You work with your lawyer and you work alone. The case takes an enormous amount of your own time and energy in investigating, fund-raising and publicity. You lose touch with

---

[3]There have been at least two instances in which a faculty member has died during the years it took for the case to inch slowly through the legal system. See *Braden v. University of Pittsburgh*, 343 F. Supp. (W.D. Pa. 1972), 477 F.2d 1 (3rd. Cir. 1975), and *Scott v. University of Delaware*, 19 FEP Cases 1730 (1979).

your real work if you have left the university; or if you are still there, you are painfully alienated. You sustain the burden of having charged your former colleagues with a truly terrible violation of academic principle.[4]

In a few instances, wrongful discharge and discrimination cases may be resolved informally or through an internal grievance mechanism. An out-of-court settlement may occur either before or after a case has gone to court. For example, the Albert Einstein College of Medicine agreed to a settlement with a former female professor after a district court denied the school's motion to dismiss the case. The professor sued the medical school for paying her less than it paid comparable male colleagues, denying her a promotion, deterring her from becoming involved in professional activities, and retaliating against her for filing charges with the U.S. Equal Employment Opportunity Commission. The professor received $900,000 in the court-approved settlement ($540,000 for pain and suffering, $325,000 for legal and other fees, and $35,000 in back pay).[5] Legal counsel who handle such litigation for institutions of higher learning quickly discover, however, that the odds of defeating a faculty member's claim are high.[6] Attorneys who represent colleges and universities may also be reluctant to accept out-of-court settlements because they fear that an unfavorable precedent will be set for future cases. Administrators at large institutions who employ full-time counsel may regard litigation as simply another cost of doing business; that is, legal expenses may be considered a sunk cost.

Nevertheless, institutions of higher learning rarely emerge from wrongful discharge and employment discrimination litigation unscathed. A race, sex, national origin, or other discrimination charge against a college or university is almost certain to generate media exposure. Students may hold public demonstrations to protest the

[4]Eleanor Swift, "Becoming A Plaintiff," *Berkeley Women's Law Journal* 4 (1989–90): 246, 248. Swift filed a gender discrimination grievance with the University Academic Senate Committee on Privilege and Tenure. The independent outside review committee of distinguished academics unanimously recommended that she be tenured and found that she satisfied the university's standards for scholarship, teaching, and service.

[5]*Weissmann v. Albert Einstein College of Medicine*, USDC SNY, 88-CIV-0458 (1994). Cited in BNA, *Fair Employment Practices*, March 28, 1994, p. 36.

[6]According to a study of sex discrimination cases in institutions of higher education between 1976 and 1986, the odds of winning a case favors the institution over the faculty member by a ratio of four to one. See Sage L. Schoenfeld and Perry A. Zirkel, "Sex Discrimination in Higher Education: An Empirical Analysis of Case Law," *Journal of Law and Education* 18 (Fall 1989): 567–81.

termination, especially if the case involves a popular professor. Charges of racism, sexism, religious bias, or blatant disregard for a faculty member's career are likely to tarnish the liberal image of the institution and may make it more difficult for the school to attract high-quality students and faculty or to generate philanthropic support and research funds. University administrators who are named in an employment discrimination suit almost always have their personal integrity called into question and run the risk of damaging their professional reputations.

Nonacademic organizations force terminated employees to leave immediately. Colleges and universities, however, usually allow a faculty member who is denied tenure to remain on the job for another nine to eighteen months. During this period, lame-duck faculty may use the hallways as a forum to "adjudicate" their cases and garner support from sympathetic colleagues. Peer review committee members, department heads, and deans are usually advised not to discuss a reappointment or denial of tenure because of potential legal repercussions. As a result, a one-sided version of a tenure denial case often emerges, which lowers faculty morale and creates internal political problems.

Faculty members in the department or college where the suit originated may split into factions, some of whom support the faculty member while others support the administration.[7] Many cases involve comparisons between the qualifications of faculty who were promoted or tenured and those who were not. Counsel for the plaintiff may attempt to belittle the research and teaching accomplishments of the faculty who have been selected for comparison. When such attacks are made public, either through the press or during a grievance hearing or trial, the damage to interpersonal relationships in a department may be irreparable. Animosity between those who support the administration and those who support the faculty member may create distractions from teaching and research or cultivate other dysfunctional behaviors.

Department heads, deans, and academic officers are forced to allocate significant amounts of time to helping attorneys gather evidence, prepare transcripts, and file motions. Time spent in these endeavors is time taken away from faculty recruitment, academic and

---

[7]Even faculty members who are sympathetic may be reluctant to openly support a plaintiff for fear of retaliation by the administration. This is especially a concern among untenured faculty.

curricular matters, alumni affairs, and fund raising. The observations of a U.S. district court judge sum up many of the problems faced by colleges and universities in employment discrimination cases:

> The court recognizes that University administrators confront an increasingly complex array of tasks in these modern times. It is difficult to strike the requisite balances between excellence in education and the constraints of a parsimonious budget; it is difficult to reconcile the competing demands of faculty and students. And, this equilibrium is especially difficult for a land-grant institution, which must also pay obeisance to the heavy burdens carried by the taxpayers. Yet, difficult or not, the juggling act must stay within the law; if the balls can be kept in the air only by trampling upon the inalienable rights of women (or blacks, or Roman Catholics, or whomever), then it is time to bring in a more dextrous troupe of jugglers.
>
> Let there be no mistake: the court does not regard the URI [University of Rhode Island] hierarchy as being comprised of blackguards and dolts, of evil or incompetent men and women. With but a few exceptions, those administrators who testified in these proceedings appeared well-intentioned, dedicated, and professional. But a certain quality of sensitivity has obviously been lacking, nourished by a struthiod tendency to see, hear, and speak no evil. To get along, one goes along. In the court's view, a reordering of administration priorities would be a healthy thing.
>
> Nor are the problems which have festered at the University and which underlay this litigation entirely attributable to the defendants. The plaintiffs, too, must share some of the responsibility. Faculty members undeniably have rights, and must be free to assert those rights. But, the AAUP [American Association of University Professors] and its members seem to have developed an unfortunate penchant for confrontation, an uncanny ability to see ghosts in the most austere of closets, a self-annihilating eagerness to tackle the administration for the sake of the battle—irrespective of the importance or insignificance of the issue or, sometimes, the merits of the administration's position. And, there are signs that faculty self-interest is, on occasion, much too far to the forefront. The faculty, too, would benefit from a reasoned reappraisal of its collective priorities.
>
> The implementation of this court's orders will—as the parties were forewarned—doubtless be expensive, time consuming, and to some extent disruptive. Yet, that is the price which must be

paid when the judiciary is forced to intrude in the groves of Academe in order to rectify demonstrable wrongs.[8]

Lawsuits that are precipitated by adverse personnel decisions are often no-win situations for both the plaintiff and the college or university that must defend itself. Prevention is clearly a superior alternative to litigation before an administrative agency or court. Although complete prevention of suits is unrealistic, there are measures that can be taken to minimize the probability of time-consuming and expensive civil suits that will leave a bitter aftertaste for both the plaintiff and the defendant. The purpose of this book is: (1) to discuss briefly the laws that are likely to be invoked in lawsuits involving adverse personnel decisions against faculty members, (2) to analyze the major issues that have arisen in such cases and the positions that the courts have taken on these issues, and (3) to recommend ways to avoid such suits.

This study is based primarily on the cases that have arisen since 1972, the year Title VII of the 1964 Civil Rights Act was amended to cover institutions of higher learning. Most of the cases involve faculty members who were terminated because their performance was inadequate or the institution's educational mission was changed. Many of the plaintiffs in these cases also brought charges of pay discrimination, a complex research issue in its own right. The focus in this book is on faculty who were either discharged or denied promotion because of alleged discrimination rooted in race, sex, national origin, or age biases. Other cases are discussed insofar as they have a bearing on illegal employment discrimination against faculty in colleges and universities.

Among the questions addressed in this book are the following:

1. What institutional mechanisms, laws, constitutional amendments, and legal doctrines are available for dealing with employment discrimination in academia?

2. Why have the courts adopted an anti-interventionist posture with regard to many discrimination suits involving colleges and universities?

3. What problems are encountered in evaluating a faculty member's competence in research, teaching, and service? How

---

[8]*Chang v. University of Rhode Island*, 40 FEP Cases 101 (1985).

are issues such as subjective criteria and academic freedom viewed by the courts?

4. How are burden of proof issues handled in discrimination suits? What role do comparative qualifications and statistical analyses play in demonstrating a discriminatory animus by an institution? Do current burden of proof standards pose insurmountable barriers for faculty who sue colleges and universities for employment discrimination?

5. To what extent are the courts requiring peer review committees, department heads, deans, and other university administrators to reveal confidential files and the content of committee deliberations associated with promotion and tenure decisions?

6. What remedies are available to faculty who win employment discrimination and wrongful discharge suits?

7. What steps can faculty members and institutions of higher learning take to minimize the possibility of discrimination suits?

3. Employment Discrimination and Relevant Legislation

FACULTY MEMBERS AND THEIR attorneys are most likely to base their claims on a federal or state civil rights (equal employment opportunity) law. The most frequently used law is Title VII of the 1964 Civil Rights Act, as amended. To a lesser extent, the Age Discrimination in Employment Act of 1967, the Rehabilitation and Americans with Disabilities Act (ADA), the post–Civil War civil rights laws, and various amendments to the U.S. Constitution are invoked. State equal employment opportunity (EEO) laws are also used in some cases. In addition to statutory law, issues of common law are raised in certain instances.

Employment discrimination cases fall into two major categories: (1) disparate treatment cases and (2) disparate impact cases. Disparate *treatment* cases arise when a racial, sexist, or other animus affects a personnel decision. That is, a member of a faculty peer review committee, a department head, a dean, or other college official harbors a bias *and* acts on that bias. Disparate treatment might occur if a department head refused to hire a candidate for a faculty position because of his or her animosity toward persons of the candidate's national origin. A peer review committee that holds female faculty to a higher standard for promotion and tenure than male faculty is also engaging in disparate treatment. Personnel decisions that are based on programmatic or budgetary considerations, so long as they are not a pretext for illegal discrimination, are not in violation of federal or state equal employment opportunity law. For this reason, the U.S. Court of Appeals (Eighth Circuit), in *Sennewald v. University of Minnesota*, held that the university's decision to grant full-time status to a male assistant women's gymnastics coach while denying full-time status to a female assistant softball coach was not the result of sex discrimination.[1]

Disparate *impact* cases typically arise when a plaintiff or class of plaintiffs believes that certain employment practices or criteria have an unfair, discriminatory impact on a protected group. For example, minimum height and weight requirements for a job may have a discriminatory impact on women, whereas some employment tests, educational requirements, and subjective criteria have allegedly excluded racial minorities from white-collar and professional jobs. Disparate impact cases originated with the landmark U.S. Supreme Court case *Griggs v. Duke Power*.[2] Before the passage of civil rights legislation in 1964, Duke Power, a public utility, openly discriminated against black employees who worked at a North Carolina facility by limiting their employment primarily to unskilled, low-paying jobs in the labor department. After Title VII of the 1964 Civil Rights Act was passed, Duke Power could no longer ban blacks from better-paying, skilled jobs. The company then decided to require all employees to have a high school diploma and pass the Wonderlic Personnel Test, an intelligence test, and the Bennett Mechanical Aptitude Test if they wanted to work in jobs outside the labor department. The U.S. Supreme Court ruled that these requirements were illegal because they were not significantly related to job performance and because they operated to disqualify black applicants at a substantially higher rate than white applicants. That jobs outside the labor department had been filled only by whites and black applicants had traditionally received an inferior education in segregated North Carolina schools before the early 1960s made it exceedingly difficult for blacks to compete for nonlabor jobs at Duke Power.[3]

The *Duke Power* case is probably the most significant of all equal employment opportunity cases because it established the concept of disparate impact and held that even unintentional discrimination may be illegal. Without the U.S. Supreme Court's *Duke Power* ruling, the civil rights laws that deal with employment discrimination would be largely ineffective. Thus, hiring or promotion criteria that are admin-

---

[1]*Sennewald v. University of Minnesota*, 46 FEP Cases 1528 (1988).

[2]*Griggs v. Duke Power*, 3 FEP Cases 175 (1971).

[3]See Irving Kovarsky, *Discrimination in Employment* (Iowa City: Center for Labor and Management, College of Business Administration, University of Iowa, 1976), pp. 75–77.

istered fairly to all job applicants or employees but which have a discriminatory impact on protected groups such as women or racial minorities may be illegal under Title VII. If an employer can show that certain employment criteria are job-relevant, however, then the criteria or qualifications are less likely to create a Title VII liability even if members of a protected group are disproportionately excluded.[4]

TITLE VII OF THE 1964 CIVIL RIGHTS ACT

Title VII of the 1964 Civil Rights Act prohibits discrimination in employment based on race, sex, religion, color, and national origin.[5] The act covers a wide range of private and public organizations and is enforced by the Equal Employment Opportunity Commission (EEOC). EEOC decisions may be appealed into the federal court system, but persons who file charges under Title VII must do so within 180 days.[6] In states that have an approved fair employment practice or human rights commission, the plaintiff must file charges with the state commission before proceeding under Title VII.[7]

[4]If a plaintiff demonstrates that an employment practice has an adverse impact on a protected group, then the employer must show that the practice is based on a legitimate business reason or business necessity.

[5]42 U.S.C., sect. 2000e-2(a) states: "It shall be an unlawful employment practice for an employer—(1) to fail or refuse to hire or to discharge any individual, or otherwise to discriminate against any individual with respect to his compensation, terms, conditions or privileges of employment, because of such individual's race, color, religion, sex, or national origin; or (2) limit, segregate, or classify his employees or applicants for employment in any way which would deprive or tend to deprive any individual of employment opportunities or otherwise adversely affect his status as an employee, because of such individual's race, color, religion, sex, or national origin."

[6]The U.S. Supreme Court has held that the limitation period runs from the time the plaintiff is notified of an adverse employment decision. See *Delaware State College v. Ricks*, 24 FEP Cases 827 (1980), *Lever v. Northwestern University*, 55 FEP Cases 1137 (1990), and *Colburn v. Trustees of Indiana University*, 739 F. Supp. 1268 (S.D. Ind. 1990). Some acts of discrimination occur at a well-defined point in time, such as on the date that notice was received of a tenure denial. Other acts of discrimination are continuing violations that occur repeatedly over a period of time. Examples of continuing violations might include daily episodes of sexual harassment or repeated denials of tenure over successive years. Under the continuing violation doctrine, where there is a pattern, policy, or practice of discrimination, the plaintiff may also recover for earlier acts of discrimination. To establish a continuing violation, a plaintiff must allege either that (1) a series of related acts occurred, at least one of which fell within the limitations period (e.g., the 180-day period under Title VII), or (2) a discriminatory system was maintained both before and during the limitations period. See *Sunshine v. Long Island University*, 65 FEP Cases 1698 (1994). Also see *Monroe-Lord v. Hytche*, 59 FEP Cases 1701 (1987).

[7]The plaintiff has three hundred days to file a Title VII complaint in states that have an approved civil rights agency; the EEOC allows the state agency up to sixty days to resolve the complaint.

Institutions of higher learning were originally excluded from coverage under Title VII.[8] In 1972, Congress amended Title VII and brought educational institutions within the purview of equal employment opportunity law. In the words of the House report:

> There is nothing in the legislative background of Title VII, nor does any national policy suggest itself to support the exemption of these educational institution employees—primarily teachers—from Title VII coverage. Discrimination against minorities and women in the field of education is as pervasive as discrimination in any other area of employment. In the field of higher education, the fact that black scholars have been generally relegated to all-black institutions, or have been restricted to lesser academic positions when they have been permitted entry into white institutions, is common knowledge. Similarly, in the area of sex discrimination, women have long been invited to participate as students in the academic process, but without the prospect of gaining employment as serious scholars.
>
> When they have been hired into educational institutions, particularly institutions of higher education, women have been relegated to positions of lesser standing than their male counterparts. In a study by Theodore Kaplow and Reece J. McGree, it was found that the primary factors determining the hiring of male faculty members were prestige and compatibility, but that women were generally considered to be outside the prestige system altogether.
>
> The committee feels that discrimination in educational institutions is especially critical. The committee can not imagine a more sensitive area than educational institutions where the Nation's youth are exposed to a multitude of ideas that will strongly influence their future development. To permit discrimination here would, more than in any other area, tend to promote misconceptions leading to future patterns of discrimination. Accordingly, the committee feels that educational institutions, like other employers in the Nation, should report their activities to the Commission [EEOC] and should be subject to the provisions of the Act.[9]

[8]Federal executive order 11246, however, which mandates affirmative action programs for organizations that either have contracts with the federal government or receive federal financial assistance, did apply to most institutions of higher learning before 1972. See *Coser v. Moore*, 36 FEP Cases 57 (1983).

[9]U.S. Congress, House, *U.S. Code Cong. and Ad. News*, 92d Cong., 2d sess., 1971, H.R. Rept. 238, cited in *Kunda v. Muhlenberg College*, 22 FEP Cases 75 (1980).

Congressional debates preceding the passage of the 1972 amendments discussed the pervasive nature of sex discrimination in university employment practices. According to the Senate *Congressional Record*:

> In the summer of 1970, Representative Edith Green, chairman of the House Special Subcommittee on Education, held extensive hearings on discrimination in education and related areas— hereafter referred to as the 1970 hearings. Over 1,200 pages of testimony document the massive, persistent patterns of discrimination against women in the academic world. Yet despite a situation which approaches national scandal, the problem has gone unnoticed for years. Today, many would deny that it exists.
>
> But discrimination against women in education does exist. Moreover, it prospers.[10]

The testimony continued by noting that women who had Ph.D.s often possessed superior academic qualifications to men yet were hired less frequently by the more prestigious schools. When hired, women were slower to advance, and their pay almost always lagged behind that of male faculty with comparable qualifications. A matched-sample study of 15,492 women and men who earned Ph.D.s in mathematics, natural sciences, social and behavioral sciences, and the humanities between 1940 and 1979 revealed that differences between men and women in academic rank and pay were not due to the commonly accepted explanations of marriage, family responsibilities, or lack of geographic mobility. Rather, the disparities were attributable to sex discrimination.[11]

Although women faculty have made progress since the 1972 amendments to Title VII, they have by no means achieved parity. "We've gotten rid of most of the horror stories, the overt policies and practices that used to harm women," said Bernice R. Sandler, director of the Association of American Colleges' Project on the Status and Education of Women. "But women are still not advancing the way they should, given the number of Ph.D.'s granted."[12]

[10]*Congressional Record*, 92d Cong., 1st sess., Feb. 28, 1972, p. 5804.

[11]Nancy C. Ahern and Elizabeth L. Scott, *Career Outcomes in a Matched Sample of Men and Women Ph.D.s: An Analytical Report* (Washington, D.C.: Committee on the Education and Employment of Women in Science and Engineering, Commission on Human Resources, National Research Council, National Academy Press, 1981), discussed in Jennie Farley, *Academic Women and Employment Discrimination: A Critical Annotated Bibliography* (Ithaca, N.Y.: New York State School of Industrial and Labor Relations, Cornell University, 1982), p. 24.

[12]Larry Rohter, "Women Gain Degrees, But Not Tenure," *New York Times*, Jan. 4, 1987, p. E9.

There is also growing concern regarding the emergence of a new class of nontenured instructors, of whom a disproportionate share are women.[13] According to recent U.S. Department of Education statistics, women comprise 32.5 percent of all faculty members, however, only 16.2 percent of all full professors and 28.7 percent of all associate professors are women. Women hold a much higher proportion of the positions in the ranks that are traditionally off the tenure track. Thus, nearly 48 percent of all instructors and 62 percent of all lecturers are women. Women appear to be well represented on education, nursing, and English faculties. Faculties in history, philosophy, and the natural sciences and some professional schools, by contrast, have relatively small percentages of females. Women are probably least represented in engineering, where they comprise only 5.9 percent of the total faculty.[14] Although women comprise an estimated 30.1 percent of business faculty, a 1992 *BusinessWeek* survey of the top twenty U.S. business schools found that only 8 percent of tenured faculty were women.[15]

Blacks account for 4.9 percent of all U.S. faculty, whereas Asians and Hispanics comprise 5.3 percent and 2.5 percent respectively. Although flagrant incidents of race discrimination among faculty members may be rare, there is evidence of an antiminority mindset in colleges and universities. This mindset can take many forms, some of which are subtle and difficult to prosecute under civil rights law. Some minority faculty members believe that they are never completely accepted by nonminority colleagues and students. They may not be sought out for collaboration on research projects or curricular matters, and they may be excluded from informal department communications and professional networking. Some faculty may be absorbed in the problems of black or other ethnic communities; yet they receive little or no recognition for their efforts at promotion and tenure time.[16] Others are unduly and harshly criticized by students

[13]The academic ranks in U.S. colleges and universities, in ascending order, are instructor, assistant professor, associate professor, and professor (sometimes referred to as full professor). Newly hired faculty who have recently completed the Ph.D. or other appropriate terminal degree are usually hired at the assistant professor rank. Faculty who have completed all requirements for the Ph.D. except the dissertation are frequently hired at the instructor level.

[14]See "Fact File: A Profile of Full-Time Faculty Members with Teaching Duties, Fall, 1992," *Chronicle of Higher Education*, Nov. 23, 1994, p. A16.

[15]Lori Bongiorno, "Where Are All of the Female B-School Profs?" *BusinessWeek*, Dec. 7, 1992, p. 40.

[16]See *Roebuck v. Drexel University*, 47 FEP Cases 752 (1988).

and faculty for their unique teaching methods or their perceived overemphasis on civil rights or race-related topics.[17] In some instances, students, faculty, and alumni resent the favored status minority faculty and students supposedly receive on college campuses.[18] In 1992, only sixty-one black professors held endowed chairs in U.S. colleges and universities; and one-fifth of these professorships were located at one institution—the University of North Carolina at Chapel Hill.[19]

During the congressional debates that preceded the passage of Title VII during the early 1960s, there was little legislative history to support the exclusion of institutions of higher learning from the act. The courts had adopted an anti-interventionist policy regarding the personnel decisions of colleges and universities, especially concerning tenure and promotions. The 1972 amendments marked a major step, however, toward changing a policy that had protected colleges and universities from charges of employment discrimination.[20]

DENOMINATIONAL COLLEGES AND UNIVERSITIES UNDER TITLE VII

Under section 703(e)(2) of Title VII, religiously affiliated educational institutions are allowed to hire and employ faculty of a particular religion. The provision requires, however, that the college or university be owned or supported in whole or in substantial part by a religious corporation, association, or society. The exemption also applies to institutions whose curricula are directed toward the propagation of a religious doctrine.

Several cases have dealt with religious discrimination in denominational institutions of higher learning. In *EEOC v. Mississippi College,* the Fifth Circuit held that the employment relationship between a religious educational institution and its faculty is not exempt from Title VII coverage. The court ruled that Title VII does not interfere

[17]See Roy L. Brooks, "Anti-Minority Mindset in the Law School Personnel Process: Toward an Understanding of Racial Mindsets," *Law and Inequality* (May 1987): 1–31.

[18]See, for example, the contemptuous letter written to Derrick Bell, a black Harvard Law School professor, by a person claiming to be a Harvard alumnus, in Derrick Bell, "The Final Report: Harvard's Affirmative Action Allegory," *Michigan Law Review* 87 (Aug. 1989): 2403–4.

[19]Liz Lucas, "UNC Leads Nation in Endowed Chairs for Black Academics," *Carolina Alumni Review* 81 (Winter 1992): 10–11.

[20]*Powell v. Syracuse University,* 17 FEP Cases 1319 (1978).

with either the establishment clause or the free exercise clause of the First Amendment. If the institution presents convincing evidence that the challenged employment practice results from religious considerations, however, Title VII deprives the Equal Employment Opportunity Commission of jurisdiction to investigate and determine whether religious discrimination was a pretext for some other type of illegal discrimination.[21]

In another case, Loyola University of Chicago attempted to reserve three tenured slots in its philosophy department for Jesuit faculty. A federal district court ruled that the university was not exempt under section 703(e)(2) of Title VII, despite its contention that it was supported, controlled, and managed by the Society of Jesus, a religious order of the Catholic Church. Although the university president and at least one-third of the board of trustees were required to be of the Jesuit faith, none of these individuals or other university administrators had received instructions from the Society of Jesus with regard to university hiring, promotion, tenure, or other matters. In addition, Loyola received only three-tenths of 1 percent of its income from Jesuit sources. The court decided that the amount of financial support by the denomination was not substantial enough to warrant an exemption under Title VII.[22]

A 1994 case of interest involved a faculty member at the Catholic University of America (CUA) who was denied tenure in the university's canon law depatment. Sister Elizabeth McDonough, who held a doctorate in law from Catholic University, was the first woman to hold a tenure-track appointment on the university's canon law faculty. Although she received a chilly reception from her department chair when she began her appointment at CUA, Sister McDonough worked diligently. She published numerous articles and taught a variety of classes, including Basic Principles of Canon Law, Religious Law, Ecclesiastical Latin, and Consecrated Life and Sanctions. Her research and service activities also centered on specialized religious topics. After six years of service, Sister McDonough was denied tenure, primarily because of alleged deficiencies in her research and

---

[21]*EEOC v. Mississippi College,* 23 FEP Cases 1501 (1980), *cert. denied,* 26 FEP Cases 64 (1981).

[22]*Pime v. Loyola University of Chicago,* 34 FEP Cases 1156 (1984), *aff'd,* 42 FEP Cases 1 (1986). See Susan J. Curry, Donald J. Manderfeld, and William H. Sullivan, "*Pime v. Loyola University of Chicago:* The Seventh Circuit Extends the BFOQ Defense," *Journal of College and University Law* 14 (1988): 607–19.

teaching. She felt that she was being held to a higher standard than other faculty because of her gender, although evidence failed to support this contention adequately.[23]

The federal district court held that the application of Title VII in this case would violate both the free exercise and establishment clauses of the First Amendment "by entangling [the] government in a primarily religious function and relationship." Citing an earlier U.S. Supreme Court ruling, the district court said that "the First Amendment requires the civil courts to defer to ecclesiastical tribunals regarding questions of 'canon or ecclesiastical law.' " The court viewed Sister McDonough's primary role in the Department of Canon Law as the "functional equivalent" of a minister.[24] The courts have developed a "ministerial function" test to determine whether a discrimination claim brought by the employee of a church or religious institution can be reviewed by a civil court: "An employee whose ' "primary duties consist of teaching, spreading the faith, church governance, supervision of a religious order, or supervision or participation in religious ritual and worship" ' must look elsewhere than to government agencies and courts for relief from race, sex, national origin, or age discrimination."[25]

The district court compared the subject matter taught in the CUA canon law department with that of a seminary, which prepares priests, ministers, and others to serve a particular religious order.[26] Furthermore, disagreements between CUA faculty and external evaluators regarding the quality of Sister McDonough's research and publications were not evaluated extensively by the court because of their ecclesiastical nature.

The few religious discrimination suits affecting faculty members have arisen at private colleges and universities. Accusations of religious discrimination against faculty by public institutions of higher learning can be adjudicated under Title VII, as well as under the Religious Freedom Restoration Act of 1993 (RFRA). Under the RFRA,

---

[23]*EEOC v. Catholic University*, 65 FEP Cases 312 (1994).

[24]*EEOC v. Catholic University*, 65 FEP Cases 320 (1994). The court cited the Supreme Court's ruling in *Serbian Eastern Orthodox Diocese v. Milivojevich*, 426 U.S. 696, 713 (1976).

[25]*EEOC v. Catholic University*, 65 FEP Cases 320 (1994), citing *Rayburn v. General Conference of Seventh-Day Adventists*, 38 FEP Cases 1641 (1985), *cert. denied* 41 FEP Cases 272 (1986), quoting Bruce N. Bagni, "Discrimination in the Name of the Lord: A Critical Evaluation of Discrimination by Religious Organizations," *Columbia Law Review* 79 (1979): 1514, 1545.

[26]See *EEOC v. Southwestern Baptist Theological Seminary*, 26 FEP Cases 558 (1981).

federal, state, and local government employers must show a compelling government interest before an individual's exercise of religion can be burdened substantially. In addition, public employers must show that there are no less restrictive means available for furthering that compelling government interest.[27]

CIVIL RIGHTS ACT OF 1991

The Civil Rights Act of 1991 reversed (in whole or in part) seven recent U.S. Supreme Court decisions and addressed other problems that had plagued the field of employment discrimination over the years.[28] The act is especially relevant to wrongful discharge and employment discrimination cases in higher education because it increases the potential financial liability that colleges and universities face if they are found guilty of intentional discrimination.

The Civil Rights Act of 1991 permits compensatory damages for victims of intentional discrimination and punitive damages (against organizations with more than five hundred employees) when the employer acts with "malice or with reckless indifference to" a victim's rights. The cap on such damages ranges from $50,000 to $300,000, depending on the number of employees in the organization. In the past, compensatory and punitive damages were available only to victims of discrimination based on race and national origin. Before 1991, damages to victims of employment discrimination based on sex, religion, and disability status were limited primarily to back pay, interest, or other "make-whole" remedies designed to return them to the economic position that they would have enjoyed in the absence of the discrimination. Under the 1991 law, victims of intentional discrimination based on sex, religion, or disability may recover compensatory damages (for pain, suffering, and mental anguish) as well as punitive damages designed to punish employers for acts of flagrant discrimination. When compensatory or punitive damages are sought in a Title VII action, any party to the case is permitted to demand a jury trial. The prospect of being able to collect large sums in damages beyond back pay, interest, and other make-whole remedies may, in

[27]BNA, "Religious Discrimination," in *Fair Employment Practices Manual* (Washington, D.C.: BNA, 1994), sect. 421. See *Bessard v. California Community Colleges*, 66 FEP Cases 507 (1994).

[28]The act is an amendment to Title VII of the 1964 Civil Rights Act. See BNA, "Civil Rights Act of 1991: Summary and Full Text," *Labor Relations Reporter* (Special Suppl.), Nov. 11, 1991.

the future, make pursuing academic discrimination cases arising under Title VII more attractive to faculty members and legal counsel. In *Boss v. Board of Education,* a federal district court held that the Civil Rights Act of 1991 does not apply retroactively.[29] Thus, faculty who were victims of discrimination prior to the effective date of the act (July 2, 1993) are currently not eligible for its more liberal remedies. The U.S. Supreme Court, however, has agreed to hear arguments on the retroactivity of the Civil Rights Act of 1991.[30] The Court's ruling in this matter could have important implications for victims of intentional discrimination.

Another important aspect of the Civil Rights Act of 1991 is the reversal (or partial reversal) of seven U.S. Supreme Court decisions that were handed down between 1989 and 1991. Several of these cases were relevant to discrimination suits in academia and are discussed in subsequent sections. Congress appears to be sending the U.S. Supreme Court a message that it will no longer tolerate its increasingly conservative, pro-employer stance in employment discrimination litigation. The nullification of these cases may make it easier for faculty to win Title VII cases when reappointment, promotion, or tenure decisions are based on a discriminatory animus.

AGE DISCRIMINATION IN EMPLOYMENT ACT OF 1967

The Age Discrimination in Employment Act (ADEA) protects persons age forty and older from adverse employment decisions based on their age rather than their qualifications or ability to perform their jobs competently.[31] Enforcement responsibility for the act is vested

[29]*Boss v. Board of Education,* 798 F. Supp. 116 (E.D.N.Y. 1992). Also see *Durrani v. Valdosta Technical Institute,* 66 FEP Cases 1333 (1992).

[30]*Harris v. Roadway Express,* 973 F.2d 490 (6th Cir. 1992), *cert. granted, sub nom., Rivers v. Roadway Express,* 113 S. Ct. 1250 (1993); and *Landgraf v. USI Film Products,* 968 F.2d 427 (5th Cir.), *cert. granted in part* 113 S. Ct. 1250 (1993), cited in Fernand N. Dutile, "The Law of Higher Education and the Courts: 1992 in Review," *Journal of College and University Law* 20 (1993): 190–91. In *Roberts v. University of South Florida,* 62 FEP Cases 247 (1993), a federal district court anticipated that the U.S. Supreme Court might rule that the Civil Rights Act of 1991 would be applied retroactively. For this reason, the court asked the jury to determine not only whether the university discriminated against the plaintiff but also whether the discrimination was with malice or reckless indifference and, if so, the amount that would reasonably compensate the plaintiff for her emotional pain, suffering, inconvenience, or mental anguish.

[31]29 U.S.C. 621(b) (1967). Section 631(d) of the ADEA contains the temporary "special rule" affecting tenured faculty members. It reads as follows: "(d) Nothing in this Act shall be construed to prohibit compulsory retirement of any employee who has attained 70 years of age, and who is serving under a contract of unlimited tenure (or similar arrangement providing for unlimited tenure) at an institution of higher education (as defined by section 1141(a) of Title 20 [Higher Education Act of 1965])."

with the EEOC. The ADEA no longer permits the involuntary retirement of tenured professors at age seventy.[32] Some observers believe a potential logjam will be created as older professors refuse to retire. If such a bottleneck occurs, it may make it difficult or impossible for younger or minority scholars to obtain academic positions.

Colleges and universities may offer financial and nonfinancial retirement incentives to older faculty. Retirement incentives are legal under the ADEA as long as they are not used to coerce a faculty member into stepping down. The Older Workers Benefit Protection Act of 1990 (OWBPA) also permits the use of most early retirement incentive programs.[33] Programs that make distinctions among employees primarily on the basis of their age, for example, by permitting only employees below a certain age to receive severance benefits, appear to be illegal unless justified by cost.[34] There may also be attempts to "decouple" a faculty member from his or her tenure status at a specific age without termination (the professor continues to work as an untenured faculty member). Any personnel policy that uses an age-based criterion, however, is fraught with legal problems.[35]

Relative to race, sex, and national origin cases, few faculty have filed age discrimination cases against colleges and universities. Many age discrimination cases focus on whether the plaintiff is physically able to continue working, an issue that arises infrequently in academia. Those age discrimination cases that do arise usually involve allegations of unfair treatment (relative to younger faculty) or pay inequities, rather than reappointment, promotion, or tenure.[36]

[32]EEOC, "EEOC: Policy Guide on Compulsory Retirement of Tenured Faculty Members at Age 70," Jan. 12, 1989, in BNA, *Fair Employment Practices Manual*, sect. 405.

[33]See Peter N. Swann, "Early Retirement Incentives with Upper Age Limits under the Older Workers Benefit Protection Act," *Journal of College and University Law* 19 (1992): 53–72.

[34]BNA, "Older Workers Benefit Protection Act," *Labor Relations Reporter* 15 (1990): S-7.

[35]See Matthew W. Finkin, "Commentary: Tenure after an Uncapped ADEA: A Different View," *Journal of College and University Law* 15 (1988): 43–60; Oscar M. Ruebhausen, "Commentary: The Age Discrimination in Employment Act Amendments of 1986: Implications for Tenure and Retirement," *Journal of College and University Law* 14 (1988): 561–74; and John H. Burton, Jr., "Tenured Faculty and the 'Uncapped' Age Discrimination in Employment Act," *Yale Law and Policy Review* 5 (Spring-Summer 1987): 450–71.

[36]See, for example, *Sischo-Nownejad v. Merced Community College District*, 56 FEP Cases 250 (1991).

AFFIRMATIVE ACTION PROGRAMS

Institutions of higher learning that receive federal funding are obligated by a series of executive orders and laws to engage in affirmative action.[37] Affirmative action programs are designed to help qualified females and members of other groups gain access to jobs that have historically been off limits to them because of discriminatory practices. To create greater diversity among faculty and to comply with affirmative action obligations, colleges and universities often appear eager to hire female and minority faculty. In some cases, funds are allocated exclusively for the hiring of black faculty. Organizations that extend preferences in hiring and promotion to women and minorities run the risk, however, of reverse discrimination suits by white males under Title VII (Section 2000e-2). The problem is compounded because the demarcation between legal affirmative action and illegal reverse discrimination is unclear.

Until 1979, discrimination in favor of females and racial minorities whose qualifications were deemed to be less impressive than their white or male counterparts was generally regarded as a violation of Title VII. In the landmark case *Steelworkers v. Weber*, however, the U.S. Supreme Court ruled that private employers may give special preference to black workers to eliminate a "manifest racial imbalance" in jobs historically dominated by whites.[38] Subsequent Supreme Court rulings have held that if blacks have been victimized by pervasive discrimination, a court order can be used to impose affirmative race-conscious relief.[39]

In a California case, the U.S. Supreme Court ruled that the promotion of a woman ahead of a man who had scored slightly higher on a promotion examination did not violate Title VII. This case is perhaps the most relevant to promotion and tenure decisions in institutions of higher learning because the employer (Santa Clara County) was attempting to use a voluntary affirmative action plan to eliminate traditional imbalances in its work force and the candidate's sex was

---

[37]Among the more prominent of these executive orders and laws are (1) Executive Order 11246, which requires federal contractors (having contracts in excess of $10,000) to take affirmative action to prevent discrimination against employees on the basis of race, sex, religion, color, or national origin and (2) Section 503 of the Rehabilitation Act of 1973, which requires contractors (in excess of $2,500) to take affirmative action to employ and promote persons with handicaps. BNA, "Additional Requirements for Federal Contractors," *Fair Employment Practices Manual*, sect. 411.

[38]*Steelworkers v. Weber*, 20 FEP Cases 1 (1979).

[39]See *U.S. v. Paradise*, 43 FEP Cases 1 (1987).

but one of a number of factors evaluated in the promotion process.[40] In a later case, however, a U.S. court of appeals held that although a person's gender may be used as a tie breaker in a competitive personnel decision, gender cannot be the only determining factor under a voluntary affirmative action plan.[41]

Although colleges and universities must make a special effort to recruit and employ female and minority faculty, affirmative action programs do not require that employers hire or promote "unqualified" females or minority group members. Unlike many jobs, the qualifications for a job in academia are nebulous and subjective. It is therefore difficult to determine whether a professor is "qualified."[42] When a minority and nonminority candidate have comparable qualifications, however, it appears permissible to give the minority candidate preference. But if a minority candidate who does not meet minimal qualifications (e.g., does not hold a terminal degree from a recognized institution) is given preference over a nonminority candidate who has the minimal qualifications, then a ruling of reverse discrimination is likely. The most difficult problem arises when both candidates possess minimal qualifications but the relative qualifications of the nonminority candidate are definitely superior. On the one hand, a college or university that hires the better-qualified nonminority candidate may be accused of failing to adhere to its affirmative action program. On the other hand, the institution may face a reverse discrimination charge if it hires the less-qualified minority candidate.

Surprisingly few of the cases analyzed here mentioned the issue of affirmative action. Colleges and universities that become too eager to hire minority faculty because of affirmative action programs, however, may become embroiled in reverse discrimination cases. The School of Social Work in the College of Arts and Sciences at the University of South Florida advertised for two positions at the assistant professor level. Two applicants, Cleora Roberts, a white female, and Aaron Smith, a black male, had equally impressive qualifications, and they emerged as the top two candidates. Roberts was offered a position as an assistant professor at a salary of $29,518. Smith told university officials that his current salary was higher and that he

---

[40]*Johnson v. Transportation Agency, Santa Clara County,* 43 FEP Cases 411 (1987).
[41]*Conlin v. Blanchard,* 51 FEP Cases 707 (1989).
[42]The issue of qualifications is discussed at length in subsequent sections.

could therefore not accept an offer as an assistant professor within the advertised range of $26,000 to $28,500. At this point, the university readvertised the position at the associate professor level. The new position was tailored to Smith's qualifications, and it carried an annual salary of $40,000.

Although Roberts did not become aware of the newly advertised position until the time for application had nearly expired, she asked the chair of the faculty whether she could apply. He told her that she could apply but that she would be competing against a highly qualified minority candidate.

Roberts then met with the dean of the College of Arts and Sciences and asked that she be employed at a higher salary than the one initially offered to her. The dean stated that additional funds were not available, and Roberts accepted the original offer of $29,518. In the meantime, Smith was offered and accepted the position as associate professor at $40,000.

The School of Social Work had no black faculty members at the time Smith was offered the position. University officials were concerned that the lack of minority faculty would jeopardize the School of Social Work's upcoming reaccreditation evaluation by the Council on Social Work Education.

Roberts filed Title VII charges against the University of South Florida, claiming intentional reverse discrimination. The university used three factors to defend the charge: (1) Smith's superior qualifications, (2) marketplace considerations, and (3) the university's mandatory affirmative action plan. The federal district court rejected these arguments, noting that Smith's qualifications were not better than those of Roberts. The court also noted that the university had never offered Smith a position as an assistant professor and that he had achieved his $40,000 salary without any negotiations with the university. Furthermore, the court said that readvertising for the position was unusual.

The jury awarded Roberts a promotion to associate professor, a salary of $45,624, benefits commensurate with those of Smith, a back-pay award of $68,212, and $250,000 in damages. The court refused to grant her tenure, however, and it also set aside a $70,000 award for pain and suffering.[43]

---

[43]*Roberts v. University of South Florida*, 62 FEP Cases 246 (1993). Also see BNA, "Unlawful Professorial Preference," *Fair Employment Practices*, July 15, 1993), p. 79.

An analysis of the major court cases that have dealt with affirmative action create the following inferences for colleges and universities:

1. Institutions of higher learning can enter into voluntary affirmative action programs to create a more favorable racial balance or diversity in the faculty as long as the plan is temporary, does not completely prevent the advancement of white or male candidates, does not set aside a specific number of positions for minorities,[44] does not force the termination of white or male candidates to make room for nonminority faculty, and emphasizes a flexible case-by-case approach to making a gradual improvement in the representation of minorities and women on the faculty.

2. Promotion and tenure decisions are usually not competitive in the sense that the favorable treatment of one faculty member will preclude the favorable treatment of another. A faculty member's sex or minority status may be used to break a tie, however, if promotion or tenure quotas are in force and the minority and nonminority faculty members' qualifications are approximately the same.

3. Institutions that use a bona fide seniority system (perhaps in conjunction with a collective bargaining agreement) cannot terminate faculty in accordance with their race or sex as a means of maintaining a specific work force composition. While hiring goals impose a diffuse burden on a potentially large number of job applicants or candidates for promotion and tenure, often foreclosing only one of several opportunities for a nonminority candidate, layoffs that are geared to race or sex impose the entire burden of achieving racial equality on particular individuals, often resulting in serious disruption to the lives of nonminority employees. For this reason, the U.S. Supreme Court has struck down preferential layoffs.[45]

REHABILITATION ACT OF 1973 AND AMERICANS WITH DISABILITIES ACT

The Rehabilitation Act of 1973 and the Americans with Disabilities Act of 1990 provide protection against discrimination in employment

---

[44]Set-aside plans by state and local governments must be justified by a compelling government interest in redressing past discrimination against a protected group, and the plan must be narrowly tailored so as not to affect unnecessarily the rights of nonminority individuals. *Richmond v. J. A. Croson*, 53 FEP Cases 197 (1989).

[45]See *Firefighters Local No. 1784 v. Stotts*, 34 FEP Cases 1702 (1984); *Wygant v. Jackson (Michigan) Board of Education*, 40 FEP Cases 1321 (1986); *NAACP v. Detroit Police Officers Association*, 43 FEP Cases 1786 (1987); and *Britton v. South Bend Community School Corp.*, 43 FEP Cases 1483 (1987).

for otherwise qualified persons with any of a broad range of physical and mental disabilities. Colleges and universities are among the many private- and public-sector organizations that must hire and promote qualified disabled persons and provide reasonable accommodation in the workplace.[46]

To date, there are few published cases involving wrongful discharge and employment discrimination against disabled faculty members.[47] Perhaps colleges and universities are more sensitive to the plight of the disabled than they are to other protected groups. As age discrimination complaints increase, it is likely that the issue of discrimination based on a person's physical or mental abilities may also increase. Faculty who have undergone drug and alcohol rehabilitation as well as those who are HIV positive will also benefit from the protection against unjust dismissals provided by the Rehabilitation Act and the Americans with Disabilities Act.[48] Faculty who engage in sexual misconduct, however, cannot use the Rehabilitation Act or the Americans with Disabilities Act for protection. The ADA specifically excludes some sexual disorders as disabilities. For example, a tenured English professor at Central Maine Technical College was fired because he violated its sexual harassment policy by kissing an eighteen-year-old female student after a sexually suggestive conversation. The professor had also been involved in four previous incidents of sexual behavior with students. He filed a lawsuit against the college, claiming that he was terminated because of his "mental handicap of sexual addiction." The court ruled that he was not protected under either state or federal disability law.[49]

One interesting aspect of the Americans with Disabilities Act is that public employees do not have to file discrimination charges with the EEOC before proceeding to federal court. Thomas Petersen worked as a business school faculty member in the University of Wisconsin's (Madison) Small Business Development Center. During the time he was recuperating from surgery for a brain tumor and taking medicine to control seizures, he was told that his contract with

---

[46]See Wayne A. Hill, Jr., "Americans with Disabilities Act of 1990: Significant Overlap with Section 504 for Colleges and Universities," *Journal of College and University Law* 18 (1992): 389–417.

[47]See *Brousard-Norcross v. Augustana College Association*, 56 FEP Cases 245 (1991), and *Sischo-Nownejad v. Merced Community College District*, 56 FEP Cases 250 (1991).

[48]See *Chalk v. U.S. District Court for Central District of California*, 46 FEP Cases 279 (1988).

[49]*Winston v. Maine Technical College*, 2 AD Cases 1228 (1993).

the university would not be renewed because his personal medical needs did not mesh with the needs of the center. In his subsequent suit, Petersen also claimed that the university failed to give him a merit raise, denied reasonable accommodation to him by refusing to reduce his work load by 20 percent, and forced him to endure a hostile work environment.

The University of Wisconsin contended that Petersen was required to first file charges with the EEOC and requested that the suit be dismissed. According to the district court, plaintiffs must exhaust administrative remedies when filing charges under Title I of the ADA. U.S. Department of Justice rules, however, permit public employees who file charges under Title II of the act to bypass the EEOC and proceed directly to federal court.[50] The Rehabilitation Act also permits nonfederal employees to circumvent administrative agencies and file charges directly in federal court. Eliminating administrative agency proceedings could reduce significantly the time needed to resolve some disability discrimination cases. This provision might be especially useful for state university faculty who are able to continue working but are forced out of their jobs by employers because of disabilities for which there is a poor prognosis.

Constitutional Amendments

The U.S. Constitution does not protect against discriminatory actions by private institutions, but the Fifth and Fourteenth amendments have been interpreted to prohibit such action by the federal and state governments respectively. Faculty members employed by state-assisted institutions may use the Fourteenth Amendment in civil rights actions against a college or university. The Fourteenth Amendment's equal protection clause may be invoked against state colleges or universities that engage in racist, sexist, or other discriminatory behavior. The due process clause of the Fourteenth Amendment may be used when a state-assisted institution fails to abide by a prescribed promotion, tenure, grievance, or other civil service procedure to the detriment of a faculty member. The U.S. Supreme Court held in *Washington v. Davis*, however, that some degree of "purposeful" conduct is required before the constitutional amendments can be applied in employment discrimination cases.[51]

---

[50]*Petersen v. University of Wisconsin Board of Regents*, 2 AD Cases 735 (1993).
[51]*Washington v. Davis*, 12 FEP Cases 1415 (1976).

There are two types of due process: (1) substantive due process and (2) procedural due process. The issue of substantive due process might arise if a faculty member believed that a state university failed to apply to interpret its faculty manual or personnel policies properly. In *Agarwal v. Regents of the University of Minnesota*, a tenured professor of East Indian Hindu origin was dismissed because of plagiarism and other unprofessional behavior. Som P. Agarwal claimed that his substantive due process rights were violated because the university failed to interpret its faculty tenure regulations properly. He also contended that his procedural due process rights were denied because he did not receive notice of the criteria by which his competence would be judged within a reasonable time before his termination. The U.S. Court of Appeals (Eighth Circuit) denied both due process claims. Agarwal's substantive due process claim was denied because he distorted the meaning of the tenure regulations. Furthermore, neither Minnesota law nor university regulations precluded consideration of his past offenses, and substantial evidence existed to support his termination. Agarwal's procedural due process claim was similarly struck down because (1) he received proper notice; (2) he was represented by legal counsel during all proceedings; (3) he took full advantage of his right to present evidence and to call and cross-examine witnesses; and (4) any procedural errors that occurred were not sufficient to establish a violation of his Fourteenth Amendment rights.[52]

In some instances, the courts require surprisingly rigorous due process standards. Rutgers University dismissed a tenured chemistry professor for taking advantage of visiting Chinese scholars and teaching assistants. The professor had used the visiting scholars to perform domestic work at his home, deducted health insurance premiums from their pay without providing medical coverage, told those who needed medical care to use the name of a third person for whom coverage had been provided, and submitted false time reports for work that was never done. Nonetheless, a federal district court said

[52]*Agarwal v. Regents of the University of Minnesota*, 40 FEP Cases 940 (1986). The court cited the four requirements of procedural due process: (1) "clear and actual notice of the reasons for termination in sufficient detail to enable him or her to present evidence relating to them"; (2) "notice of both the names of those who have made allegations against the teacher and the specific nature and factual basis for the charges"; (3) "a reasonable time and opportunity to present testimony in his or her own defense"; and (4) "a hearing before an impartial board or tribunal."

that although the professor clearly violated Rutgers University's ethical standards, he did not fail to maintain "standards of sound scholarship and competent teaching," a basis for dismissal set forth in a separate university regulation. The chemistry professor was granted summary judgment by the court because Rutgers University's regulation was held to be "void for vagueness."

The U.S. Court of Appeals (Third Circuit), however, reversed the lower court's decision and remanded the case to the district court for further proceedings. Ultimately, the federal district court granted summary judgment on September 30, 1993, in favor of the university. The professor, who had been detenured in 1988 and was no longer employed at Rutgers, then appealed to the Third Circuit, which affirmed the due process issues but reversed and remanded on the professor's First Amendment claims that he had been detenured in retaliation for filing previous grievances and lawsuits against Rutgers. In August 1994, the Third Circuit refused to reconsider its opinion. The case is still pending, and the next step will be for the pretrial rulings of the Third Circuit to be appealed to the U.S. Supreme Court.[53]

Although the equal protection clause of the Fourteenth Amendment to the U.S. Constitution requires the government to treat similarly situated individuals in a similar manner, individual mistakes in the evaluation of a faculty member's credentials or relatively insignificant deviations from the prescribed evaluative procedure are

---

[53]Information on the current status of this case was supplied by David Scott, university counsel of Rutgers University. See *San Filippo v. Bongiovanni*, 961 F.2d 1125 (3d Cir., *cert. denied*, 113 S. Ct. 305 (1992), cited and discussed in Fernand N. Dutile, "The Law of Higher Education and the Courts: 1990 in Review," *Journal of College and University Law* 18 (1991): 234–35. The Third Circuit noted that the void-for-vagueness doctrine was based on "fairness" and was meant to provide notice of prohibited conduct. The court stated that a "reasonable, ordinary person using his common sense and general knowledge of employer-employee relationships would have fair notice" that San Filippo's actions would constitute grounds for dismissal. See Fernand N. Dutile, "The Law of Higher Education and the Courts: 1992 in Review," *Journal of College and University Law* 20 (1993): 188. According to Arval A. Morris, "Dismissal grounds such as 'moral turpitude' or 'uncooperativeness' or 'improper professional attitude,' etc. seem equally vulnerable to due process of law challenges of vagueness or lack of relatedness, because such bare grounds, by themselves, neither tie the dismissal ground to professional capacities, nor convey sufficient information to qualify as 'adequate notice' required by due process of law." See Arval A. Morris, *Dismissal of Tenured Higher Education Faculty: Legal Implications of the Elimination of Mandatory Retirement* (Topeka, Kans.: National Organization on Legal Problems of Education, 1992), p. 53. Also see Carolyn J. Mooney, "Dismissals 'for Cause,'" *Chronicle of Higher Education*, Dec. 7, 1994, pp. A17, A19–20.

not grounds for judicial review, however. According to the U.S. Supreme Court:

> The federal court is not the appropriate forum in which to review the multitude of personnel decisions that are made daily by public agencies. We must accept the harsh fact that numerous individual mistakes are inevitable in the day-to-day administration of our affairs. The United States Constitution cannot be feasibly construed to require federal judicial review for every such error. In the absence of any claim that the public-employer was motivated by a desire to curtail or to penalize the exercise of an employee's constitutionally protected rights, we must presume that official action was regular and, if erroneous, can best be corrected in other ways. The Due Process Clause of the Fourteenth Amendment is not a guarantee against incorrect or ill-advised personnel decisions.[54]

The U.S. Supreme Court in *Regents of the University of Michigan v. Ewing* made it clear that the courts may override a decision under substantive due process only if that decision is "such a substantial departure from accepted academic norms as to demonstrate that the person or committee responsible did not actually exercise professional judgment."[55] Intentional racial, sex, or other form of discrimination by a peer review committee, department head, dean, or other official at a state-assisted institution would constitute a substantive due process violation of the equal protection clause under the Fourteenth Amendment.[56]

Faculty in public colleges and universities rely on constitutional amendments and statutory law for varying degrees of protection, but those in private institutions must often depend primarily on principles of contractual law to safeguard due process and tenure rights. In the absence of illegal race, sex, age, or other form of discrimination, a faculty member at a private school cannot usually rely on constitutional guarantees to ensure adequate notice of dismissal or a fair and impartial hearing—the two hallmarks of due process. Instead, he or

---

[54]*Bishop v. Wood*, 96 S. Ct. 2074, quoted in *Gutzwiller v. Fenik*, 48 FEP Cases 413 (1988).

[55]*Regents of the University of Michigan v. Ewing*, 106 S. Ct. 513 (1985). In this case, the court granted university faculty broad deference with regard to student academic dismissals. Presumably, the same logic would apply to the termination or tenure denial of faculty members. See Jayna Jacobson Partain, "A Qualified Academic Freedom Privilege in Employment Litigation: Protecting Higher Education or Shielding Discrimination?" *Vanderbilt Law Review* 40 (1987): 1402.

[56]*Gutzwiller v. Fenik*, 48 FEP Cases 405 (1988).

she will typically file a breach of contract suit, which will lead to an examination of the faculty member's written contract as well as personnel documents and other institutional policies and procedures that deal with promotion, tenure, and grievance hearings.[57]

RECONSTRUCTION-ERA CIVIL RIGHTS ACTS

A plaintiff in a civil rights case may elect to use one of the post–Civil War acts instead of Title VII. The Civil Rights Acts of 1870 and 1871 were passed to give effect to the Thirteenth, Fourteenth, and Fifteenth amendments of the U.S. Constitution, which granted rights to former slaves. The 1870 Act (sometimes referred to as the 1866 Act) prohibits race discrimination in the making and enforcing of contracts and applies to both public and private employers. The 1871 act bars anyone acting "under color of any" state or local law from depriving an individual of rights "secured by the Constitution and laws."[58] Until 1991, the Reconstruction-era civil rights acts were narrowly interpreted to apply only to the formation and enforcement of contracts. An amendment to the law by the Civil Rights Act of 1991 clarified the "make and enforce contracts" provision to include "the making, performance, modification, and termination of contracts, and the enjoyment of all benefits, privileges, terms, and conditions of the contractual relationship."[59]

These statutes have been used in recent years in job discrimination suits. The Reconstruction-era civil rights acts can be used against firms that have fewer than fifteen employees and are not covered under Title VII. These laws are most likely to be used against colleges and universities when the plaintiff has not filed within the time period allowed under Title VII. Furthermore, the post–Civil War laws impose no limit on compensatory or punitive damages.[60] As with the Fourteenth Amendment, the use of Reconstruction-era civil rights acts requires proof of discriminatory intent.

---

[57]See Morris, *Dismissal of Tenured Higher Education Faculty*, pp. 27–30.

[58]In the case of an Iraqi-born professor who was denied tenure at St. Francis College and sued the college under the Civil Rights Act of 1877, the U.S. Supreme Court noted that Congress intended, when it enacted the law, to protect from discrimination identifiable classes of persons who are subjected to intentional discrimination solely because of their ancestry or ethnic characteristics. See *St. Francis College v. Al-Khazraji*, 43 FEP Cases 1305 (1987).

[59]BNA, "Reconstruction-Era Civil Rights Acts," *Fair Employment Practices Manual*, sect. 411.

[60]BNA, "Reconstruction-Era Civil Rights Acts," *Fair Employment Practices Manual*, sect. 411.

TITLE IX OF THE EDUCATION AMENDMENTS OF 1972

Title IX of the Education Amendments of 1972 provides that no person shall be subjected to sex discrimination under any educational program or activity receiving federal financial assistance. The U.S. Supreme Court has ruled that Title IX applies to employees as well as students and therefore prohibits employment discrimination on the basis of sex in federally funded educational programs.[61] According to the Court, the ban on employment discrimination applies only to educational programs and activities that use federal funds. Since the Court did not define "program or activity," a great deal of controversy arose over the exact meaning of these terms.

In its 1984 decision, *Grove City College v. Bell*, the U.S. Supreme Court held that Title IX's coverage was limited to the specific program within an institution that received federal funds.[62] The Civil Rights Restoration Act of 1987 overturned the *Grove City* decision, however, and specified that the entire institution receiving federal funds must comply with Title IX and other civil rights laws.[63]

[61]*North Haven Board of Education v. Bell*, 28 FEP Cases 1393 (1982).

[62]*Grove City College v. Bell*, 465 U.S. 555 (1984).

[63]See BNA, "Federal Law, Prohibitions, the Basic Laws, Title IX of the Education Amendments of 1972," *Fair Employment Practices Manual*, sect. 411.

4. THE REAPPOINTMENT, PROMOTION, AND TENURE PROCESS

ROMOTION AND TENURE DECISIONS at U.S. colleges and universities are usually the outcome of a formal process that begins with a peer evaluation in the faculty member's department and concludes with a rubber-stamp vote of approval by the institution's board of trustees.[1] From start to final decision, the process is often intense and typically consumes the better part of an academic year. Most reappointment, promotion, and tenure decisions involve inputs from peer review committees, department heads, college deans, and other academic administrators. Many of the cases analyzed here were also referred to faculty grievance or appeals committees, which evaluated the decisions and then made recommendations to the institutions' chief academic officers.

PEER REVIEW AND BEYOND

In 1940, the Association of American Colleges and the American Association of University Professors promulgated a "standard" tenure plan, which was embodied in the AAUP's Statement of Principles on Academic Freedom and Tenure.[2] Today, many institutions subscribe to the AAUP's "seven-year, up-or-out rule," which provides a faculty member with a six-year probationary period. During the sixth

---

[1] Reappointment decisions that involve no adverse action are often confined to officials within a faculty member's college and are not reviewed by upper-level administrators or governing boards.

[2] Commission on Academic Tenure in Higher Education, *Faculty Tenure: A Report and Recommendations by the Commission on Academic Tenure in Higher Education* (San Francisco: Jossey-Bass, 1973), pp. ix, x.

year of employment (sometimes referred to as the penultimate year), an evaluation is made regarding the faculty member's teaching, scholarship, and service. If the faculty member's performance is meritorious and his or her research and teaching expertise meet institutional needs, then tenure is granted. Should the peer review committee and administration decide that the faculty member is not deserving of tenure, he or she is usually put "on notice" with a one-year terminal contract.[3]

Department peer review committees composed of tenured senior faculty typically make initial recommendations on reappointment, promotion, and tenure. The courts have granted a great deal of deference to the opinions of these committees, primarily because of their specialized expertise in an academic discipline and their knowledge of faculty members' scholarly potential, teaching effectiveness, and collegiality. In *Johnson v. University of Pittsburgh*, the U.S. district court noted, "The peer review system has evolved as the most reliable method for assuring promotion of the candidates best qualified to serve the needs of the institution."[4]

This position was echoed in *EEOC v. University of Notre Dame du Lac.*

> It is clear that the peer review process is essential to the very lifeblood and heartbeat of academic excellence and plays a most vital role in the proper and efficient functioning of our nation's colleges and universities. The process of peer evaluation has evolved as the best and most reliable method of promoting academic excellence and freedom by assuring that faculty tenure decisions will be made objectively on the basis of frank and unrestrained critiques and discussions of a candidate's academic qualifications.[5]

Despite their long tradition in promotion and tenure decisions, peer review committees are not universally favored. They are usually made up of tenured faculty with established academic records, and, to the extent that scholars with well-defined research programs are

---

[3]Colleges and universities that follow AAUP guidelines usually grant their faculty members a one-year notice before permanent termination. See John Anthony Palombi, "The Ineffectiveness of Title VII in Tenure Denial Decisions," *DePaul Law Review* 36 (Winter 1987): 259.

[4]*Johnson v. University of Pittsburgh*, 15 FEP Cases 1530 (1977).

[5]*EEOC v. University of Notre Dame du Lac*, 32 FEP Cases 1057 (1983), cited in *EEOC v. Franklin and Marshall College*, 39 FEP Cases 221 (1985).

skeptical of untested areas of research, there is concern that peer review committees may stifle innovation and creativity among junior faculty.[6] The fear that peer review committees may create a barrier to faculty whose ideas are unorthodox has not been a major factor, however, in wrongful discharge or employment discrimination suits.

Once the peer review committee has made its recommendation about a faculty member, his or her dossier is forwarded to the department head and then to the dean of the college. Recommendations by the committee, department head, and dean are usually nonbinding. The institution's chief academic officer (provost, vice chancellor, vice president for academic affairs) normally has (for all practical purposes) the final authority to reappoint, promote, or grant tenure.[7] But it is rare for the chief academic officer to reverse a recommendation of a peer review committee, department chair, or dean except in the case of a split vote. The primary objective of the peer review committee's evaluation is to assess the faculty member's professional competencies; by contrast, the evaluation conducted by the institution's top academic officers is more likely to focus on the financial and institutional ramifications of granting a promotion or tenure. Notwithstanding this distinction, the relative influence of administration and faculty in reappointments, promotion, and tenure decisions remains an area of potential conflict. Academic institutions also vary with regard to the degree of power vested in peer review committees, department heads, deans, and other academic officers to make appointments.[8]

Although most wrongful discharge and employment discrimination suits in academia have their origins at the department or college level, suits are occasionally precipitated by decisions made at higher levels of a university. In *Faculty of the City University of New York Law School at Queen's College v. Murphy*, the chancellor decided not to forward to the board of trustees the applications of two candidates who had not received the unanimous approval of a joint law school–Queen's College review committee. The New York Supreme Court

[6]The potential of peer review committee bias also exists in the review of grant applications. See "Peer Review System Plans Being Reevaluated," *Boston Globe*, June 23, 1987, p. 1, quoted in Ieuan G. Mahony, "Title VII and Academic Freedom: The Authority of the EEOC to Investigate College Faculty Tenure Decisions," *Boston College Law Review* 28 (May 1987): 567.

[7]The final decision is usually made by the president or board of trustees of the college or university. The board's approval is usually automatic.

[8]Peter M. Blau, *The Organization of Academic Work* (New York: Wiley, 1973), p. 167.

ruled that the chancellor had acted beyond the scope of his power in the tenure review process when he failed to forward the applications to the higher level.[9] This case was decided under New York law, rather than under federal law. The New York court made the point, however, that a board of trustees (or equivalent body) of a state-assisted institution has an exclusive, nondelegable power to grant promotions and tenure. Any attempt to truncate the review process may jeopardize a faculty member's entitlement to due process.

Most institutions use three major criteria for evaluating faculty performance: (1) teaching effectiveness; (2) research and publications; and (3) service to the public, profession, or institution. To a lesser extent, a faculty member's ability to work in harmony with others is also evaluated. The standards for reappointment, promotion, and tenure vary, often substantially, from one institution to another. Large public and private institutions, especially those with doctoral programs, have traditionally placed significant emphasis on research and scholarly activities. Smaller liberal arts schools often emphasize excellence in teaching and a faculty member's willingness to work closely with students. But even within the same institution, standards will vary among departments or colleges. For example, faculty members in a college of agriculture at a land-grant institution may be evaluated on the extent to which they provide services through extension programs. Engineering faculty at the same institution may be evaluated largely on their ability to obtain external funding through government agencies or research foundations. Business and social science faculty may be judged on the extent to which they publish their research findings in scholarly journals. The diversity of expectations within a single campus makes it difficult and even undesirable for top academic officers to use a standard set of criteria in evaluating faculty. For this reason, a great deal of credence must be given to the recommendations of peer review committees, department heads, and deans.

Some institutions require that nontenured faculty be evaluated for reappointment annually, whereas others require evaluations biannually or less frequently. Some schools require such faculty to submit a

[9]*Faculty of the City University of New York Law School at Queen's College v. Murphy*, 49 FEP Cases 859 (1989), quoted in Fernand N. Dutile, "Higher Education and the Courts: 1988 in Review," *Journal of College and University Law* 16 (1989): 246–47. The New York Supreme Court held that the two faculty members did not establish a prima facie case of race and sex discrimination.

dossier that documents and summarizes their teaching, research, and service activities. And in institutions where research, publications, or other scholarly activity are weighted heavily, letters of evaluation may be solicited from respected scholars at other institutions.

Once the evaluation process begins, the proceedings are conducted in private and the faculty member is usually not privy to either the deliberations of the peer review committee or other academic officers. The faculty member is usually kept informed of the status of the review process and normally is aware of whether the peer review committee, department head, and dean support his or her application for reappointment, promotion, or tenure. But rarely do faculty members have detailed knowledge of the deliberations of the peer review committee or know the precise reasons behind a particular recommendation to reappoint, promote, or grant tenure.

Faculty members whose performance is regarded as unsatisfactory or whose prospects of tenure are especially bleak may be terminated before their sixth year. Likewise, nontenured faculty who show considerable promise may be promoted during their probationary period.[10] And, finally, faculty members whose contracts are renewed during their probationary period will not necessarily be regarded as tenurable at the end of their sixth year of service, especially if the college or university is undergoing changes in its leadership or mission. According to a federal district court in Pennsylvania:

> The fact that an individual's first three-year contract may be renewed for an additional three-year period does not indicate that [the] faculty member's performance is satisfactory or in accord with the long range goals of the department. Under the rules of the medical school, a non tenured, [sic] faculty member must be notified in the second year of his first three year contract whether his contract will be renewed. Thus, the department chairman does not have a substantial opportunity to observe the performance of the faculty member or to assess his qualification; therefore the decision of the chairman to renew the appointment is of no particular importance. As stated by Dr. Youngner, a faculty member barely has time to establish his research program or his presence in the department by the time the notice is required, so the appointment is almost automatically renewed in all cases.[11]

[10]The most common scenario, however, is to grant tenure and promotion to the rank of associate professor simultaneously.

[11]*Johnson v. University of Pittsburgh*, 15 FEP Cases 1525 (1977).

It appears that increasingly fewer institutions are willing to grant tenure before a faculty member's penultimate year. This reluctance seems to stem from several causes. First, the growing fiscal conservativeness at many colleges and universities means that institutions are hesitant to make permanent commitments to faculty until their sixth year of employment. Second, the increasing emphasis on research at many institutions of higher learning and the high degree of competition and selectivity associated with publishing in top-tier academic journals make it more difficult for junior faculty to establish impressive publication records within the first few years of their academic careers. Third, many college officials are reluctant to establish a precedent of early tenure and thus adopt a rigid rule that they will not grant tenure before a faculty member's sixth year of service. By adopting such a policy, institutions guard against a gradual erosion of standards.

GRIEVANCE PROCEDURES

Most colleges and universities have grievance procedures that allow a faculty member to appeal an unfavorable reappointment, promotion, or tenure decision. Typically, a grievance committee is established, and is composed of faculty who are not associated with the faculty member's department or the individual filing the suit; it may be a subcommittee of the faculty senate, formed as an independent committee, or established based on a procedure that is part of a collective bargaining agreement. The committee's chief functions are to help resolve the dispute between the faculty member and the institution, to determine whether the faculty member was afforded due process, and to ensure that the adverse personnel decision was made without regard to the faculty member's race, sex, or age or for other potentially illegal reasons. Although a grievance committee does not abide by legal rules of evidence, it typically admits evidence such as the faculty member's dossier and hears testimony from interested parties. The committee then makes a recommendation to the chief academic officer, who may either sustain or reverse the personnel action. Concern has been expressed that top academic administrators are more likely to uphold the position of other administrators such as department heads and deans to the detriment of faculty. A survey of university grievance procedures indicates that such biases vary from one institution to another.[12]

[12]Marten Estey, "Faculty Grievance Procedures Outside Collective Bargaining: The

Establishing clear internal grievance procedures is important for several reasons. First, they help ensure due process. They give a faculty member who has been denied reappointment, promotion, or tenure the opportunity to present his or her case and, perhaps, to learn more about the deliberations that culminated in the adverse decision.[13] That college or university administrators often ignore or reverse the recommendations of grievance committees raises serious doubts, however, as to whether such committees do, in fact, create a climate for fair treatment.

Second, internal grievance committees sometimes defuse serious conflicts that could lead to expensive and lengthy civil suits. A hearing before a grievance committee may also provide a faculty member with an assessment of the strengths and weaknesses of his or her case. This assessment will undoubtedly affect whether the grievant will pursue litigation.

Third, in some states, a faculty member forfeits his or her right to action in state court unless an attempt is made to resolve the case through an internal grievance procedure. In *Dahlman v. Oakland University*, the Court of Appeals of Michigan held that an employee who was demoted could not bring a breach of contract suit against his employer because he had failed to exhaust his options under the university's grievance procedure.[14]

Fourth, a college or university's failure to follow an established pretermination or grievance procedure may raise questions regarding institutional due process. In *Page v. DeLaune*, the U.S. Court of Appeals (Fifth Circuit) found that Texas A&M University failed to follow pretermination procedures adequately. The employee had received a memorandum discussing matters "not clearly related to the termination," which ended with a statement that "a repeat performance will necessitate termination." According to the Fifth Circuit, this statement did not provide sufficient notice to the employee or allow him an adequate opportunity to respond.[15] In another

---

Experience at AAU Campuses," *Academe* 71 (May–June 1986): 13–14. It was also noted that "administrators, for their part, fear that grievance committee members may be biased in favor of fellow faculty grievants and against [department] chairs and deans."

[13]Failure to follow all steps of a grievance procedure may be regarded as a lack of procedural due process.

[14]*Dahlman v. Oakland University*, 172 Mich. App. 502, 432 N.W.2d 304 (1988), cited in Dutile, "Higher Education and the Courts," p. 251.

[15]*Page v. DeLaune*, 837 F.2d 233 (1988), cited in Dutile, "Higher Education and the Courts," p. 253.

case, however, two tenured professors at the University of Washington who were terminated during a period of financial exigency failed to convince a state appeals court that they were denied due process even though an internal grievance committee failed to comply with procedural guidelines.[16] Since the grievance committee review afforded the professors a "meaningful opportunity to argue why the proposed termination should not occur," the state court ruled that their procedural due process rights were not violated.[17]

Fifth, having an internal grievance procedure helps keep the parties honest. Members of peer review committees as well as department heads, deans, and chief academic officers usually want to be known for making personnel decisions that are both reasonable and based on a complete review of all relevant information. A grievance hearing can prove embarrassing if it exposes faculty and administrators who allow vendettas, internal politics, favoritism, or discriminatory attitudes to influence their performance evaluations and personnel decisions.

Unionized faculty who are covered by collective bargaining agreements may have the option of using binding arbitration during the final stage of a grievance concerning reappointment, promotion, or tenure. Although the U.S. Supreme Court has been reluctant to allow grievants to appeal arbitration decisions in a state or federal court, it has made a notable exception in discrimination cases. In *Alexander v. Gardner-Denver*, the U.S. Supreme Court ruled that race discrimination claims heard by arbitrators could be relitigated by the EEOC or courts.[18] Furthermore, *Gardner-Denver* allows the EEOC or courts to determine what weight, if any, they want to place on the arbitrator's opinion. The essence of *Gardner-Denver* is that, because of the highly personal and sensitive nature of discrimination, collective bargaining agreements containing arbitration clauses cannot be used to deprive an employee of his or her Title VII rights.

Conversely, collective bargaining agreements that preclude faculty from using an internal grievance mechanism if they have filed a suit

---

[16]For a somewhat different set of outcomes, see *Texas Faculty Association v. University of Texas at Dallas*, 946 F.2d 379 (5th Cir. 1991), and *Johnston-Taylor v. Gannon*, 907 F.2d 1577 (6th Cir. 1990).

[17]*Christensen v. Terrell*, 754 P.2d 1009 (Wash. App. Ct. 1988), cited in Dutile, "Higher Education in the Courts," p. 253. See also *Newman v. Burgin*, 930 F.2d 955 (1st Cir. 1991).

[18]*Alexander v. Gardner-Denver*, 415 U.S. 36 (1974).

with the EEOC or courts may be regarded as an illegal form of retaliation. *EEOC v. Board of Governors of State Colleges and Universities* concerned Raymond Lewis, who was denied tenure at Northeastern Illinois University.[19] He filed a grievance under a procedure that was part of a collective bargaining agreement between the Board of Governors of State Colleges and Universities and the University Professionals of Illinois Union. A provision of the agreement permitted the board to cancel a grievance hearing if a college or university employee brought action on the grievance through another forum such as the EEOC. Shortly before the arbitration hearing, and unknown to the board, Lewis filed an age discrimination suit with the EEOC. The arbitration hearing was held, but upon learning about the suit, the board instructed the arbitrator not to render his decision.[20] A federal district court ruled in favor of the board, stating that the provision not to allow litigants using other forums access to the grievance procedure was promulgated in good faith and was not retaliatory. The Seventh Circuit, however, held that the provision was a form of retaliation that constituted a per se violation of section 4(d) of the Age Discrimination in Employment Act. The court reasoned that the board had retaliated against Lewis and other similarly situated faculty "for the sole reason that the employee has engaged in protected activity" by filing an ADEA claim.[21]

EMPLOYMENT CONTRACTS, PERSONNEL POLICIES, AND FACULTY HANDBOOKS

The duration of employment for untenured faculty is usually one to three years. Once the employment contract has expired, the institution is free to either terminate or reappoint the faculty member for another academic year or longer. A faculty member who is terminated during the life of his or her employment contract is normally entitled to a remedy such as reinstatement or compensa-

[19]*EEOC v. Board of Governors of State Colleges and Universities*, 957 F.2d 424 (7th Cir. 1992), *cert. denied*, 113 S. Ct. 299 (1992).

[20]Lewis reached a settlement with the board and with the university. The EEOC, however, brought suit against the board and union seeking injunctive relief on behalf of other similarly situated employees.

[21]See Fernand N. Dutile, "The Law of Higher Education and the Courts: 1992 in Review," *Journal of College and University Law* 20 (1993): 196–97, and Edward C. Lyons, "*EEOC v. Board of Governors of State Colleges and Universities:* Collective Bargaining Agreements and Age Discrimination in Employment Act Claims: What Counts as Retaliation under ADEA Section 4(D)?" *Journal of College and University Law* 20 (1993): 241–59.

tion, unless the institution can demonstrate that the faculty member breached the terms and conditions of the contract.

Institutional or state personnel policies often require timely notification or permit faculty members a formal hearing if their contracts are not being renewed. In *Zuelsdorf v. University of Alaska at Fairbanks*, for example, two nontenured assistant professors sued the institution after they were notified in May 1986 that they would not be retained after the following academic year (1986–87). They claimed that the administration at the University of Alaska at Fairbanks did not provide them with timely notice of the termination in accordance with personnel policies and regulations. The university had recently changed the deadline for notifying faculty members of nonrenewals from March to June. Since the two faculty members were notified in May, the university claimed that it had provided timely notification. The Alaska Supreme Court held, however, that the original March deadline was a legally enforceable part of the contract for the two faculty (since they were appointed when the original March deadline was in effect). The court held that the university was not entitled to amend the terms of the contract without the consent of the faculty members who would potentially be affected.[22]

Questions may also arise over whether a college or university's faculty handbook affects the contractual relationship between faculty and their institution. In *Arneson v. Board of Trustees*, a faculty member was terminated without notice. A state court ruled, however, that the faculty manual was part of the employment contract and that Arneson should therefore have received a twelve-month notice of termination.[23] When the language of the faculty handbook is broad or general or a disclaimer in the handbook specifically states that no contractual relationship is created, college and university administrators may have a sufficient degree of discretion in making personnel decisions.[24] An assistant professor of German at the University of Houston was dismissed at the end of his fifth year of employment. The professor claimed that his due process rights were violated, and

[22]*Zuelsdorf v. University of Alaska, Fairbanks*, 794 P.2d 932 (Alaska 1990), cited and discussed in Fernand N. Dutile, "The Law of Higher Education and the Courts: 1990 in Review," *Journal of College and University Law* 18 (1991): 229.

[23]*Arneson v. Board of Trustees*, 569 N.E.2d 252 (Ill. App. 1991), cited and discussed in Fernand N. Dutile, "Higher Education in the Courts: 1991 in Review," *Journal of College and University Law* 19 (1992): 132–33.

[24]See *De Simone v. Skidmore College*, 553 N.Y.S.2d 240 (App. Div. 1990).

a jury found that the university's rules and regulations created a reasonable expectation of continued employment. Nevertheless, the district court found in favor of the university, and the Fifth Circuit Court of Appeals affirmed. The Fifth Circuit said that (1) the Texas courts have held consistently that employee handbooks do not create contractual rights unless there is specific language to the contrary, and (2) the preface of the University of Houston faculty handbook contained a statement that it was intended to be only a guide for faculty and not a comprehensive, self-contained policy document.[25] Thus, a faculty handbook that has been carefully written may permit college administrators to make personnel decisions without violating an expressed or implied contractual agreement with its faculty.

Personnel policies or state laws can also create de facto tenure for faculty. De facto tenure can arise if an institution continues to reappoint (or fails to terminate) a faculty member after a specified number of years. Although faculty have not usually been successful in convincing the courts that they are entitled to de facto tenure, the issue has been raised frequently enough to convince administrators to compare their reappointment and tenure procedures with relevant personnel policies and laws to avoid "accidentally" granting tenure to a faculty member who does not meet performance standards.[26]

---

[25]*Spuler v. Pickar*, 958 F.2d 103 (5th Cir. 1992), cited and discussed in Dutile, "The Law of Higher Education and the Courts: 1992 in Review," p. 185.

[26]See *Dugan v. Stockton State College*, 586 A.2d 322 (N.J. Super A.D. 1991), in which a faculty member claimed that she had achieved tenure under New Jersey's State and County College Tenure Act. See also *Edinger v. Board of Regents of Morehead State College*, 906 F.2d 1136 (6th Cir. 1990); *King v. Board of Regents of the University of Wisconsin System, University of Wisconsin at Milwaukee*, 52 FEP Cases 816 (1990); *Scagnelli v. Whiting*, 30 FEP Cases 1693 (1982); and *Carton v. Trustees of Tufts College*, 25 FEP Cases 1117 (1981).

5. Judicial Intervention in Promotion and Tenure Disputes

ADMINISTRATIVE AGENCIES AND COURTS have traditionally been reluctant to impose their judgments on the personnel actions of colleges and universities. This hands-off policy can be traced to the latter part of the eighteenth century (circa 1790) when a court refused to issue a writ of mandamus sought by several grammar school teachers who were seeking reinstatement.[1] Despite the 1972 amendments to Title VII, the courts have continued to defer to the judgments of institutional officers and have claimed that they do not have the expertise to evaluate academic qualifications and standards.[2] The three reasons cited by the courts for their deferential attitude toward faculty personnel decisions are (1) the courts' professed lack of expertise regarding the teaching, research, and service criteria associated with promotion and tenure decisions; (2) the long-term economic and institutional implications of tenure decisions; and (3) the sanctity of academic freedom in institutions of higher learning. The federal courts have occasionally detoured from their anti-interventionist position to examine more carefully university employment practices. Cases such as *Sweeney v. Board of Trustees of Keene State College*, *Powell v. Syracuse University*, *Kunda v. Muhlenberg College*, *Brown v. Trustees of Boston University*, and *Fisher v. Vassar College* all

---

[1]*Bracken v. Visitors of William and Mary College*, 7 Va. (3 Call.) 573, 581 (1790), cited in Elizabeth Kluger, "Sex Discrimination in the Tenure System at American Colleges and Universities: The Judicial Response," *Journal of Law and Education* 15 (Summer 1986): 325.

[2]Kluger, "Sex Discrimination in the Tenure System," pp. 324–25.

represent instances in which the federal courts have been willing to question reappointment, promotion, and tenure decisions.[3] But when viewed in relation to dozens of similar court cases, *Sweeney, Powell, Kunda, Brown,* and *Fisher* appear to represent little more than periodic short excursions off the well-beaten anti-interventionist path. This judicial posture has made it exceedingly difficult for women and minority faculty members to use Title VII or other laws in employment discrimination suits.[4] Whether the cases cited above mark a turning point for federal courts in abolishing their anti-interventionist posture remains uncertain.

LACK OF JUDICIAL EXPERTISE

University employment discrimination cases have always created a dilemma for the courts. Judges have repeatedly expressed reservations about becoming involved in academic personnel matters primarily because they feel ill equipped to question the subjective and scholarly evaluations that must be made regarding reappointment, promotion, and tenure decisions.[5]

In a 1974 case, *Faro v. New York University,* the U.S. Court of Appeals (Second Circuit) demonstrated considerable judicial deference to the university. The plaintiff, a female medical school instructor, alleged unlawful sex discrimination when New York University terminated her after a research grant expired. The court denied relief, stating that the courts are poorly suited to supervise faculty personnel decisions at the university level.[6]

---

[3]*Sweeney v. Board of Trustees of Keene State College,* 18 FEP Cases 520 (1978); *Powell v. Syracuse University,* 17 FEP Cases 1319 (1978); *Kunda v. Muhlenberg College,* 22 FEP Cases 73 (1980); and *Brown v. Trustees of Boston University,* 51 FEP Cases 815 (1989); *Fisher v. Vassar College,* 64 FEP Cases 1346 (1994).

[4]See, in general, John Anthony Palombi, "The Ineffectiveness of Title VII in Tenure Denial Decisions," *DePaul Law Review* 36 (Winter 1987): 259–83. The Civil Rights Act of 1991 (P.L. 102–6) amended Title VII to provide plaintiffs with the right to a jury trial when compensatory or punitive damages are sought. Jury trials have long been available to plaintiffs under the Age Discrimination in Employment Act, and juries are often sympathetic to older workers. If the number of jury trials increases for race, sex, and other types of discrimination, the judicial deference given to academic decision makers at colleges and universities may diminish. There is, however, a growing public skepticism about tenure in U.S. colleges and universities, and some jurors may have little sympathy for faculty who are litigating an adverse tenure decision. It will probably take several years before we can assess the impact of jury trials on promotion and tenure cases.

[5]*Smith v. University of North Carolina,* 23 FEP Cases 1758 (1980).

[6]Andrew M. Staub, "Title VII in Academia: A Critical Analysis of the Judicial Policy of Deference," *Washington University Law Quarterly* 64 (Summer 1986): 622.

Of all fields which federal courts should hesitate to invade and take over, education and appointments at the University level are probably the least suited for federal court supervision. Dr. Faro would remove any subjective judgment by her faculty colleagues in the decision-making process by having the courts examine "the university's recruitment, compensation, promotion and termination and by analyzing the way these procedures are applied to the claimant personally." . . . Such a procedure, in effect, would require a faculty committee charged with recommending or withholding advancements or tenure appointments to subject itself to a court inquiry at the behest of unsuccessful and disgruntled candidates as to why the unsuccessful was not as well qualified as the successful.[7]

The courts are generally loathe to function as super–tenure review committees.[8] In tenure cases, perhaps more than in any other employment decisions, the courts must take special care to preserve the college or university's autonomy while simultaneously protecting the civil rights of faculty.[9] The subjective aspects of evaluating a faculty member's performance have made tenure decisions an enigma for the courts. The following observation by Chief Judge Campbell of the U.S. Court of Appeals (First Circuit) is illustrative.

I believe that courts must be extremely wary of intruding into the world of university tenure decisions. These decisions necessarily hinge on subjective judgments regarding the applicant's academic excellence, teaching ability, creativity, contributions to the university community, rapport with students and colleagues, and other factors that are not susceptible of quantitative measurement. Absent discrimination, a university must be given a free hand in making such tenure decisions.[10]

The importance of allowing colleges and universities to exercise a great deal of discretion and latitude in making tenure decisions was

[7]*Faro v. New York University*, 8 FEP Cases 609 (1974). For other examples of cases in which the courts have expressed reservations about considering the merits of faculty complaints, see *Brousard-Norcross v. Augustana College Association*, 56 FEP Cases 245 (1991); *Villanueva v. Wellesley College*, 55 FEP Cases 1061 (1991); *Clark v. Whiting*, 607 F.2d 634 (4th Cir. 1979); *Huang v. College of the Holy Cross*, 15 FEP Cases 706 (1977); *Johnson v. University of Pittsburgh*, 15 FEP Cases 1516 (1977); *Keddie v. Pennsylvania State University*, 412 F. Supp. 1264 (M.D. Pa. 1976); and *Green v. Texas Tech University*, 335 F. Supp. 249 (N.D. Tex., 1971), *aff'd*, 474 F.2d 594 (5th Cir. 1973), *reh. denied*, 475 F.2d 1404 (5th Cir. 1973).

[8]See *Johnson v. University of Pittsburgh*, 15 FEP Cases 1516 (1977).

[9]*Brown v. Trustees of Boston University*, 51 FEP Cases 824 (1989).

[10]*Kumar v. Board of Trustees, University of Massachusetts*, 38 FEP Cases 1742 (1985).

stated with clarity by the U.S. Court of Appeals (Second Circuit) in *Zahorik v. Cornell University.* The court noted that tenure decisions are unique among employment decisions for five reasons:

First, tenure contracts entail commitments both as to length of time and collegial relationships which are unusual. Lifetime personal service contracts are uncommon outside the protected civil service but even there difficulties in collegial or professional relationships can be eased by transfers among departments. Professors of English, however, remain in that department for life and cannot be transferred to the History Department.

Second, academic tenure decisions are often non-competitive. Whereas in other employment settings a decision not to hire one person is usually the flip side of a decision to hire another, a decision to grant or not grant tenure to a particular person does not necessarily affect the future of other tenure candidates. In some cases, of course, the number of tenure slots is fixed and an affirmative tenure decision necessarily excludes other candidates. Even in such cases, however, the effect on those excluded is uncertain since the immediate alternate candidates have no assurance that they would have received tenure had a slot been available. For the same reason, a denial of tenure to one person does not necessarily lead to tenure for another. The number of tenure slots available may be flexible and, even where fixed, there may be no pressing need to fill vacancies since teaching chores can be discharged by non-tenured faculty.

Third, university tenure decisions are usually highly decentralized. The decision at the departmental level is of enormous importance both because of the department's stake in the matter and its superior familiarity with the field and with the candidate. Authority to overrule departmental decisions may exist, particularly in the case of affirmative decisions since the downside risk of affirmative decisions is greater than that of negative ones, but the deference given to departmental decisions grows as a case travels up the chain of authority.

Fourth, the number of factors considered in tenure decisions is quite extensive. The particular needs of the department for specialties, the number of tenure positions available, and the desired mix of well known scholars and up-and-coming faculty all must be taken into account. The individual's capacities are obviously critical. His or her teaching skills, intelligence, imagination, willingness to work, goals as a scholar and scholarly writing must be evaluated by departmental peers and outsiders asked to render advice. The evaluation does not take place in a vacuum, however, but often in the context of generations of scholarly work in the same area and always against a background of current scholarship and current reputation of others. Moreover, universities and departments within them occupy different positions in the academic pecking order and the standard of "excellence" may vary widely according to the ability to attract faculty.

Fifth, tenure decisions are a source of unusually great disagreement. Because the stakes are high, the number of relevant variables is great and there is no common unit of measure by which to judge scholarship, the dispersion of strongly held views is greater in the case of tenure decisions than with employment decisions generally. As the present record amply demonstrates, arguments pro and con are framed in largely conclusory terms which lend themselves to exaggeration, particularly since the stauncher advocates on each side may anticipate and match an expected escalation of rhetoric by their opponents. Moreover, disagreements as to individuals may reflect long standing and heated disputes as to the merits of contending schools of thought or as to the needs of a particular department. The dispersion of views occurs within departments themselves but is accentuated by the solicitation of opinion from students, faculty from other departments and faculty from other universities. Where a broad spectrum of views is sought and the candidate suggests certain persons as referents, a file composed of irreconcilable evaluations is not unusual.[11]

The court continued by stating that the context and nature of tenure decisions rarely benefit Title VII plaintiffs who seek to prove that a denial of tenure was rooted in sex, race, or other form of illegal discrimination. The court also acknowledged, however, that "a resort to illegitimate considerations can be hidden in the weighing of the numerous factors which are relevant to a tenure decision."[12] For this reason, it indicated a willingness to examine Cornell University's procedures to ensure that they were not inherently discriminatory.

Three of the five points of contention made by the Second Circuit in *Zahorik* provide only part of the story surrounding reappointment, promotion, and tenure decisions. First, although tenure contracts

[11]*Zahorik v. Cornell University*, 34 FEP Cases 169, 170 (1984).
[12]*Zahorik v. Cornell University*, 34 FEP Cases 170 (1984).

represent long-term employment commitments, tenured faculty can be terminated for gross misconduct, negligence, moral turpitude, or institutional financial emergencies.[13] Tenured professors have also resigned under duress after it was discovered that they engaged in unprofessional conduct or were linked to other improprieties.[14] Tenure, however, can provide substantial protection for faculty whose teaching, research, and service record is poor but does not border on gross negligence or incompetence. Tenured professors at state colleges and universities who are discharged must generally be afforded due process through an internal grievance hearing that takes into account mitigating circumstances.[15] Nontenured faculty at such institutions are not usually entitled to a hearing if their contracts are not renewed unless "liberty" or "property interests" are at stake.[16]

Second, tenure decisions are not necessarily noncompetitive. Some institutions, as noted in *Zahorik*, have quotas on the number or percentage of faculty who can be tenured.[17] In addition to a faculty member's scholarly and teaching abilities, tenure decisions may hinge on a candidate's academic specialty and department teaching and research needs. A department with a large tenured faculty may limit the number of faculty it will tenure to ensure there will be room for newer and more promising faculty. This can pose almost insurmount-

---

[13]See Jerome W. D. Stokes and Christopher J. Reese, "Tenure at Harvard Med: No Immunity from Ill Treatment," *Journal of Law and Education* 18 (Fall 1989): 583–92, and Timothy B. Lovain, "Grounds for Dismissing Tenured Postsecondary Faculty for Cause," *Journal of College and University Law* 10 (1983–84): 419–33. "The theory of academic freedom and tenure has also been interpreted to require financially strained institutions to place tenured professors in other suitable positions before terminating their contracts." *Browzin v. Catholic University of America*, 527 F.2d 843 (1975), quoted in Johnny C. Parker and Linda C. Parker, "Affirmative Action: Protecting the Untenured Minority Professor during Extreme Financial Exigency," *North Carolina Central Law Journal* 17 (1988): 122.

[14]See Constance Holden, "Stanford Psychiatrist Resigns under a Cloud," *Science*, July 31, 1987, pp. 479–80.

[15]*McConnell v. Howard University*, 818 F.2d 58 (1987). See also *Perry v. Sindermann*, 408 U.S. 593 (1972).

[16]*Board of Regents v. Roth*, 408 U.S. 564 (1972). The Fourteenth Amendment recognizes three areas in which due process rights arise: life, liberty, and property. A professor at a public college or university may claim a denial of liberty interests if a termination causes damage to his or her professional reputation. Deprivation of a property interest occurs when a professor has demonstrated a vested property right in a faculty position and is removed without being given the opportunity to appear before the appropriate reviewing body. Tenured college professors, in all likelihood, have a legitimate property interest in their faculty positions, as do professors who work under a written or implied contract. See William J. Holloway and Michael J. Leech, *Employment Termination: Rights and Remedies* (Washington, D.C.: BNA, 1985): 165–66.

[17]*Sola v. Lafayette College*, 42 FEP Cases 170 (1986).

able barriers to tenure when there is an abundant supply of qualified faculty in an academic specialty. Under these conditions, a department can establish rigorous promotion and tenure standards that reflect the highly competitive, survival-of-the-fittest labor market. Thus, tenure decisions may be competitive although the identities of specific competitors may be unknown to the untenured professor whose job is on the line.

Third, an examination of the cases indicates that there is probably less disagreement among peer review committees, department heads, deans, and other academic officers than is suggested in *Zahorik*. When disagreements do arise, they usually occur at the college level among peer review committees, department heads, and deans. Only rarely does the chief academic officer veto a promotion or tenure decision when there is unanimity at department and college levels. An analysis of the cases reveals that judges are more likely to rule in favor of a faculty member when the faculty member's promotion or tenure request was supported by the departmental peer review committee.

LONG-TERM IMPLICATIONS OF TENURE DECISIONS

The courts are cognizant of the far-reaching implications of a college or university's decision to grant tenure.[18] The primary purpose of tenure is to uphold academic freedom and to prevent retaliatory termination of faculty who hold or espouse unpopular ideas.[19] Unlike other employment decisions, conferring tenure not only binds the institution to a long-term employment and financial commitment, it also affects its academic mission. One of the most eloquent statements regarding the perils of tenure was made by a New York State court:

> Although permanency of employment has advantages, it has its evils as well. With employment secured permanently, an incentive for diligence disappears. Tenure can provide a haven for competent, though dull and unimaginative, instructors. At worst, tenure may protect the marginally competent from replacement by the more qualified. Moreover, tenure tends to freeze the university into a designated number of faculty posi-

---

[18]*Keyishian v. Board of Regents*, 385 U.S. 589 (1967).
[19]James H. Brooks, "Confidentiality of Tenure Review and Discovery of Peer Review Materials," *Brigham Young University Law Review* (Fall 1988): 709.

tions in each academic department. For example, if two young mathematics professors with similar specialties are granted tenure at a prestigious university today, the university must act on the reasonable likelihood that they will still be there 30 years later, though the university may no longer require two instructors with the same technical expertise. Thus, tenure is not an item lightly to be conferred, for the granting of tenure is likely to shape the university's future for years to come.[20]

In contrasting the termination of an employee from an "ordinary job" with the demise of tenure of a faculty member at a state university, the New Jersey Supreme Court stated that granting tenure to a faculty member who is not qualified "is plainly contrary to sound educational administration" and is not in the best interests of the public.[21] Judicial deference toward institutions of higher learning is incongruous with the fact that there are other nonacademic jobs that guarantee job security comparable to tenure. Employees of state or federal civil service agencies who are no longer on probationary status have traditionally enjoyed job security equivalent to that of tenured college professors.[22] Yet the courts have not granted the same special treatment to federal and state government agencies under Title VII that they have afforded colleges and universities.

The debate over the wisdom and effects of tenure will probably continue. The Commission on Academic Tenure in Higher Education has delineated several arguments for and against tenure.[23] Arguments favoring the tenure system include the position that tenure is an essential condition of academic freedom and that it creates a faculty that has a long-term commitment to the institution. Proponents of tenure also believe that the system minimizes competitive economic incentives among faculty, encourages faculty to concentrate on their basic obligations of teaching and research, and helps offset the lower financial rewards of a career in higher education. Achieving tenure should be regarded as a career *milestone* rather than as a career *objective*.

[20]*New York Institute of Technology v. State Division of Human Rights*, 35 FEP Cases 1125 (1976).

[21]*Countiss v. Trenton State College*, 34 FEP Cases 1548 (1978).

[22]George R. Kramer, "Title VII on Campus: Judicial Review of University Employment Decisions," *Columbia Law Review* 82 (1982): 1206.

[23]See Commission on Academic Tenure in Higher Education, *Faculty Tenure: A Report and Recommendations by the Commission on Academic Tenure in Higher Education* (San Francisco: Jossey-Bass, 1973), pp. 13–20.

Tenure is kind of a paradox. It is both an ending and a beginning. For the academic who has endured a grueling six- to eight-year doctoral program, the ordeal of a job search and then, once hired, a probationary period of another six or seven years, attaining tenure is a culmination. It is a rite of passage that bestows a well-earned recognition and success, as well as relief from job uncertainty. But at the same time, it signals—or should signal—the onset of a long and fruitful career, one that may bring further promotions and rewards.[24]

The tenure system also forces colleges and universities to make "hard" rather than tentative decisions about faculty retention. If tenure were replaced with a series of multiyear contracts, peer review committees, department heads, and deans might be tempted to give marginal faculty members the benefit of the doubt when their contracts came up for renewal. Hampshire College in Amherst, Massachusetts, originally offered faculty three- to five-year contracts instead of tenure. It found, however, that short-term contracts made it tempting to procrastinate in making difficult personnel decisions. Frederick Weaver, a professor of economics and history at Hampshire, has stated that "some people were being retained on very short leashes who should have been let go" because there was always the "soft option" of another three-year contract. In the 1980s, Hampshire College moved toward the more traditional tenure system by offering faculty two initial three-year contracts followed by ten-year contracts.[25]

Arguments against tenure include the contention that academic due process, rather than academic freedom, is the essential condition of employment. Tenure systems are also accused of imposing financial burdens on colleges and universities, fostering mediocrity and "dead wood" in faculty ranks, and encouraging litigation when a decision is made to deny tenure. The tenure system has also been attacked for lowering the standards of undergraduate teaching (tenured faculty often want to teach graduate courses only) and providing a sanctuary for political activists who encourage disruptions on campuses. Perhaps the most critical charge against tenure is that it not only fails to ensure academic freedom but actually discourages it.

[24]Karen C. Blansfield, "The Tenure Debate," *Carolina Alumni Review* 82 (Spring 1993): 19–20.
[25]Amanda Bennett, "Tenure: Many Will Decry It, Few Deny It," *Wall Street Journal,* Oct. 11, 1994, p. B1.

The following comments made by a physics professor at Columbia University who was offered tenure but turned it down summarize this view:

> I turned down tenure because I believe that the university tenure system should be abolished. Tenure is rooted in the premise that academic freedom and review of performance are somehow antithetical. It is, however, used more often to deprive young academics of freedom than to defend the senior faculty it is designed to protect. It can exclude productive, energetic scholars from the system, maintain unproductive, unmotivated teachers in our universities, and discourage our best young minds from pursuing academic careers. Finally, it attracts and protects faculty members more concerned about preserving their job security than in defending their convictions, a group carefully selected to nurture established norms rather than one committed to the vigorous pursuit of knowledge.[26]

During the past decade, the percentage of tenured faculty in the United States remained at about 63 percent, although the percentage is expected to decline slightly. This decline will likely occur as a small number of colleges and universities abolish tenure or institute a system of renewable faculty contracts. Other institutions are replacing departing tenured faculty with part-time or nontenure-track instructors. Still other institutions are offering early retirement incentives to older tenured faculty.[27] Despite the projected declines, most faculty covet tenure and are willing to go to great lengths to attain and protect it. When tenure is denied, the record provides ample illustration of the willingness of some faculty to pursue wrongful discharge and employment discrimination litigation.

ACADEMIC FREEDOM: IMPLICATIONS FOR PROMOTION AND TENURE DECISIONS

Academic freedom looms large among the reasons federal and state courts maintain an anti-interventionist posture regarding reappointment, promotion, and tenure decisions.[28] According to the courts,

[26]David Helfand, "I Turned Down Tenure: Why Other Professors Should, Too," *Washington Monthly*, June 1986, p. 13.

[27]William H. Honan, "Wary of Entrenchment in the Ranks, Colleges Offer Alternatives to Tenure," *New York Times*, April 20, 1994, p. B13.

[28]When the 1972 amendments to Title VII were being debated by Congress, Senator James Browning Allen, a Democrat from Alabama, voiced concern that "objective criticism, independent judgment, the search for truth unhampered by transient political interests—all of which are vital to academic freedom—could be altered or reshaped by the EEOC." *Congressional Record*, 92d Cong., 1st sess., Feb. 28, 1972, pp. 946, 949.

academic freedom furthers society's interest in the uncensored development and availability of ideas.[29] The concept of academic freedom is based on the rationale that there may be no undue interference by special-interest groups with the promotion of scholarship, the exchange of ideas and the pursuit of truth, the discovery of new knowledge, and the transmission of that knowledge through teaching.[30] The U.S. Supreme Court has fostered academic freedom because of the important societal interest in the uninhibited flow of ideas.[31] Although academic freedom is not a specifically enumerated constitutional right, it has long been a special concern under the First Amendment.[32] The extent and importance of academic freedom was promoted by Justice Felix Frankfurter in *Sweezy v. New Hampshire* when he spoke of the "four essential freedoms" of universities: (1) who may teach, (2) who may be taught, (3) how it may be taught, and (4) who may be admitted to study.[33] Some faculty and college officials argue that academic freedom is fundamental to achieving academic excellence.[34]

[29]"Comment: Drawing the Line on Academic Freedom: Rejecting an Academic Peer Review Privilege for Tenure Committee Deliberations," *Washington University Law Quarterly* 64 (1986): 1272.

[30]See George R. Kramer, "Title VII on Campus: Judicial Review of University Employment Decisions," *Columbia Law Review* 82 (1982): 1223, n. 103: "[Academic freedom's] historic roots lie in the independence of academic institutions from other centers of power. The medieval university first shielded freedom to teach and learn. The economic power acquired by universities, and the respect that learning commanded both for its own sake and as an adjunct to theology, gave universities influence and leeway against encroachment by [the] state or church. Amid the decentralized and conflicting powers of medieval Europe, the universities were able to foster a free spirit of inquiry among their students and faculties, within whatever margin spiritual belief allowed.

"After the emergence of strong nation-states, universities no longer inhabited a power vacuum. In many places, the development of learning and the proper subjects of scholarship evolved into matters of national policy and expediency, as they remain today. Paradoxically, academic freedom was transformed in the autocratic atmosphere of nineteenth-century Germany. Freedom for faculty and students won wide acceptance under the concepts of *Lernfreiheit* and *Lehrfreiheit*. The former term referred to the freedom of a university professor to research, teach, and publish as a professional prerogative. *Lehrfreiheit* meant the freedom of students to pursue their studies as they saw fit free of administrative constraints on courses, attendance, or grades.

"The perceived virtues of German academic freedom worked a cathartic effect on American academia, which adopted the idea of academic freedom as an individual right of professors to speak and teach on matters within their scope of expertise free of extramural pressure. The traditional institutional safeguard for this freedom is tenure." (Citations omitted)

[31]See *Keyishian v. Board of Regents*, 385 U.S. 589 (1967).

[32]*Dixon v. Rutgers, the State University of New Jersey*, 52 FEP Cases 1625 (1988), quoting *Regents of the University of California v. Bakke*, 17 FEP Cases 1000 (1978).

[33]*Sweezy v. New Hampshire*, 77 S. Ct. 1203 (1957).

[34]James H. Brooks, "Confidentiality of Tenure Review and Discovery of Peer Review

Legal scholars have delineated two strands of academic freedom—individual and institutional. The individual strand concerns a faculty member's freedom to teach, express his or her thoughts, and explore new ideas without fear of censorship by the government or special-interest groups.[35] Individual academic freedom has been asserted frequently and is firmly entrenched as a constitutional right.[36] *Sweezy* deals with the second and less developed institutional strand. A university's ability to grant or deny tenure, for example, falls under the rubric of this strand; the right of colleges and universities to select and retain only those faculty whose performance clearly warrants tenure is well within the bounds described by Justice Frankfurter.

> It does not follow that because academic freedom is inextricably related to the educational process it is implicated in every employment decision of an educational institution. Colleges may fail to promote or grant tenure for a variety of reasons, such as anticipated decline in enrollment, retrenchment for budgetary reasons, termination of some departments, or determination that there are higher priorities elsewhere. These are decisions which may affect the quality of education but do not necessarily intrude upon the nature of the educational process itself.[37]

The courts have held, however, that academic freedom should not be construed as a license to engage in illegal discrimination.[38] In a

---

Materials," *Brigham Young University Law Review* (Fall 1988): 712. Also see "Academic Freedom and Federal Regulation of University Hiring," *Harvard Law Review* 92 (Feb. 1979): 879–97.

[35] A faculty member's right to academic freedom is not without limits. Faculty have the right, as citizens, to act or speak on matters of public concern. The faculty member at a state-assisted institution must demonstrate that his or her speech was a substantial motivating factor in the college's decision to dismiss or deny tenure. When a faculty member at a state school speaks out about matters that are only of a personal interest (e.g., complaints about class assignments or other internal department matters), then such statements may not be regarded by the courts as constitutionally protected free speech. The courts must balance two considerations: (1) the faculty member's right to speak freely on public issues and (2) the institution's right to manage its affairs efficiently and without disruption. The faculty member must demonstrate that his or her termination was motivated substantially by an action or speech that was a matter of public concern. See *Pickering v. Board of Education*, 391 U.S. 563 (1968). If these burdens are met, then the college or university may still terminate the faculty member if it can show, by a preponderance of the evidence, that it would have taken the same action in the absence of the protected activity (i.e., the faculty member would have been terminated anyway because of poor teaching and an inadequate number of scholarly publications). See *Mt. Healthy Board of Education v. Doyle*, 429 U.S. 274 (1977).

[36] Charles J. Stevens, "Preventing Unnecessary Intrusions on University Autonomy: A Proposed Academic Freedom Privilege," *California Law Review* 69 (1981): 1546.

[37] *Kunda v. Muhlenberg College*, 22 FEP Cases 73 (1980).

[38] See *Bob Jones University v. United States*, 461 U.S. 575 (1983), and *Regents of the University of California v. Bakke*, 438 U.S. 265 (1978).

controversial case at the University of Georgia, a faculty member, James A. Dinnan, refused to reveal his vote in a promotion and tenure decision and was held in contempt of court. The court was forced to determine where the line existed between academic freedom and a faculty member's right to delve into the reasons she was denied a promotion and tenure.[39] The court summarized its position as follows:

> Though we recognize the importance of academic freedom, we must also recognize its limits. The public policy of the United States prohibits discrimination; Professor Dinnan and the University of Georgia are not above that policy. To rule otherwise would mean that the concept of academic freedom would give any institution of higher learning a *carte Blanche* to practice discrimination of all types.[40]

There has been increasing concern by the EEOC and courts regarding the wisdom of some academic personnel decisions that offer the potential to conceal illegal discrimination behind the protection of academic freedom. In *Powell v. Syracuse University*, the U.S. Court of Appeals (Second Circuit) noted:

> In recent years, many courts have cited the Faro opinion for the broad proposition that courts should exercise minimal scrutiny of college and university employment practices. Other courts, while not citing Faro, have concurred in its sentiments.
>
> This anti-interventionist policy has rendered colleges and universities virtually immune to charges of employment bias, at least when that bias is not expressed overtly. We fear, however, that the common-sense position we took in Faro, namely that courts must be ever-mindful of relative institutional competences, has been pressed beyond all reasonable limits, and may be employed to undercut the explicit legislative intent of the Civil Rights Act of 1964. . . .
>
> It is our task, then, to steer a careful course between excessive intervention in the affairs of the university and the unwarranted tolerance of unlawful behavior. *Faro* does not, and was never intended to, indicate that academic freedom embraces the freedom to discriminate.[41]

[39]The issues of discovery and the confidentiality of peer review committee proceedings is discussed in a subsequent section of this monograph.
[40]*In re Dinnan*, 27 FEP Cases 292 (1981). Also see *Blaubergs v. Board of Regents of the University of Georgia*, 27 FEP Cases 287 (1980).
[41]*Powell v. Syracuse University*, 17 FEP Cases 1319 (1978).

A prime example of an attempt by the courts to walk carefully the line between wanting to avoid involvement in the academic matters of a university and ensuring that a faculty member is not the victim of illegal discrimination came in *Brown v. Trustees of Boston University*.[42] This case marked one of the few times that the courts were willing to challenge directly the substantive merits of a university's decision to deny tenure. Boston University English professor Julia Prewitt Brown was denied tenure despite the unanimous support of a department peer review committee. The president of the university refused to grant her tenure on the basis of the unfavorable recommendations from scholars outside the school and the mixed reviews of a book she had written. The U.S. Court of Appeals (First Circuit) undertook an extensive review of Brown's qualifications, including the quality of her teaching and her publications. The court also compared Brown's qualifications with those of other faculty who were granted tenure and discovered that her credentials were superior. Although the court paid homage to the concept of academic freedom and said that the judiciary should be "extremely wary of intruding into the world of university tenure decisions," the court also stated that "the University's prerogative to make tenure decisions must be subordinated to the goals embodied in Title VII." In making its decision, the First Circuit also rejected Boston University's contention that an award of tenure to Brown would infringe on the institution's right to determine who may teach. The court stated that "we respect universities' judgment only so long as they do not discriminate."[43]

In a subsequent section I discuss the increased willingness of federal courts to invade the sanctity of college and university personnel decisions by examining the documentation and deliberations surrounding reappointment, promotion, and tenure decisions.[44] It is one thing, however, to require a peer review committee, department head, or dean to submit confidential documents and reveal individual votes to a court for judicial scrutiny and quite another to infer an illegal race, sex, or other animus from such documents.

The courts are also mindful that faculty who challenge promotion and tenure decisions impose a tremendous burden on both academic

---

[42]*Brown v. Trustees of Boston University*, 51 FEP Cases 815 (1989).

[43]James E. Brammer, Dina L. Lallo, and Sarah Ney, "*Brown v. Trustees of Boston University*: The Realization of Title VII's Legislative Intent," *Journal of College and University Law* 17 (1991): 560–61.

[44]See *University of Pennsylvania v. EEOC*, 51 FEP Cases 1118 (1990).

administrators, who must defend their decisions, and the judicial system, which must process their complaints. The court's position in this regard was evident in *Lieberman v. Gant*, a case involving a female English professor who was denied tenure by the University of Connecticut, allegedly because of her weak scholarship. She claimed that the adverse decision was made because she was a woman and an advocate of women's rights.[45]

> This [case] produced a transcript of nearly 10,000 pages and almost 400 exhibits and consumed 52 days of court time. The docket entries stretch over 32 pages. Trial concluded on May 26, 1978. Briefs were directed to be filed no later than July 31, but the court later granted an extension until March 5, 1979, a deadline which [the] defendants met. . . .
>
> We do not understand how either the federal courts or universities can operate if the many adverse tenure decisions against women or members of a minority group that must be made each year are regularly taken to court and entail burdens such as those here incurred. This is not the first lengthy trial in a case of this sort.[46]

The court made it clear at the outset that its task was to determine whether the university's evaluation of the plaintiff was procedurally fair and substantively reasonable. Additionally, the court suggested that it would give deference to the professional judgment of the university officials who made tenure decisions. The court emphasized, however, that it would still scrutinize subjective evaluations of the faculty member's teaching, scholarship, and service to ensure that the motives behind the denial of tenure were not discriminatory.[47]

Colleges and universities should be allowed a sufficient degree of autonomy to ensure that they are able to maintain academic integrity and chart their own courses. But a crucial question that remains largely unanswered is under what conditions the courts should be willing to drop their anti-interventionist posture and examine pro-

---

[45]For a detailed discussion of this case, see "A Faculty Wife Who Was Not a Gentleman," in George R. LaNoue and Barbara A. Lee, *Academics in Court: The Consequences of Faculty Discrimination Litigation* (Ann Arbor: University of Michigan Press, 1987), pp. 51–88.

[46]*Lieberman v. Gant*, 23 FEP Cases 506 (1980).

[47]Elizabeth Kluger, "Sex Discrimination in the Tenure System at American Colleges and Universities: The Judicial Response," *Journal of Law and Education* 15 (Summer 1986): 329.

motion and tenure decisions. It has been suggested that the courts should place a faculty member's interests above the institution's interests in autonomy under three conditions.[48] First, the faculty member shows that the institution did not comply with its own written reappointment, promotion, and tenure procedures. In state-assisted colleges and universities, a significant deviation from internal personnel procedures might be viewed by the state as a lack of due process. Denial of procedural or substantive due process by a state institution might also run afoul of the Fourteenth Amendment to the U.S. Constitution.

Second, the faculty member demonstrates that written procedures, even if followed, do not provide adequate protection against illegal discrimination. For example, if too much power over promotion and tenure decisions is vested in one person, or if peer review committees are not given sufficient input, then the faculty member may argue that the institution's interests in autonomy have been eroded and judicial deference is not warranted.

Third, the faculty member is able to produce substantial evidence of a racist, sexist, or other illegal bias. Burden of proof considerations regarding such biases are discussed in a subsequent section.

The courts appear to be attempting to strike a balance between preserving the academic freedom of colleges and universities and protecting faculty from invidious discrimination. This posture may eventually result in a shift from the subjective application of vague criteria by colleges and universities in their reappointment, promotion, and tenure decisions to a more objective and extensively documented set of criteria. To date, however, the scales have been tipped decidedly in favor of the institution. Unless a faculty member can demonstrate a substantial procedural irregularity or blatant evidence of discrimination, the odds of reversing a negative reappointment, promotion, or tenure decision remain low.

[48]Kramer, "Title VII on Campus," pp. 1229–32.

6. CRITERIA FOR MAKING PROMOTION AND TENURE DECISIONS

REAPPOINTMENT, PROMOTION, AND TENURE decisions hinge on two categories of criteria. The first category includes the personal accomplishments or characteristics of the individual faculty member, such as his or her effectiveness as a teacher, research and publications record, service activities, and collegiality. The second category includes institutional needs as dictated by financial constraints, departmental growth or decline, and curricular or program changes. Personnel decisions involving faculty members are affected primarily by personal criteria and to a lesser extent by institutional concerns.

An important aspect of the criteria on which reappointment, promotion, and tenure decisions are based is their measurability. Employment criteria can be divided into objective and subjective measures. Objective measures are those that can be readily observed and counted; they include the type of degree held by a faculty member, years of service, the number of books and journal articles published, the incidence of committee assignments, and the frequency of public service activities.

Subjective measures are those that are open to varying degrees of interpretation by peer review committees, department heads, and others. Such measures include the quality of the institution from which a faculty member received his or her graduate degree, the reputation and quality of the journals in which a faculty member's work appears, the quality of a faculty member's teaching, the significance of the service activities performed by a faculty member, and a faculty member's ability to work in harmony with colleagues.

A primary difficulty in dealing with wrongful discharge or employment discrimination cases in academia is that such cases almost always hinge on *personal* attributes that must be evaluated *subjectively*. This issue was summarized in *Lewis v. Chicago State College*: "A professor's value depends upon his creativity, his rapport with students and colleagues, his teaching ability, and numerous other intangible qualities which cannot be measured by objective standards."[1]

A U.S. district court in Texas expressed similar sentiments on subjective promotion and tenure standards:

> The qualities of a good university professor simply cannot be reduced to a rigid formula to be applied uniformly to each candidate. This observation does not apply only to universities and is not intended to carve a special exception for them. It is made simply to emphasize that subjectivity is not in itself illegal. While obviously presenting a *potential* for discrimination, subjective evaluations still have an important role in decision-making processes. This is another way of saying that we know there are prediction factors which as yet we have not quantified. Of course such subjectivity must withstand the test of nondiscriminatory impact.[2] (Emphasis in the original)

An analysis of court cases indicates that subjective judgments of a faculty member's teaching and research pose a difficult dilemma. The U.S. Court of Appeals (Seventh Circuit), in *Namenwirth v. Board of Regents of the University of Wisconsin System*, concluded that the inherent subjectivity of the tenure process creates an irresolvable problem. Marion Namenwirth was the first woman to be hired by the Department of Zoology at the University of Wisconsin campus in Madison in thirty-five years, and she was also the first woman to be denied tenure by the department. Although the court recognized a history of sex discrimination at the university, it refused to second-guess the university's evaluation of Namenwirth's academic potential relative to that of a male faculty member who was granted tenure. The court concluded that it could not infer illegal discrimination from collegial judgments about a faculty member's worth or potential.[3]

---

[1]*Lewis v. Chicago State College*, 2 FEP Cases 96 (1969).

[2]*Cooper v. University of Texas at Dallas*, 22 FEP Cases 1070 (1979). See also *Wilkins v. University of Houston*, 26 FEP Cases 1241 (1981).

[3]Andrew M. Staub, "Title VII in Academia: A Critical Analysis of the Judicial Policy of Deference," *Washington University Law Quarterly* 64 (Summer 1986): 624–25.

To allow the decision-maker also to act as the source of judgments of qualification would ordinarily defeat the purpose of the discrimination laws. But in the case of tenure decisions we see no alternative. Tenure decisions have always relied primarily on judgments about academic potential, and there is no algorithm for producing those judgments. Given the similar research output of two candidates, an experienced faculty committee might— quite rightly—come to different conclusions about the potential of the candidates. It is not our place to question the significance or validity of such conclusions.

But to say all that is only to face up to the problem. The problem remains: faculty votes should not be permitted to camouflage discrimination, even the unconscious discrimination of well-meaning and established scholars. The courts have struggled with the problem since Title VII was extended to the university, and have found no solution. Because of the way we have described the problem—the decision-maker is also the source of the qualifications—there may be no solution; winning the esteem of one's colleagues is just an essential part of securing tenure. And that seems to mean that in a case of this sort, where it is a matter of comparing qualification against qualification, the plaintiff is bound to lose.[4]

It is telling in *Namenwirth* that "winning the esteem of one's colleagues" is seen as "an essential part of securing tenure." Faculty acquire the respect of their senior colleagues on the basis of such criteria as research and teaching performance. "Citizenship," as evidenced by a faculty member's willingness to serve on department committees or help with faculty and student recruitment and fund raising, is also a legitimate, nondiscriminatory criterion in promotion and tenure decisions. But, if "winning the esteem of one's colleagues" means being of the same gender or race as members of the peer review committee, department heads, or deans, then a serious problem exists. Unfortunately, the courts' "hands-off" posture in cases such as *Namenwirth* may allow the use of illicit criteria to creep into promotion and tenure decisions.

In response to the majority opinion in *Namenwirth*, Senior Circuit Judge Swygert wrote the dissent that criticized the anti-interventionist attitude that has been taken by state and federal courts in employ-

---

[4]*Namenwirth v. Board of Regents of the University of Wisconsin System*, 38 FEP Cases 1161 (1985).

ment discrimination cases involving college and university faculty members:

> I do not see a qualitative distinction between a tenure decision and any other employment decision. The subjective esteem of colleagues and supervisors is often the key to any employment decision. Yet, especially in the blue-collar context, the courts have not hesitated to review with great suspicion subjective judgments that adversely affect minorities. . . . And because all lawyers are trained in academia, courts are better equipped to scrutinize academic decisionmaking than decisionmaking in the perhaps less familiar blue-collar context.[5]

Judge Swygert also appealed to the use of common sense in inferring discrimination against Namenwirth because of past discriminatory acts at the University of Wisconsin. The judge wrote that the courts could correct for their lack of academic expertise by relying on outside experts, especially when attempting to assess the quality of a faculty member's research and scholarship.

In *Pace College v. Commission on Human Rights of the City of New York*, the court noted that educational institutions "are not 'businesses' where employees are all fairly fungible unskilled or semiskilled workers" but places where "subjective judgments necessarily have a proper and legitimate role."[6] Furthermore, reappointment, promotion, and tenure standards change over time as a result of changes in institutional leadership and mission.[7] There is no need for an institution to exhibit perfect consistency in subjective matters such as promotion or tenure decisions as long as such decisions are not tainted by an illegal discriminatory animus.[8] A Massachusetts federal district court, for example, recognized that colleges and universities have the right to raise promotion and tenure standards to reflect changing institutional needs. The court made the following comment in the case of Dawn Hooker, the physical education instructor who was denied tenure at Tufts University:

---

[5]*Namenwirth v. Board of Regents of the University of Wisconsin System*, 38 FEP Cases 1162 (1985).

[6]*Pace College v. Commission on Human Rights of the City of New York*, 19 FEP Cases 431 (1975), cited in *New York Institute of Technology v. State Division of Human Rights*, 35 FEP Cases 1125 (1976).

[7]See *Jamerson v. The Board of Trustees of the University of Alabama*, 27 FEP Cases 441 (1981), and *Scott v. University of Delaware*, 19 FEP Cases 1734 (1979).

[8]*Langland v. Vanderbilt University*, 36 FEP Cases 220 (1984), and *Rios v. Board of Regents of the University of Arizona*, 43 FEP Cases 237 (1987).

The fact is that achieving tenure at a major academic institution is a highly selective and elitist process. Certain pedestrian concepts of fairness, for example, that one should be rewarded for a job well done, are inapposite in this context. The institution has broad discretion to set very high standards and thus to decline to retain exceedingly talented people. Similarly, it has broad discretion to waive its own standards when the needs of the institution so dictate, so long as such decisions do not run afoul of the mandate of Title VII or other applicable law.[9]

Cases concerned with whether faculty deserved a promotion or tenure have also focused on whether they did more than meet the initial set of criteria set forth in their institution's faculty manual or handbook. As a general rule, the courts have held that merely meeting the minimum standards does not necessarily warrant a favorable decision. For example, the U.S. Court of Appeals (First Circuit), which reversed a U.S. district court and ruled in favor of the University of Massachusetts, stated:

> It seems to us that the district court . . . treated Title VII of the Civil Rights Act of 1964 as though it were an affirmative action statute, and so proceeded on the theory that once a candidate was "qualified" under the standards of the university, it would be pretextual for the university's administrator not to appoint him on the ground that he did not measure up to the administrator's vision of the ideal teacher. But this overlooks the difference between the selection of a craftsman and of a professional. A bricklayer who can properly lay a specified number of bricks in a specified period is ordinarily as good as any other bricklayer likely to appear. But in the selection of a professor, judge, lawyer, doctor, or Indian chief, while there may be appropriate minimum standards, the selector has a right to seek distinction beyond the minimum indispensable qualities.[10]

Nevertheless, the element of subjectivity in reappointment, promotion, and tenure decisions creates the possibility "that discriminatory attitudes may be hidden subtly behind subjective standards."[11] When Congress decided in 1972 to include academic institutions under Title VII, there was extensive discussion of the fact that the

[9]*Hooker v. Tufts University*, 37 FEP Cases 518 (1983).
[10]*Kumar v. Board of Trustees, University of Massachusetts*, 38 FEP Cases 1742 (1985).
[11]*Johnson v. Michigan State University*, 30 FEP Cases (1982).

central problem of employment discrimination was not overt discrimination but covert bias and the systematic exclusion of women and minorities from certain jobs because of facially neutral hiring and promotion criteria.[12] According to Harvard law professor Elizabeth Bartholet, the elitist nature of higher-level jobs has apparently created a differential standard between selection and promotion systems "primarily on the basis of the social and economic status of the jobs involved."

> Judges defer to the employers with whom they identify, and they uphold the kinds of selection systems from which they have benefited. When they deal with prestigious jobs, the courts show an appreciation of the apparent rationality of the employment procedures at issue and a respect for the decisionmakers involved that can only be explained by the fact that these cases confront the courts with their own world. Judges have a personal investment in traditional selection procedures on the upper level. By contrast, courts can readily strike down a civil service test or a . . . subjective system because, not knowing or caring much about how blue collar workers are chosen or promoted, judges find it easy to focus on the social harm of racial exclusion.
>
> In deferring to upper level employers, courts often profess their lack of expertise. Only the universities, the courts say, are competent to assess teacher qualifications and to design appropriate selection and promotion systems. But courts are surely more qualified to intervene in academic decisions, with which they have some familiarity, than to decide who is qualified to serve in highly skilled blue collar jobs or how they should be chosen. It is the courts' expertise, rather than the lack of it, that makes them reluctant to interfere at the upper level. They know these decisionmakers; they sympathize and identify with their concerns and their use of traditional selection methods.[13]

One New York attorney, Judith P. Vladeck, who is a veteran of several major sex discrimination cases involving female faculty, of-

---

[12]Elizabeth Bartholet, "Application of Title VII to Jobs in High Places," *Harvard Law Review* 95 (March 1982): 982.

[13]Bartholet, "Application of Title VII," pp. 979–80. Also see Amy B. Ginensky and Andrew B. Rogoff, "Subjective Employment Criteria and the Future of Title VII in Professional Jobs," *Journal of Urban Law* 54 (1976): 165–236, and Lois Vanderwaerdt, "Higher Education Discrimination and the Courts," *Journal of Law and Education* 10 (Oct. 1981): 467–83.

fered the following observation regarding the typical judge's knowledge of academic employment practices.

> The terminology—the *deans*, and the *provosts*, and the *adjuncts*, and the *tenure track*—is such mystical language that it creates a problem for the ordinary judge trying to understand the employment practices of universities. This has caused a certain hands-off policy. If they don't understand it, they want to leave it alone.[14] (Emphasis in the original)

Reference has been made to a "sliding scale" in which the courts are more willing to defer to the judgments of personnel decision makers as the courts' estimation of a particular job's mental difficulty, educational requirements, prestige, and social importance increases. As a job becomes more complex, it appears that the courts are requiring more convincing evidence before ruling that an employer engaged in illegal employment discrimination.[15]

Employment discrimination cases often hinge on whether the criteria for hiring or promotion are job-related. But in cases involving colleges and universities, job relevance rarely, if ever, is discussed. The three traditional criteria—research, teaching, and service—that are evaluated by peer review committees when making reappointment, promotion, and tenure decisions appear to be well established and beyond reproach. The courts apparently have taken the position that traditional Title VII standards are inappropriate for complex jobs such as college professor because of the special difficulties in linking the criteria for promotion and tenure to job-relatedness and business necessity. Furthermore, the courts have taken the stance that defining and measuring effective performance for upper-level jobs is either impractical or too difficult.[16] Faculty who have challenged negative promotion or tenure decisions have not focused on the legitimacy of the teaching, research, and service requirements per se. Instead, they have primarily attacked the fairness with which colleges and universities have administered these criteria. Likewise, the "seven-year up-or-out rule" that is used by most colleges and universities has also withstood the test of legitimacy.[17]

---

[14]Judith P. Vladeck, "Litigation: Strategy of Last Resort," in Jennie Farley, ed., *Sex Discrimination in Higher Education: Strategies for Equality* (Ithaca, N.Y.: New York State School of Industrial and Labor Relations, Cornell University, 1981), p. 7.

[15]"Tenure and Partnership as Title VII Remedies," *Harvard Law Review* 94 (1980): 472.

[16]Bartholet, "Application of Title VII," pp. 984–85.

[17]*Carpenter v. Board of Regents of the University of Wisconsin System,* 34 FEP Cases 252 (1984).

The courts may be more willing to evaluate subjective factors in employment decisions somewhat differently since the U.S. Supreme Court's decision in *Watson v. Fort Worth Bank & Trust*.[18] Clara Watson, who is black, was employed by Fort Worth Bank & Trust. She was rejected for promotion to supervisory positions on four occasions, and each time a white employee was promoted instead. In court, Watson produced evidence that the bank (1) had never had a black officer or director, (2) paid black employees lower salaries than white employees for equivalent work, and (3) evaluated black employees less favorably than whites on performance reviews. These disparities were analyzed and found to be statistically significant. There was no dispute that the white supervisors at the bank made hiring and promotion decisions using subjective criteria.

As noted earlier, there are two types of discrimination cases: disparate treatment and disparate impact. Under the disparate treatment theory, an *intent* to discriminate must be shown. Because of the statistical proof that supported the claim of disparate impact and because intentional discrimination is often difficult (if not impossible) to prove, Watson's case was pursued as one of disparate impact discrimination. The use of subjective employment criteria in this case broke new legal ground in civil rights cases.

Both the district court and the U.S. Court of Appeals (Fifth Circuit) had ruled that the bank was not racially discriminatory in using subjective criteria in its decision not to promote Watson. The U.S. Supreme Court granted certiorari in *Watson* to determine whether the lower courts had properly held that the disparate impact theory was inapplicable to a subjective or discretionary promotion system.[19] The Court determined that subjective criteria could be used in a disparate impact analysis and remanded the case back to the lower courts for further consideration.

In spite of *Watson*, it is difficult to measure the critical but intangible qualities that contribute to the effectiveness of supervisory and professional employees. As the Court noted:

---

[18]*Watson v. Fort Worth Bank & Trust*, 47 FEP Cases 102 (1988).

[19]Certiorari is an order or writ from a higher court demanding that a lower court send up the record of a case for review. Most cases that reach the U.S. Supreme Court do so because the Court has issued such a writ or has "granted certiorari." If certiorari is denied by the U.S. Supreme Court, it means that the justices are content to let the lower court's decision stand. Adapted from Jay M. Shafritz, *Dictionary of Personnel Management and Labor Relations* (Oak Park, Ill.: Moore, 1980), p. 48.

Respondent [Ft. Worth Bank & Trust] warns, however, that "validating" subjective selection criteria in this way is impracticable. Some qualities—for example, common sense, good judgment, originality, ambition, loyalty, and tact—cannot be measured accurately through standardized testing techniques. Moreover, success at many jobs in which qualities are crucial cannot itself be measured directly. Opinions often differ when managers and supervisors are evaluated, and the same can be said for many jobs that involve close cooperation with one's coworkers or complex and subtle tasks like the provision of professional services or personal counseling.[20]

The Court wrote that business necessity can be established in a number of ways and "will vary with the type and size of the business in question."[21] Business necessity may be established through formal validation studies, expert testimony, and prior successful experience. In mentioning the latter, the Court quoted *Zahorik* and the "generations of experience reflecting job-relatedness of [a] decentralized decisionmaking structure based on peer judgments in the academic setting." The reference to *Zahorik* indicates that according to the Court, colleges and universities have amply demonstrated business necessity. Furthermore, it could be a signal that the Court has no immediate interest in allowing challenges to the methods that colleges and universities have traditionally used to make reappointment, promotion, and tenure decisions.

Since most academic employment discrimination cases are based on the disparate treatment theory instead of the disparate impact theory, the impact of *Watson* on colleges and universities may not be significant. That the Supreme Court is willing to expand its view of subjective employment criteria could result, however, in more disparate impact and class-action claims against institutions of higher education in the future. The bright side of the *Watson* decision for colleges and universities is that it does not pose a strong evidentiary burden on employers to validate selection devices that are used in promotion and tenure decisions.

---

[20]*Watson v. Fort Worth Bank & Trust*, 47 FEP Cases 102 (1988).

[21]Business necessity is defined as "justification for an otherwise prohibited employment practice based on [an employer's] proof that: (1) the otherwise prohibited employment practice is essential for the safety and efficiency of the business, and (2) no reasonable alternative with a lesser impact exists." See BNA, "Glossary of Terms," *Fair Employment Practices Manual* (Washington, D.C.: BNA, 1979), sec. 400.

RESEARCH, PUBLICATIONS, AND SCHOLARSHIP

IMPORTANCE OF RESEARCH

Research and scholarly activities, sometimes referred to collectively as "scholarship," are critical functions at nearly all major colleges and universities. Further, there is ample evidence that promotion, tenure, and compensation decisions at many four-year institutions are influenced primarily by a faculty member's research and publications.[22] The litmus test for such activities is the publication of research results in journals, especially those that are refereed.[23] Manuscripts submitted to refereed journals are anonymously reviewed (blind reviewed) by scholars who are either members of the journal's editorial review board or who are selected on an ad hoc basis by the journal editor because of their specialized expertise in a particular discipline.[24]

The debate over the appropriate balance between research and teaching has been hotly contested for years. Several reasons are frequently cited to support the value of research and publications by faculty members.[25] First, colleges and universities have a responsibility both to create knowledge through research and to disseminate knowledge through teaching. The rapid advancement of knowledge requires that professors stay abreast of current developments in their fields. Professors who are active researchers are more likely to be aware of new ideas and breakthroughs in their discipline than are those who do little, if any, research.

[22]Howard P. Tuchman, "The Academic Reward Structure in American Higher Education," in Darrell R. Lewis and William E. Becker, Jr., eds., *Academic Rewards in Higher Education* (Cambridge, Mass.: Ballinger, 1979), pp. 165–90.

[23]Ernest L. Boyer, *Scholarship Reconsidered: Priorities of the Professorate* (Princeton, N.J.: Carnegie Foundation for the Advancement of Teaching, 1990), p. 28. As one court noted, "One usually can assume that publications in refereed sociological journals are of good quality." See *Cussler v. University of Maryland*, 15 FEP Cases 1299 (1977).

[24]The degree of prestige afforded "refereed" journals may be somewhat misplaced. A journal may be refereed in the sense that it uses a group of reviewers who are located at different institutions. Such an arrangement does not necessarily ensure that the articles appearing in the journal are of high quality. Other journals use an in-house editorial staff that rigorously screens manuscripts and selects only those that meet high standards and make a significant contribution to an academic discipline. Some institutions may not regard the latter arrangement as a refereed process. Perhaps a more valid approach to assessing the quality of a journal would be to examine such factors as its manuscript acceptance rate, the extent to which its articles stimulate further research by other authors, the number of citations that a journal receives in other research outlets, and its general reputation for publishing high-quality work.

[25]See Peter Seldin, *Successful Faculty Evaluation Programs* (Crugers, N.Y.: Coventry Press, 1980), pp. 128–29.

Second, research and teaching are not necessarily mutually exclusive endeavors. A professor who is an active researcher often brings new knowledge and ideas to the classroom. Research sharpens a professor's intellectual powers and improves his or her teaching abilities. This is especially true if the professor teaches in a department with a doctoral program.

Third, research and publications bring a degree of recognition to both the professor and the institution that is not attainable through teaching excellence alone. Articles in prestigious journals are read by scholars at other educational and research institutions. The academic prestige of a major university is based largely on the research prowess of its faculty and, only to a lesser extent, on its reputation for high-quality teaching. The enhancement of an institution's prestige through its faculty's extensive research activities helps a college or university attract high-caliber faculty and graduate students and increases the likelihood of obtaining grants and external funding.

Proponents of the view that research and publications should be emphasized believe that the creation of knowledge lies at the heart of most major institutions of higher learning. Publications make the results of research generally available for challenge and subsequent improvement by other experts and scholars. The results of research are also used by educational and health-care institutions, corporations, and government agencies to develop social programs and establish policy. Disparaging references to the "publish-or-perish" syndrome have been compared with a form of output restriction that stems from the same origins as "rate busting" among factory workers or "curve bending" among students.[26] As Christopher Jencks and David Riesman have noted:

> Publication is the only way a man can communicate with a significant number of colleagues or other adults. Those who do not publish usually feel they have not learned anything worth communicating to adults. This means that they have not learned much worth communicating to the young either. There are, of course, exceptions: men who keep learning but cannot bring themselves to write. . . . Still, these are exceptions.[27]

[26]Peter M. Blau, *The Organization of Academic Work* (New York: Wiley, 1973), p. 103.
[27]Christopher Jencks and David Riesman, *The Academic Revolution* (Garden City, N.Y.: Anchor Doubleday, 1969), p. 532, quoted in Blau, *Organization of Academic Work*, p. 103.

Proponents of the importance of research output have argued that it is a superior and more objective measure of faculty performance than teaching effectiveness. Luis R. Gomez-Mejia and David B. Balkin, in their discussion of research productivity and faculty pay, make the following observation:

> First, research productivity can be efficiently evaluated both externally and internally. . . . Teaching performance is primarily assessed internally. Given limited resources, unless teaching-related rewards are made contingent on research performance, a university will lose ground to competing institutions. . . .
>
> Second, although those who do a good job in the classroom serve an important university constituency, the evaluation of teaching performance is much more subjective, ambiguous, and controversial than that of research productivity, for which outcome measures are readily available. Therefore, evidence of research productivity serves as an inexpensive quality control check on assessments of teaching performance. The superior classroom performance of a top scholar, however measured, is more immune from questioning because his or her mastery of the subject has been independently established. Indicators of high teaching performance for an individual who is not engaged in scholarship may be subject to alternative interpretations; a teacher may be credited with being an entertainer, or with repackaging publicly available information but not disseminating cutting-edge knowledge, or with having superior platform or delivery skills but a lack of depth or rigor. Monitoring these different effects in the absence of a strong scholarly record is labor intensive and uncertain at best. [Colleges and universities] may reduce performance uncertainties by relying on scholarly publications to verify or correct potential errors in teaching-related judgments.[28]

Opponents of the ever-increasing emphasis on research and publications in U.S. institutions of higher learning are quick to note that such endeavors detract from high-quality teaching, especially at the undergraduate level. They argue that the skills required to perform competently in the classroom are vastly different from those required to conduct effective research. Most professors engage in highly specialized research that has, at best, only limited use in the classroom.

[28]Luis R. Gomez-Mejia and David B. Balkin, "Determinants of Faculty Pay: An Agency Theory Perspective," *Academy of Management Journal* 35 (Dec. 1992): 926–27.

Thus, opponents of the publish-or-perish orientation contend that research robs the professor of the time and energy needed for teaching. Several studies and position papers have examined the relationship between measures of a professor's research productivity and his or her teaching effectiveness. The results have been mixed; some studies have shown that research does detract from teaching, whereas others have reported positive (but low) correlations between research productivity and teaching effectiveness.[29]

The heavy emphasis on research has also been attacked on the grounds that it is often highly specialized and of little relevance in addressing major societal concerns. U.S. corporations, for example, face challenges from global competitors in an increasingly complex economic, social, and regulatory environment. Yet there is concern that much of the research that is generated by faculty at U.S. business schools has little impact on corporate executives who make major business decisions.[30] Furthermore, those who fear that research has become too critical in promotion and tenure decisions argue that the number of academic journals has proliferated primarily in response to the increased pressures imposed on faculty to publish rather than because of intellectual curiosity and a thirst for new knowledge.

Concern has also been expressed that the scholarship a faculty member must produce to receive a promotion or tenure has become too narrowly defined. Because of this narrow definition of acceptability, scholarly activities are likely to be driven more by the desire to adhere to a proper form and methodology than by the need to address important intellectual issues. Paul Woodring, a professor who has written a number of books on higher education in the United States, made the following observation on research, promotion, and tenure.

> James' *Principles of Psychology*, which appears on some of the
> lists of "100 Great Books," was written as a textbook. It contains

---

[29]Perhaps K. E. Elbe said it best: "Some good researchers are good teachers; some good researchers are poor teachers." Elbe concluded by saying that "the majority of both researchers and teachers are mediocre." See Elbe, *The Craft of Teaching* (San Francisco: Jossey-Bass, 1976), pp. 18–19, cited in Seldin, *Successful Faculty Evaluation Programs*, p. 131.

[30]The dean of the graduate school of business at New York University, after reading articles from a recent edition of a prestigious management journal, commented that "It's often crap. . . . They say nothing in these articles, and they say it in a pretentious way. If I wasn't the dean of this school, I'd be writing a book on the bankruptcy of American management education." See John A. Byrne, "Is Research in the Ivory Tower 'Fuzzy, Irrelevant, Pretentious'?" *Business Week*, Oct. 29, 1990, p. 62.

few footnotes and rarely mentions the research evidence that supports the author's conclusions. If James were an assistant professor at a minor American university today and submitted this book as evidence of his scholarship—it was just about the only thing he had to offer at the age of forty-eight—he would probably be denied promotion while some third-rate pedant who used more footnotes and had done more research would move up the ladder.

If Plato were a graduate student today and submitted his *Republic* as a doctoral dissertation, no graduate committee would even consider it. The philosophy department would deny that it is philosophy. Political scientists would call it fantasy rather than a scholarly treatise. Departments of literature would almost certainly reject it, and professors in all disciplines would complain about the lack of documentation and Plato's failure to include a survey of the previous literature.[31]

MEASURING AND EVALUATING SCHOLARLY OUTPUT

The assessment of scholarship has both objective as well as subjective elements. Counting the number of journal articles or books that a faculty member has published provides a quantitative summary of his or her output but little insight into the quality or impact of the research.[32] Compounding the problem, research and scholarly activities are often dichotomized by labels such as "basic" versus "applied," "empirical" versus "theoretical," or "analytical" versus "descriptive." Many peer review committees, department heads, and deans are more impressed by faculty who publish in journals that have a scholarly, empirical, or quantitative focus than in those that have a qualitative, theoretical, or practical orientation.[33] Further, some departments permit faculty members to receive credit for publishing in a wide variety of journals, whereas others carefully rank-order journals or define a select few in which faculty must publish if they aspire to a promotion or tenure. As a general rule, most disciplines have a well-defined hierarchy of journals.[34] The prestige hierarchy

[31]Paul Woodring, *The Higher Learning in America: A Reassessment* (New York: McGraw-Hill, 1968), pp. 191–92.

[32]According to Peter Seldin, "Many institutions rely on a nose-count of a professor's published articles in evaluating the professor's performance, a hazardous procedure at best. Some professors can write 10 articles while others rewrite the same article 10 times. Some professors can churn out lightweight articles (not worth the sacrifice of a tree) while others spend years on a seminal monograph." Seldin, *Successful Faculty Evaluation Programs*, p. 134.

[33]Boyer, *Scholarship Reconsidered*, p. 29.

[34]See, for example, Marian M. Extejt and Jonathan E. Smith, "The Behavioral Sciences

often places a higher value on journals that are selective and have acceptance rates of less than 10 percent. Scholarly books that advance the state of knowledge or suggest new avenues of research are also generally held in high regard, especially if they receive favorable reviews.[35]

The impact that a faculty member's research has on an academic discipline is being given increased attention by peer review committees, department heads, and others, as determined by the number of times that the work is cited by other authors. One method that is used to distinguish between meaningful research of enduring value and articles that are merely "journal filler" is to count the number of times other scholars cite a particular article or author. Indexes such as the *Social Science Citation Index*, the *Arts and Humanities Citation Index*, and the *Science Citation Index* provide means by which such counts can be made.

Proponents of citation analysis argue that the true test of a faculty member's impact or eminence is the frequency with which researchers and writers cite his or her work. Advocates of this approach argue that the acceptance of an article for publication in a leading journal depends on the opinions of a few editorial reviewers but does not guarantee that the article will have a significant impact on future research. Frequencies of citation are also objective in that they eliminate the problem of race or sex bias.[36] In *Fisher v. Vassar College*, a federal district court in New York discussed the *Science Citation Index* (SCI) and the manner in which it provides an assessment of the prestige of scientific journals. Cynthia Fisher, a biology professor, was denied tenure at Vassar in 1985 and subsequently filed charges of sex and age discrimination against the college. The court appeared to rely heavily on the fact that Fisher had fifty citations to her papers in the SCI, whereas other recently tenured biology faculty at Vassar

---

and Management: An Evaluation of Relevant Journals," *Journal of Management* 16 (1990): 539–51; R. K. Coe and I. Weinstock, "Evaluating the Management Journals: A Second Look," *Academy of Management Journal* 27 (1984): 660–66; and T. Vocino and R. Elliott, "Public Administrative Journal Prestige: A Time Series Analysis," *Administrative Science Quarterly* 29 (1984): 43–51.

[35]Scholarly books should be distinguished from textbooks in that the former advance knowledge through the dissemination of research results, whereas the latter package existing knowledge and present it in a fashion that permits its use in undergraduate or graduate classes. Because the writing and publishing of a textbook is a very time-consuming activity that requires several years of work, most faculty members who write textbooks do so only after they have received tenure.

[36]Farley, *Sex Discrimination in Higher Education*, pp. 42–44 and 56–58.

had fewer SCI citations. It ruled in favor of Fisher and concluded that her publication record was superior to that of the four males who received tenure between 1984 and 1987. The court also said that Fisher's publication record was approximately the same as that of an unmarried female professor who was promoted during this time. (Fisher is married, and the biology department at Vassar was accused of discriminating against married female professors.)[37]

Opponents of citation analysis argue that a work may be cited for negative reasons (that is, as an example of poor-quality research) rather than because of its contribution to an academic field. Furthermore, the length of time required to publish articles in prestigious journals often makes the use of citation analysis unfair in tenure decisions. Several years may pass between the time a journal article is first submitted for publication and the time the printed article is first read by other scholars.[38] If another author subsequently cites this work, it may take several additional years before the initial work appears in print as a citation.[39] Finally, at least one court has viewed citation analysis with skepticism:

> None of the studies based on the Science Citation Index, including the Lifetime Citation Index which was devised by Dr. Davies

---

[37]*Fisher v. Vassar College*, 64 FEP Cases 1351 (1994).

[38]When a manuscript is submitted to a prestigious journal, it receives an initial screening; at this point, it will either be summarily rejected by the editor or, if the article has merit, it will be sent to two or more external reviewers for evaluation. The external reviewers may take several months (or longer) to submit their recommendations to the editor. The article then may be rejected, tentatively accepted pending revisions, or accepted with no further revisions. If the article is tentatively accepted (and few receive outright acceptances after the initial submission), moderate to extensive revisions may be required. It is not unusual for the external reviewers to have mixed opinions on the publishability of an article. The editor may break the tie and either accept or reject the article based on the reviewers' comments or submit the manuscript to additional reviewers. If the latter option is used, more time is needed to make an editorial decision. Mixed reviews and revisions usually require that the author address the reviewers' criticisms and resubmit the manuscript. Revising and resubmitting may require several iterations before a final publication decision is made. If the article is accepted for publication, backlogs of accepted articles and printing schedules may create a delay of an additional year or more before it is actually published.

[39]Many published papers are never cited. The citation frequency distribution data from the 1978 *Science Citation Index* show that of more than 3,800,000 cited articles, 70 percent were cited only once, and 23 percent were cited two to four times. Articles with five to nine citations were in the 98.7th percentile; seventeen to twenty-five, the 99.62d percentile; twenty-six to fifty, the 99.81st percentile; fifty-one to one hundred, the 99.96th percentile. These figures do not vary significantly from one year to the next. See E. Garfield, *Essays of an Information Scientist*, 2 vols. (Philadelphia: Institute for Scientific Information Press, 1977), cited in Farley, *Sex Discrimination in Higher Education*, p. 44.

for the purpose of this trial, can be used to measure the quality of the plaintiff's research, either absolutely or in relation to other members of the biochemistry department and Dr. Diven, or to assess the importance of the plaintiff's work. The court finds that the reliability of this method in individual cases has not been shown.[40]

A number of employment discrimination cases have dealt with faculty whose records of scholarship were insufficient to merit favorable reappointment, promotion, or tenure decisions. The use of scholarship as a facially neutral, job-relevant requirement for making such decisions is clearly acceptable from a legal standpoint. Colleges and universities that equate the quality of a faculty member's scholarship with the number of refereed journal articles that he or she has published may also afford themselves a degree of protection from charges of illegal discrimination. Thus, a federal district court in Rhode Island made the following observation about the role of a refereed publication:

> First, it provides some outward indication of quality of research: a book will usually not be published if it is meritless; acceptance of an article by a refereed journal is a tangible indicator of some intrinsic worth; it is unlikely that an individual will be requested to present a paper at a recognized scholarly conference if certain standards have not been met. Because academic research, to be worthy of the appellation, is by its very nature subjected to outside review at some point, a model pivoting off this fact avoids the possibility that internal peer review may be biased against one group or another. And, the model adapts to judgments at the department, dean, or president level of review. Similarly productive individuals should be treated comparably at all stages. If they are not, and if the inequality works consistently to the disadvantage of an identifiable class, then evidence of discrimination exists.[41]

The above argument can be taken one step further insofar as a manuscript submitted to a refereed journal is usually blind reviewed. That is, the anonymity of the author is preserved from reviewers, and vice versa, until after the article is accepted for publication; the author and reviewers remain mutually anonymous if the article is

[40]*Johnson v. University of Pittsburgh*, 15 FEP Cases 1529 (1977).
[41]*Chang v. University of Rhode Island*, 40 FEP Cases 78 (1985).

rejected. The blind-review system should enhance fairness and objectivity and enable a faculty member to build a record of scholarship free from invidious discrimination.[42]

Most colleges and universities place heavier weight on research *output* (articles and books published or accepted for publication) than on research *input* (articles and books in process or under review). Nonetheless, a candidate's research input may be considered under some circumstances.[43] For example, a candidate for promotion or tenure may receive credit for a journal article or book that has been tentatively accepted for publication pending minor revisions. Many faculty members have developed an inventory of manuscripts or projects that are in various stages of completion or revision. Peer review committees, department heads, and deans may recognize research input of this type, especially if the faculty member has already established a track record for having manuscripts accepted for publication. The key to evaluating research input, however, is to do so consistently.

Some peer review committees and department heads are more impressed with a candidate for tenure who has a few articles in top journals than with one who has more publications in less prestigious journals. And some departments have a minimum number of articles that they require before they will recommend faculty for promotion or tenure. Most peer review committees and department heads, however, refuse to specify the minimum, preferring instead to evaluate both the quantity and the quality of the candidates' articles.[44] Furthermore, a marginal record of research may be offset by excellence in teaching and service.[45]

Many institutions also solicit letters from scholars at other universities who assess the quality and impact of the tenure candidate's research. In a case involving a female professor in the Department of Classics at the University of Cincinnati, the U.S. Court of Appeals (Sixth Circuit) noted:

[42]Some well-known scholars have developed highly specific lines of research. In such instances, a reviewer may be able to make an educated guess as to the identity of the author of a manuscript.

[43]See, for example, *Coser v. Moore*, 36 FEP Cases 68 (1983).

[44]There may be concern when a faculty member has collaborated extensively with a mentor. The question that arises is whether the faculty member has demonstrated the requisite independence of scholarship to merit promotion or tenure. See *Jew v. University of Iowa*, 57 FEP Cases 653 (1990).

[45]See *Kumar v. Board of Trustees, University of Massachusetts*, 32 FEP Cases 316 (1983), and 38 FEP Cases 1740 (1985).

Scholarship, as evidenced by the quality of a candidate's published works, was a factor upon which the Department placed primary importance. The Department's subjective assessment of a candidate's scholarship was assisted by evaluations obtained from a number of scholars outside the University. Generally, five outside evaluators were selected for each candidate. Because the quality of published work was such a significant factor in the tenure decision, the outside evaluations were a very important part of the process. Tenure candidates understandably wanted their work to be evaluated by scholars who were familiar with their particular academic specialty and who would give a fair and unbiased evaluation of their work.[46]

A college or university may benefit from the use of outside reviewers in several ways. First, faculty at large research universities often develop highly specialized and even esoteric research agendas. In such cases, peer review committees or department heads may not feel completely confident in their ability to evaluate a faculty member's scholarship.[47]

Second, accusations of racial, sexist, or other forms of discrimination by a faculty member are likely to be believed less when persons outside a department or college are involved in the peer review process. At the same time, review committees or department heads who want to engage in illegal discrimination can select outside reviewers who are known to be unreasonably critical and "springloaded" to evaluate harshly even the most stellar research record. Bias can also creep into the process if peer review committee members indicate to the outside evaluator that they believe the record of a candidate for promotion or tenure is marginal.

Third, faculty members who are allowed to submit a list of prospective evaluators to a peer review committee or department head are more likely to perceive that the promotion or tenure review process is fair. If reviewers from the list are not used, however, a faculty member may become highly suspicious of the entire process.

There are several points that emerge regarding the courts' position

[46]*Gutzwiller v. Fenik*, 48 FEP Cases 399 (1988).

[47]Peer review committees must decide when the use of outside evaluations is appropriate. Some departments use such evaluations for all promotion and tenure decisions. Other departments use them only when they lack the expertise to make an informed judgment about the line of research of a particular faculty member. Still other departments restrict the use of outside evaluations to tenure decisions only or, perhaps, for promotion to the rank of full professor.

on evaluating a faculty member's scholarship. In the absence of invidious discrimination or substantial procedural irregularities (from which discrimination may be inferred), the courts are reluctant to substitute their judgment for the institution's judgment regarding the merits of scholarship. The courts clearly recognize the difficulties inherent in measuring research output and in comparing the output of one faculty member with another.

> One proxy for direct evidence of bias is the likelihood of promotion of comparably productive individuals. Since research is the prime consideration in the evaluation of promotion candidates, it seems fair to assume that faculty with equally impressive research credentials and the same seniority . . . will enjoy an equal probability of promotion. If equally productive candidates do not garner comparable advancement in rank, the promotion scenario becomes suspect. Yet, the proposition is easier stated than implemented. An examination of faculty research credentials requires the compilation of articles published in refereed and non-refereed journals, books published or edited, and papers presented at various conferences. Once this data has been assembled, some formula must be devised to give weight to the different types of publication. This, in itself, is no easy task. Not only are there differences *between* classifications (a book carries different weight than a journal article) but there are subtle shadings *within* classifications (some journals are more selective and/or prestigious than others). And, publications in journals may, as a generic matter, be more impressive in some fields than in others. E.g. Langland v. Vanderbilt University, 589 F.Supp. 995, 1011, 36 FEP Cases 200 (M.D. Tenn 1984) (contrasting journal articles in the sciences and in the humanities). If this data can be meaningfully assembled, an analysis of it will then show whether equally productive researchers are being treated comparably by the institution.[48]

Furthermore, the state and federal courts have granted colleges and universities a wide latitude in which to evaluate scholarship as it relates to the institution's mission, faculty composition, and academic orientation. Finally, the courts recognize a compensatory approach to faculty evaluation, in which strengths in one area may compensate for deficiencies in other areas.

---

[48]*Chang v. University of Rhode Island*, 40 FEP Cases 78 (1985).

Although research and publications are the primary measures of a faculty member's scholarship, they are not the only measures. The Carnegie Foundation for the Advancement of Teaching has encouraged colleges and universities to expand their definitions of scholarship:

> As a first step, we urge that faculty assessment take into account a broader range of writing, especially in advancing the scholarship of integration. While articles in refereed journals and scholarly books are of great value, writing a textbook also can be a significant intellectual endeavor. Of course, textbooks, like journal articles, differ greatly in quality, and must be evaluated as rigorously as any other form of scholarly work. Still, such writing, if well done, can reveal a professor's knowledge of the field, illuminate essential integrative themes, and powerfully contribute to excellence in teaching, too.
>
> Writing for nonspecialists—often called "popular writing"— also should be recognized as a legitimate scholarly endeavor. In the past, such work has frequently been dismissed as "mere journalism," but this misses, we believe, a larger point. To make complex ideas understandable to a large audience can be a difficult, demanding task, one that requires not only a deep and thorough knowledge of one's field, but keen literary skills, as well. Such effort, when successful, surely should be recognized and rewarded. The writings of Stephen Jay Gould in Natural History, the essays of Lewis Thomas, and Stephen Hawking's brilliant little book on the history of time illustrate, at the highest level, the kinds of contributions we have in mind. . . .
>
> Let's also acknowledge that scholarship often finds expression in other ways as well. Preparing quality computer software, for example, is increasingly a function of serious scholars, and even videocassette and television offer opportunity for communicating ideas to nonspecialists in creative new ways. This potential was used by Jacob Bronowski, the British scholar, in his series "The Ascent of Man," which was broadcast on American public television in the early 1970s—a presentation of Western intellectual history in which Bronowski, educated as a mathematician, could extend brilliantly his insightful talents as poet, inventor, and playwright.[49]

Some liberal arts disciplines may assess a faculty member's scholarship from the standpoint of plays written and produced, poetry

[49]Boyer, *Scholarship Reconsidered*, pp. 35–36.

published in literary reviews, music recitals, or juried exhibitions of art. Some institutions include as scholarly activity serving on the editorial boards of journals, chairing dissertation committees, reviewing research grants for national research organizations such as the National Science Foundation, and presenting papers at scholarly meetings.

Many research institutions also place significant weight on a faculty member's ability to attract external funding for research projects. University administrators are especially pleased with externally funded research because a portion of these funds is applied to the institution's overhead costs. When evaluating a faculty member's scholarly activities, three issues arise with regard to external research funds. First, agencies that grant research funds often evaluate the publication record of the applicant, thereby putting junior faculty at a distinct disadvantage. Second, peer review committees, department heads, and deans must decide whether to count research funding as scholarly activity or wait until the product of the research (e.g., a manuscript, journal article, or technical report) is completed before giving credit for the sake of promotion or tenure. Third, many externally funded research projects involve a research team. Peer review committees, department heads, and deans must then determine the contribution a candidate for a promotion or tenure made toward the overall research project.[50]

TEACHING EFFECTIVENESS

THE ROLE OF TEACHING IN PROMOTION AND TENURE DECISIONS

Teaching effectiveness is clearly an important formal criterion for promotions and tenure at most colleges and universities. According to the U.S. Court of Appeals (Eighth Circuit), "Student reaction [to a professor's teaching] is a legitimate, nondiscriminatory factor on which to evaluate tenure candidates."[51] Teaching effectiveness can be difficult to evaluate, however. According to educational psychologist Kenneth O. Doyle, Jr., "There is no perfect way to evaluate teaching.

---

[50]Many refereed journal articles, scholarly books, and technical reports are written by multiple authors. In many cases, the authors do not contribute equally. Peer review committees and other decision makers must determine the relative contributions of each author. See, for example, J. S. Long and R. McGinnis, "On Adjusting Productivity Measures for Multiple Authorship," *Scientometrics* 5 (1982): 379–87.

[51]*Brousard-Norcross v. Augustana College Association*, 56 FEP Cases 245 (1991).

There may not even be a really excellent way. There are, however, good and responsible ways to evaluate teaching that are within the reach of any college or university."[52]

Teaching occurs in a classroom or laboratory setting away from the direct observation of peer review committees, department heads, and deans. The criteria used to measure its contributions and effectiveness are often poorly designed and lacking in reliability and validity. Students who complete teaching effectiveness questionnaires may not take the time to complete them in a thoughtful manner, either because they believe that the administration ignores student input or because they regard them as a bother.

There is also concern regarding the actual weight that is attached to teaching. Few college presidents and administrators, even at major research institutions, would publicly state that teaching is not important. Yet faculty often perceive that teaching remains far less important than research and scholarship insofar as promotion and tenure evaluations are concerned.

Colleges and universities typically have a variety of teachers, some of whom are excellent and make lasting impressions on their students and some of whom are dull and apathetic toward their classroom responsibilities. There have been several cases in which poor teaching contributed to an unfavorable promotion and tenure decision.[53] In some of these cases, the faculty member's ineffectiveness in the classroom bordered on gross incompetence or negligence and was forcefully brought to the attention of college or university administrators through student complaints. One of the most extreme of these cases arose in the Department of Biochemistry at the University of Pittsburgh School of Medicine. The plaintiff, Dr. Sharon Johnson, worked as an assistant professor in the department. First-year medical students became so frustrated with her teaching that they cursed at her, made rude noises and audible complaints, and walked out during her lectures. Dr. Johnson was denied tenure and subsequently filed sex discrimination charges against the University of Pittsburgh.

[52]Kenneth O. Doyle, Jr., "Use of Student Evaluations in Faculty Personnel Decisions," in Lewis and Becker, *Academic Rewards in Higher Education*, p. 145.

[53]See, for example, *Fields v. Clark University*, 43 FEP Cases 1247 (1987); *Kumar v. Board of Trustees, University of Massachusetts*, 38 FEP Cases 1734 (1985); *Meehan v. New England School of Law*, 27 FEP Cases 1111 (1981); *Wilkins v. University of Houston*, 26 FEP Cases 1230 (1981); *Mosby v. Webster College*, 16 FEP Cases 521 (1977); *Johnson v. University of Pittsburgh*, 15 FEP Cases 1516 (1977); and *Jawa v. Fayetteville State University*, 19 FEP Cases 1252 (1976).

A U.S. district court held that she failed to show that the reason for her dismissal was illegal discrimination; rather, the court found that the university denied her tenure because her research and teaching were inadequate.[54] Vocal dissatisfaction such as that expressed by the medical students at the University of Pittsburgh is rare. In most cases, poor teaching is reflected in student responses on teaching evaluations completed at the end of a course or in complaints to department heads or college deans.

Student complaints of poor teaching usually stem from a professor's lack of organization or preparedness in the classroom, unfairness in grading, or bad attitude and disrespectful treatment of students.[55] In *Meehan v. New England School of Law*, for example, the dean of the law school stated that he had received numerous complaints from students about Dorothy K. Meehan's teaching. Other students complained directly to the school's board of trustees. The students "complained that Meehan was condescending, incoherent, unresponsive to questions, and that she dealt with the material only superficially." They also complained that Meehan canceled classes and rescheduled them at inconvenient times. The law school dean claimed that he discussed Meehan's teaching problems with her on several occasions, but her performance failed to improve. Meehan was ultimately denied tenure and filed sex discrimination charges under Title VII against the law school. A U.S. district court in Massachusetts ruled that the institution was entitled to terminate Meehan because she was not an effective teacher.[56]

The administration of a college or university may also believe that a faculty member's teaching is unacceptable because he or she overemphasizes a particular school of thought. An attempt to censor the faculty member's ideas and expressions in the classroom could encroach on individual academic freedom unless the institution can demonstrate another reason for a negative personnel action. In *Peters v. Middlebury College*, the faculty member was told that she was too heavily involved in the women's movement and that her teaching was too feminist in orientation. She was not reappointed by the college and subsequently filed suit. Counsel for Middlebury argued

[54]*Johnson v. University of Pittsburgh*, 15 FEP Cases 1522 (1977).

[55]See *Kumar v. Board of Trustees, University of Massachusetts*, 38 FEP Cases 1741 (1985); *Meehan v. New England School of Law*, 27 FEP Cases 1111 (1981); and *Fields v. Clark University*, 43 FEP Cases 1249 (1987).

[56]*Meehan v. New England School of Law*, 27 FEP Cases 1111 (1981).

that her lack of expertise in literature was the real reason for her termination, a defense the court accepted.[57]

Some faculty have had their teaching effectiveness questioned on the grounds that they were inaccessible to students or otherwise neglected their teaching responsibilities.[58] In *Thomasko v. University of South Carolina*, a psychology professor was denied tenure in part because her private practice in clinical psychology detracted from her teaching responsibilities. She filed sex and national origin discrimination charges (she is of Hungarian-German origin) against her institution under Title VII. A U.S. district court held that the University of South Carolina (Coastal Carolina College campus) had denied Thomasko tenure for legitimate professional reasons and not because of her sex or national origin.[59]

Faculty from foreign countries may experience teaching difficulties because of their heavy accents or poor skills in spoken English.[60] Since accent and national origin are often inextricably linked, some faculty who are terminated because of complaints about their inability to communicate effectively in the classroom end up filing discrimination charges.

Mohsen Hassan, a faculty member who was Egyptian in national origin, was hired as a visiting professor by Auburn University's business school to teach courses in operations management. During his visiting professorship, he taught eight classes. Although he was required to conduct student evaluations in all his classes, he did so in only three. His evaluations were below the department average for each of these three classes. He received particularly low ratings on a question that dealt with the instructor's ability to speak audibly and clearly. Students also complained about Hassan's communications skills, and his faculty colleagues expressed similar concerns.

When the Auburn business faculty decided to hire a permanent senior faculty member with a background in the management of technology (MOT) field, Hassan was not hired for the position and the funding for his temporary position was eliminated. The dismissal was based both on Hassan's lack of training and interest in the MOT field as well as on his difficulties with spoken English. The federal

[57]*Peters v. Middlebury College*, 12 FEP Cases 295 (1974).
[58]See *O'Connor v. Peru State College*, 39 FEP Cases 1240 (1985).
[59]*Thomasko v. University of South Carolina*, 41 FEP Cases 1032 (1985).
[60]See comments of Father Keegan in *Bina v. Providence College*, 64 FEP Cases 409 (1994).

district court rejected his claim that remarks about his accent by Auburn faculty and administration were direct evidence of discrimination: "In the present case, the written and oral remarks concerning Plaintiff's accent were made in the context of his ability to communicate in a classroom, a factor that even Plaintiff concedes is a proper hiring consideration."[61]

Both Hassan and Auburn University made reference to a nonacademic case, *Fragante v. City and County of Honolulu*, which involved a Filipino native who scored high on an employment exam but was rejected for a clerical job because of his heavy accent. The Ninth Circuit Court of Appeals found that Fragante "was passed over because of the deleterious *effect* of his Filipino accent on his ability to communicate orally, not merely because he had such an accent" (emphasis in original).[62] According to the Ninth Circuit, "An adverse employment decision may be predicated upon an individual's accent when—but only when—it interferes materially with job performance. There is nothing about an employer making an *honest* assessment of the oral communications skills of a candidate for a job when such skills are reasonably related to job performance."[63] (Emphasis in original)

Hassan argued that this standard means that an accent, or an accent's effect on communication skills, can be a factor in a hiring decision only if the accent is so heavy as to make a candidate completely unqualified for the position. The district court held that this argument was without merit and the employer has a right to select the candidate whose communications skills are superior.

> To accept Plaintiff's argument would be equivalent to saying that an employer could consider whether a foreign national candidate was completely unable to communicate, but could not consider whether a foreign national candidate's ability to communicate was merely poorer than that of a competitor candidate. *Fragante* itself refutes this argument. The plaintiff in *Fragante* was a job candidate who, according to two experts, could communicate effectively in English. The court assumed that the plaintiff was qualified for the job and that he had established a prima facie case. Notwithstanding the assumption that Plaintiff was quali-

[61]*Hassan v. Auburn University*, 64 FEP Cases 1386 (1993).
[62]*Fragante v. City and County of Honolulu*, 51 FEP Cases 195 (1989), *cert. denied*, 52 FEP Cases 848 (1990).
[63]*Fragante v. City and County of Honolulu*, 51 FEP Cases 193 (1989).

fied, the Court held that the employer could legitimately consider the plaintiff's communication skills in relationship to that of his competitors and that, after such consideration, the plaintiff "failed to get the job because two competitors had superior qualifications with respect to the relevant task."[64]

Although an academic department may have a limited number of faculty positions, quotas limiting the number or percentage of tenured faculty are rare. Thus, reappointment and tenure decisions do not usually involve pitting two or more faculty against each other to determine who wins tenure. *Fragante* would be applicable to reappointment and tenure decisions, however, for two reasons. First, communications skills are an integral part of teaching. Second, a college or university may decide that there are applicants for a faculty position who have superior language skills and better teaching potential than an incumbent but untenured faculty member. The federal district court ruled that Auburn University's motive for not offering Hassan a permanently funded position was based on nondiscriminatory reasons (his lack of MOT expertise and his poor communications skills) rather than on his national origin.

Measuring and Evaluating Teaching Effectiveness

Defining what constitutes good teaching and then designing measures to assess effectiveness is an arduous task because a good teacher possesses many characteristics, some of which are imponderable. After studying several teaching evaluation instruments, it was proposed that an effective teacher should possess eight characteristics. He or she (1) considers the rights and needs of students, (2) contributes to students' intellectual growth, (3) evaluates students' performances fairly, (4) has command of the subject, (5) stimulates students, (6) has professional integrity, (7) sets forth course objectives, and (8) transmits subject matter.[65] Other studies of teaching effectiveness have included such attributes as "empathy," "professional maturity," "rapport," "professional impression," and "instructor competence."[66]

---

[64]*Hassan v. Auburn University*, 64 FEP Cases 1386 (1993), quoting *Fragante v. City and County of Honolulu*, 51 FEP Cases 195 (1989).

[65]Ronald C. Wimberly, Gary L. Faulkner, and Robert L. Moxley, "Dimensions of Teaching Effectiveness," *Teaching Sociology* 4 (Oct. 1978): 9.

[66]See James A. Kulik and Wilbert J. McKeachie, "The Evaluation of Teachers in Higher Education," in Fred N. Kerlinger, ed., *Review of Research in Education*, vol. 3 (Itasca, Ill.: Peacock, 1975), pp. 211–13.

Teaching and learning are unique, individualized functions. Variations in educational philosophies and pedagogical approaches among professors is the rule rather than the exception. Furthermore, professors and students in U.S. colleges and universities are economically and culturally diverse. Any experienced professor will attest that students vary widely in their abilities, willingness to participate in class discussions, level of preparation, motivation, and seriousness of purpose. Each class takes on its own personality, and the rapport a professor enjoys in a morning section of a course may be conspicuously absent with a different group of students taking the same course in the afternoon. Further, the diversity among professors and students can create a wide range of expectations in the classroom.

It seems obvious that good teachers will receive good ratings from students, whereas poor teachers will receive poor ratings. But, according to James A. Kulik and Wilbert J. McKeachie, much more than good teaching goes into a good rating.[67] First, it might be assumed that ratings of a professor's teaching effectiveness will vary depending on who is involved in the rating process. Research has shown, however, that factors such as a student's sex, age, grade level, and major are of little value in predicting the teaching effectiveness rating a student will give a professor.[68]

Second, teaching conditions such as class size and location may have a significant impact on student ratings of teaching effectiveness. In a University of Illinois study, professors who taught lower-level courses received less favorable ratings from students than professors who taught upper-level courses. Professors who taught either large or small classes fared better on evaluations than professors who taught moderate-size classes. Furthermore, professors assigned to off-campus courses or to elective courses tended to receive higher ratings than those teaching on-campus or required courses.[69] This research illustrates an important point: many factors affecting the perceived quality of a professor's teaching may be beyond the professor's control. In fact, one study indicates that charisma and verbal

[67]Kulik and McKeachie, "Evaluation of Teachers," pp. 214–15.

[68]N. F. Rayder, "College Student Ratings of Instructors," *Journal of Experimental Education* 37 (1968): 76–81, cited in Kulik and McKeachie, "Evaluation of Teachers," pp. 214–15. Also see Lawrence M. Aleamoni, "Student Ratings of Instruction," in Jason Millman, ed., *Handbook of Teacher Evaluation* (Beverly Hills, Calif.: Sage, 1981), pp. 110–45.

[69]N. L. Gage, "The Appraisal of College Teaching: An Analysis of Ends and Means," *Journal of Higher Education* 32 (1961): 17–22.

fluency may be the most important attributes of teaching effectiveness as rated by students.[70] Furthermore, research on the numerous facets of teaching effectiveness has not always yielded consistent results. For example, studies of whether a professor's gender affects his or her teaching evaluations have not been conclusive.[71]

End-of-course student questionnaires are the primary means by which teaching effectiveness is assessed at nearly all U.S. colleges and universities.[72] The practice of allowing students to judge the value of courses and the competency of their professors has been supported by some academicians and viewed with disdain by others. Proponents of the questionnaires claim that students are capable of making sound judgments and offering useful suggestions for improving a particular course. Students can usually detect if a course is poorly organized or if the professor is not adequately prepared. Proponents also claim most students are able to assess a professor's ability to communicate, as well as his or her fairness in grading.

Opponents of teaching evaluations believe that students do not possess the maturity or expertise to judge the accuracy or quality of course content. In addition, they note that teaching evaluations reflect a professor's charisma rather than his or her competence in the classroom.[73] Nevertheless, it is the students who have firsthand knowledge of a professor's teaching performance. Members of peer review committees, department heads, deans, and other college

[70]D. H. Naftulin, J. E. Ware, Jr., and F. A. Donnelly performed a study that employed an actor who was totally ignorant of his subject matter. The actor was instructed to teach "charismatically and nonsubstantively" on a topic about which he knew nothing. His audience was not a relatively unsophisticated group of undergraduate students but rather fifty-five professionals who served as students (they included psychiatrists, social workers, and educators). This group rated both the lecture and the lecturer favorably. D. H. Naftulin, J. E. Ware, Jr., and F. A. Donnelly, "The Doctor Fox Lecture: A Paradigm of Education Seduction," *Journal of Medical Education* 48 (1973): 630–35. If being a good teacher depends on being a good talker, then there may be some truth to the accusation that form is more important than substance when it comes to evaluating teaching effectiveness.

[71]See Ellyn Kaschak, "Sex Bias in Student Evaluations of College Professors," *Psychology of Women Quarterly* (Spring 1978): 235–43, and Marlene Mackie, "Student Perceptions of Female Professors," *Journal of Vocational Behavior* 8 (1976): 337–48.

[72]"It is obvious that the explosive growth of student ratings is directly attributable to the campus unrest in the 1960s. Historically, however, the origins can be traced to the Middle Ages. Then, for instance, at the University of Padua, in Italy, students hired and fired their own teachers. And it was common at the great universities in Paris, Bologna, and Heidelberg for students to express appreciation of a professor by pressing coins into his hand or dropping them into the hood of his gown." Seldin, *Successful Faculty Evaluation Programs*, p. 36.

[73]Seldin, *Successful Faculty Evaluation Programs*, p. 45.

officials rarely, if ever, visit the classes of candidates for promotion or tenure. When they do visit, it is usually by invitation only or with advance notice. A one-time visit to a class provides only a limited view of the course. Students, by contrast, are present in a class throughout an entire academic quarter or semester and are in a much better position to see the range of behaviors a professor exhibits.

Some questionnaires solicit essay responses that allow students to discuss, in their own words, the professor's strengths and weaknesses in teaching. Such responses are not amenable, however, to statistical analyses or comparisons among faculty. For this reason, many student questionnaires consist of multiple-choice questions that require the students to fill in a form that can be processed by an optical scanner.[74] Statistics can then be generated and summarized by comparing a professor's mean scores on each question or teaching dimension with course, department, or college norms.

Even when evaluative criteria for teaching effectiveness can be agreed upon by students, faculty, and administrators, designing the instruments to measure such criteria is difficult. To be useful, standardized questionnaires must be both reliable and valid. Errors of observation, perception, communication, or sampling reduce the reliability, or consistency, of a questionnaire. For example, the reliability can be diminished if students who complete the questionnaire have not attended class regularly. Students who either want to help or, conversely, sabotage a professor's chances for tenure can provide less than candid responses, which will also reduce the reliability of a questionnaire.[75] In at least two recent employment discrimination cases in academia, the plaintiffs contended that a biased sample of students completed teaching evaluations as a means of dismissing the faculty members. In neither case, however, was the plaintiff able to convince the court that the biased sample was used to engage in illegal discrimination.[76]

Most estimates of reliability focus on the extent to which students

---

[74]These forms may request that a student answer a series of questions that deal with course content, grading procedures, assigned readings, the professor's treatment of students, classroom and laboratory facilities, and other factors. Teaching effectiveness questionnaires often use a five- or seven-point response scale (e.g., very good to very poor, strongly agree to strongly disagree, etc.).

[75]Doyle, "Use of Student Evaluations," pp. 147–48.

[76]*Fields v. Clark University*, 59 FEP Cases 129 (1992), and *Brousard-Norcross v. Augustana College Association*, 56 FEP Cases 246 (1991).

give similar responses to similar questions regarding a professor's teaching effectiveness.[77] They also focus on consistency (or degree of agreement) among students who evaluate a particular professor and course. Research indicates that college students are only moderately consistent in their ratings of professors and courses, although composite ratings are substantially reliable when the ratings of twenty to twenty-five students in a class are averaged together.[78]

The reliability of a teaching effectiveness questionnaire may also be affected if the instrument is administered under nonstandard conditions. Some institutions do not permit the professor to be present in the classroom when students are completing the form. And to quell student fears of retaliation, many institutions do not allow the professor to examine the results of a teaching evaluation until the course is completed and final grades have been determined. If these conditions are violated, then the reliability of the instrument may be affected.

Validity pertains to the extent to which the questionnaire deals with the relevant aspects of a course and a professor's teaching methods.[79] The validity of the items on a teaching effectiveness questionnaire is often based on subjective judgments regarding five criteria: (1) the manner in which the professor presents the subject matter (expositional skills), (2) the extent to which the professor relates well to students (interpersonal skills), (3) the degree to which the professor

---

[77]For example, a questionnaire designer might expect that students would rate a professor the same on the following two questions: (1) "The professor was not accessible outside of class" and (2) "The professor kept office hours and was available to meet with students outside of class." If students claimed that the professor was not accessible outside of class (question 1) yet stated that he or she kept office hours and was available to meet with students at his or her office (question 2), then serious doubts might arise regarding the reliability of the questionnaire. The lack of reliability might stem from the fact that the students did not take the questionnaire seriously and completed it in a hurried fashion without reading the questions carefully.

[78]Kenneth A. Feldman, "Consistency and Variability among College Students in Rating Their Teachers and Courses: A Review and Analysis," *Research in Higher Education* 6 (1977): 256. According to Feldman: "The estimates of average reliabilities are probably somewhat inflated, however, since there is a sense in which students in a class do not rate their teachers and courses with complete independence: The objects of the ratings (particular teachers or courses) are the very entities about which students, in part, mutually influence each other's assessments as the semester progresses."

[79]Validity is much more difficult to assess than reliability. Most student rating forms have been validated by the judgment of experts that the items and subscales measure important aspects of instruction." Aleamoni, "Student Ratings of Instruction," p. 113. A measure can be reliable but not necessarily valid. A valid measure must always be reliable, however.

challenges and stimulates students (motivational skills), (4) the frequency and thoroughness with which the professor informs students of their progress (feedback skills), and (5) the amount of work that the professor gives students.[80] A valid measure of teaching effectiveness also reflects the content and structure of a course. If chemistry students in a laboratory course are asked to complete a questionnaire that fails to address such issues as the professor's helpfulness in demonstrating the use of equipment or safety procedures, then the validity of the questionnaire as a measure of teaching effectiveness is diminished. Colleges and universities that use standardized questionnaires for all disciplines (from classes in the liberal arts to engineering to the agricultural sciences) are likely to encounter validity problems because the questions must, by necessity, be general enough to accommodate a wide range of academic disciplines, pedagogical methods, and teaching environments.[81]

Another concern is that students may not completely understand all of the questions being asked.[82] To the extent that students do not understand the content of the questionnaire, both reliability and validity are jeopardized.

In short, the selection and design of a measure of teaching effectiveness is a critical but subjective process. Faculty, students, and administrators are likely to have differing opinions about the attributes of a good teacher and, hence, the proper questions to ask on a teaching effectiveness questionnaire. One academic expressed this dilemma as follows:

> What is a good teacher? Who decides? Perhaps a dean or other administrator. More likely a faculty committee with substantial student input. Whatever criteria they choose, such groups necessarily favor those teacher qualities that enable them to reach a consensus and deemphasize those that are controversial. And when students have input, they tend to avoid defining the good

[80]Doyle, "Use of Student Evaluations," pp. 149–50.

[81]See Herbert W. Marsh, "Validity of Students' Evaluations of College Teaching: A Multitrait-Multimethod Analysis," *Journal of Educational Psychology* 74 (1982): 264–79; Elizabeth L. Harris, "Student Ratings of Faculty Performance: Should Departmental Committees Construct the Instruments?" *Journal of Educational Research* (Nov.-Dec. 1982): 100–106; and Oren Harari and Sheldon Zedeck, "Development of Behaviorally Anchored Scales for the Evaluation of Faculty Teaching," *Journal of Applied Psychology* 58 (1973): 261–65.

[82]See Thomas Bertsch and Linda Peek, "Determination of Measurement Scales for Revising or Developing Teacher Evaluation Instruments," *Journal of Marketing Education* 4 (Spring 1982): 15–24.

teacher as one whose assignments are difficult, whose examinations are demanding, and whose standards of performance are high. Consequently, criteria that challenge students rarely appear on rating forms, or, when they do, they represent only a minor element in a vast array of qualities used to identify the ideal. Instead, clarity of expression, arousal of interest, and stimulation of thinking are emphasized most frequently.[83]

There are concerns that problems exist even with well-developed standardized teaching evaluations. First, there is a widely held belief that professors who are lenient graders receive higher evaluations than those with harsher grading standards.[84] Considerable controversy has centered on the relationship between student ratings of teaching effectiveness and their actual or expected course grades. According to Lawrence M. Aleamoni, "Correlational studies have reported widely inconsistent grade-rating relationships." And even when the research indicates a relationship, it has been relatively weak.[85] It would behoove a peer review committee, department head, or dean, however, to request copies of a professor's grade distributions, especially if the professor's teaching evaluations are either very good or very poor.

Second, teaching effectiveness tends to be viewed in accordance with the "journeyman principle." According to this principle, the majority of professors are assumed to be competent at routine teaching tasks. Evaluations of teaching effectiveness are best used to determine performance at the ends of the continuum; that is, to identify teachers who are clearly gifted and exceptional and those who are clearly incompetent.

Do college faculty members fit the definition of journeyman? Can one assume, in other words, that they represent a selected group, the vast majority of whom are knowledgeable in their subject matter and able to convey it in an organized manner to their students?

There are many reasons to believe that the assumption is true. In the first place, members of a college faculty have usually successfully completed some amount of graduate training, which

---

[83]Richard R. Renner, "Comparing Professors: How Student Ratings Contribute to the Decline in Quality of Higher Education," *Phi Delta Kappan* (Oct. 1981): 128.

[84]Miriam J. Rodin, "By a Faculty Member's Yardstick, Student Evaluations Don't Measure Up," *Chronicle of Higher Education*, May 5, 1982, p. 64.

[85]Aleamoni, "Student Ratings of Instruction," p. 115.

may be taken to certify a certain high level of intellectual competence and mastery of subject matter. The ability to present material in a clear and organized fashion is generally a prerequisite for successfully completing a graduate degree. There is, furthermore, an additional process of self-selection: Those who dislike teaching, or feel inarticulate or uncomfortable addressing groups, tend to avoid choosing teaching as a profession.[86]

Because the self-selection process eliminates those who are not suited to teaching, distinguishing among faculty members based on small statistical differences on standardized teaching evaluations is probably unrealistic. Professors who score below department norms on teaching effectiveness measures may, in fact, be very good teachers, especially in departments in which the faculty is renowned for its teaching excellence.

Third, the use of essay questions as a supplement to multiple-choice questions allows students to elaborate on specific aspects of a professor's teaching behavior or course content. Their responses may be especially useful to peer review committees attempting to assess either very good or very poor teaching evaluations for a particular professor.

Although student evaluations of teaching effectiveness may provide insights into a professor's classroom performance, they should not be used in isolation. An additional, but universally neglected, way to evaluate teaching is to poll alumni who have had several years to reflect on the quality of their education but whose memories of their college experience has not yet been dulled or distorted by time. Alumni who have had the opportunity to mature and gain experience may be in a better position to evaluate objectively the teaching effectiveness of a former professor than are students who are currently completing a course. The latter group may be less objective because of time and work pressures or because a low (or high) grade biases their evaluation. Research indicates no significant differences, however, between ratings by current students and those given by alumni who have been out of school for five to ten years.[87]

Once the major hurdle of designing a sound instrument for measuring teaching competence is overcome, a decision must be made as

[86]Rodin, "By a Faculty Member's Yardstick," p. 64.
[87]Aleamoni, "Student Ratings of Instruction," pp. 112–13.

to the weight to assign to good teaching relative to research, publications, and professional service.[88] According to the Carnegie Foundation for the Advancement of Teaching:

> The question of how to evaluate *teaching* remains a mare's nest of controversy. The problem relates not only to procedures but also to the weight assigned to the endeavor. Teaching, as presently viewed, is like a currency that has value in its own country but can't be converted into other currencies. It may be highly regarded on a sizable campus and yet not be a particularly marketable skill. Thus, for faculty members whose primary loyalty is to their careers rather than to their institutions, teaching now counts little in increasing prospects to move on and move up. Consequently, excellence in the classroom all too often is undervalued.[89] (Emphasis in the original)

An evaluation of the teaching effectiveness of a candidate for promotion or tenure should not be limited to student ratings. The professor's course syllabi as well as evidence of pedagogical innovations, development of new courses or changes in the curriculum, service on graduate student committees, and involvement in writing or editing textbooks, instructors' manuals, or test banks should be included in the evaluation. Whether a faculty member advised students or served as a sponsor for a student professional or academic association might also be part of the evaluation.

UNIVERSITY, PROFESSIONAL, AND COMMUNITY SERVICE

Most colleges and universities require their faculty to engage in service activities. Service is usually mentioned as a requirement in

[88]The extent to which teaching evaluations affect promotions and tenure decisions appears to vary from one institution to another. Teaching and related activities such as student advising appear to be of primary importance at institutions that depend heavily for survival on student enrollments and retention. See Seldin, *Changing Practices in Faculty Evaluation,* p. 38. Professors at institutions that emphasize research and publications appear to perceive teaching as less important. One study, which surveyed twenty senior faculty at the University of Michigan, indicated that quality of teaching was considered to be relatively unimportant in evaluating candidates for promotion and tenure. See Timothy A. Salthouse, Wilbert J. McKeachie, and Yi-Guang Lin, "An Experimental Investigation of Factors Affecting University Promotion Decisions," *Journal of Higher Education* 49 (March-April 1978): 177–83. A study of Stanford University faculty yielded similar results. See Sanford M. Dornbusch, "Perspectives from Sociology: Organizational Evaluation of Faculty Performance," in Lewis and Becker, *Academic Rewards in Higher Education,* pp. 50–51.

[89]Boyer, *Scholarship Reconsidered,* p. 37.

faculty handbooks and is part of the formal appraisal process. Service activities are typically divided into (1) service to the university, (2) service to one's profession, and (3) service to the community. Service to the university might include participation on various committees, fund-raising efforts, or involvement with a task force. Professional service encompasses such activities as serving as an officer in a professional association, acting as a reviewer for scholarly journals, or organizing academic conferences or meetings. Community service typically involves serving on government and corporate advisory boards, giving speeches at community functions, or participating in other activities that promote the relationship between the institution of higher learning and the public at large.

Compared with research and teaching, service activities do not carry a great deal of weight in promotion and tenure decisions at most colleges and universities. I found no examples of wrongful discharge or employment discrimination cases in which a professor's failure to perform adequately university, professional, or community service activities per se led to an unfavorable personnel decision. There was at least one instance, however, in which a faculty member's inadequate university and professional service record contributed to an unfavorable promotion decision. In *Ottaviani v. State University of New York at New Paltz*, a faculty member was not promoted allegedly, in part, because her record of university service was weak. But she was also deemed to be weak in the areas of "scholarly ability" and "continuing growth."[90]

Several plaintiffs claimed their excessive service activities and responsibilities prevented them from establishing adequate levels of scholarship or teaching. Two cases involved black faculty members who were denied tenure because they spent too much time on service activities and failed to achieve adequate standards of scholarship. James Roebuck, a faculty member at Drexel University, was hired largely because the university wanted to establish better relations with the nearby, predominantly black community of West Philadelphia. Roebuck devoted a great deal of his time to a variety of community organizations as well as several university committees.

---

[90]*Ottaviani v. State University of New York at New Paltz*, 50 FEP Cases 275 (1989). The plaintiff, Susan Puretz, did, in fact, have a record of "strong service" according to the court. She was not granted tenure primarily because of her lack of acceptable scholarship.

Administrative officials at Drexel praised Roebuck for his community service and his contributions toward improving the institution's relations with the surrounding community. When Roebuck was evaluated for tenure, however, his scholarship, teaching, and service were regarded as only "satisfactory." He was denied tenure and filed a charge of race discrimination against Drexel. A U.S. district court ruled in favor of the university, but the U.S. Court of Appeals (Third Circuit) reversed and remanded the case for further proceedings. The Third Circuit cited evidence that university officials may have held a discriminatory animus that resulted in Roebuck's relatively low ratings and his being denied tenure.[91]

Another black faculty member who was denied tenure, at the University of Wisconsin at Milwaukee, claimed he was unable to achieve an acceptable record of scholarship because of the heavy administrative burdens associated with being part of the Department of Afro-American Studies and his work within the community. A U.S. district court did not find evidence of racial discrimination because, according to Senior District Judge Doyle: "No findings were sought by [the] plaintiff that agents of [the university] placed obstacles in plaintiff's tenure track in an act of conscious racism, and the evidence does not permit me to make such a finding."[92]

WORKING RELATIONSHIPS

Faculty members have a general, but usually unwritten, obligation to display a spirit of goodwill and cooperation in their working relationships with colleagues, students, and administrators. Cases have arisen in which faculty were denied promotions or tenure because of "personality problems." Some of these cases involved disagreements over schools of thought or professional issues. Others

---

[91]*Roebuck v. Drexel University*, 47 FEP Cases 755 (1988). Evidence of a potential discriminatory animus was based on (1) comments by the university president that "blacks cost more," (2) the department head's claim that community service was not relevant, even though Roebuck was hired for the purpose of establishing better relations between the university and the nearby black community, (3) holding Roebuck to standards that differed from university promotion and tenure guidelines, (4) discounting the use of student teaching evaluations in assessing Roebuck's teaching effectiveness, even though it was standard procedure to assess teaching performance from student evaluations, and (5) discounting favorable recommendations on Roebuck's scholarly activities by the department peer review committee and external reviewers.

[92]*Carpenter v. Board of Regents of the University of Wisconsin System*, 30 FEP Cases 1421 (1983).

involved faculty who disrupted working relationships and created ill will among colleagues, students, or staff. Disputes have arisen over faculty members who have attacked college officials over curricular or other educational matters. Interpersonal clashes have also involved a combination of professional and personal issues.

The U.S. Court of Appeals (Sixth Circuit) has said that "professional disagreements with members of an academic department are sufficient, nondiscriminatory reasons to deny tenure."[93] The Ninth Circuit echoed this position in *Lam v. University of Hawaii*.[94] Although it is acceptable to make an adverse employment decision for reasons of collegiality, the court noted the importance of evaluating case facts and circumstances carefully to ensure that interpersonal difficulties are not rooted in an illegal discriminatory motive.

> The university setting—in which, as in this case, employment decisions are made by a group, and collegiality and personal relationships are often significant factors—presents an especially difficult one in which to evaluate allegations of discrimination. As with all group decisionmaking, a complex of motives may exist. Personal animus, factional infighting and politics may influence and even determine certain faculty employment decisions, and are legally permissible if not praiseworthy bases for such decisions. Without a full factual inquiry, however, it may be extremely difficult to distinguish these types of permissible, though relatively personal, motivations from unlawful ones.[95]

In *Huang v. College of the Holy Cross*, a faculty member in a department of political science was denied tenure partly because of his professional opinion regarding core courses in his department as well as his alleged failure to help the department recruit outstanding faculty members. The executive committee at Holy Cross cited these factors as evidence of inadequate departmental service and voted unanimously to deny tenure to Huang. Administrators at Holy Cross felt that the political science department was weak and in need of better faculty and students as well as a stronger curriculum. Huang was perceived as a potential roadblock in improving the quality of

[93]*Poddar v. Youngstown State University*, 6 FEP Cases 456 (1973), quoted in *Perham v. Ladd*, 20 FEP Cases 129 (1977).

[94]*Lam v. University of Hawaii*, 66 FEP Cases 74 (1994).

[95]*Lam v. University of Hawaii*, 66 FEP Cases 83 (1994). A U.S. district court in Rhode Island noted that "rapport with students and colleagues is a legitimate inquiry." *Bina v. Providence College*, 64 FEP Cases 412 (1994).

the department, in part because he apparently prevented an outstanding faculty member from being hired and instead supported a candidate with less impressive qualifications. A U.S. district court held that Holy Cross's administration was motivated by legitimate academic reasons and not by race, color, or national origin bias when it denied tenure to Huang.[96]

Faculty members who are terminated or denied a promotion because of their unpopular or radical ideas or because they support certain causes or organizations may invoke the First Amendment of the U.S. Constitution to preserve their academic freedom.[97] As the president of Yale University stated in 1972, "In strong universities, assuring freedom from intellectual conformity coerced *within* the institution is even more of a concern than is the protection of freedom from external interference"[98] (emphasis in the original). A conflict may exist, however, between the ideologies of a faculty member and the research and teaching needs of an academic unit. The courts may thus have to untangle the individual and institutional strands of academic freedom when a faculty member claims tenure was denied because of his or her research and teaching interests, whereas the institution claims that the faculty member's academic specialty did not mesh with its research and teaching needs.

Faculty who chronically complain or create interpersonal problems may also jeopardize their employment status. *Johnson v. Michigan State University*, discussed earlier, involved a black female faculty member at a medical school who complained repeatedly about her office facilities and secretarial support. She was described by colleagues as abrasive, intimidating, authoritarian, and incapable of accepting constructive criticism. Her personality led to confrontations with both faculty and students. These characteristics, plus her failure to pass medical board examinations, ultimately led to her being denied tenure at Michigan State, a decision that was upheld in U.S. district court.[99]

A similar problem arose in *Jawa v. Fayetteville State University*. In

[96]*Huang v. College of the Holy Cross*, 15 FEP Cases 720 (1977).

[97]Faculty members in most private colleges and universities who support labor organizations are protected under the National Labor Relations Act, as amended. Faculty in public institutions may seek protection through state collective bargaining legislation, executive orders, court decisions, or attorney general opinions.

[98]Quoted in Perry A. Zirkel, "Personality as a Criterion for Faculty Tenure: The Enemy It Is Us," *Cleveland State Law Review* 33 (1984–85): 230.

[99]*Johnson v. Michigan State University*, 30 FEP Cases 265 (1982).

this case, a tenured professor of education psychology was terminated because of his harsh treatment of students (grading unfairly and screaming at them in class) and frequent conflicts with administrators and faculty (creating disruptions during faculty meetings). Jawa, a native of India, filed charges of race and national origin discrimination against the university.[100] In supporting the university's right to terminate him, even though he was tenured, a U.S. district court noted:

> This court finds as fact that [the] plaintiff was a poor teacher who was apparently unwilling to prepare for class; that he had difficulty interacting with students and had little interest in his students; that he failed to keep office hours and to advise properly his students; that he was uncooperative with his colleagues and the administration; that he was unwilling or unable to follow the appropriate and proper directives of his superiors and comply with University policies and procedures; and that plaintiff's reckless disregard for the truth resulted in accusing his superiors of incompetence and discriminatory practices against him.[101]

Faculty members who are denied tenure because of poor working relationships with colleagues or administrators may claim that either the institution's promotion and tenure guidelines or its employment contracts made no reference to such criteria as "collegiality," "cooperativeness," or "leadership potential." Robert Bresnick, a faculty member in Manhattanville College's dance and theater department, was denied tenure because of concerns about his "unwillingness to work with colleagues 'in a sufficiently collegial and collaborative manner,' raising 'doubts about his ability to offer necessary leadership.' " Bresnick and the American Association of University Professors (AAUP) argued that collegiality and working relationships with

---

[100]Fayetteville State University, a state-assisted institution in North Carolina, has traditionally had a predominantly black faculty and student body.

[101]*Jawa v. Fayetteville State University*, 19 FEP Cases 1256–57 (1976). A plaintiff's demeanor in court may also work against him or her in a personality case. In a case in which a professor was denied tenure and filed charges of discrimination based on national origin against Tarleton State University, a U.S. district court in Texas noted: "Additionally, the Court notes that from observing the personality and demeanor of Plaintiff as a witness it was evident that Plaintiff would be a difficult person with whom to work. Throughout the trial, it was evident that Plaintiff's personality could create a number of conflicts in the workplace." *De Weist v. Tarleton State University*, 48 FEP Cases 490 (1987).

colleagues were not listed as performance criteria in Manhattanville College's faculty evaluation guidelines. A federal district court in New York, however, disagreed and stated that cooperation and collegiality "are essential to a department" that must work with other departments and train groups of students to orchestrate dance and drama programs. The court cautioned against the "tyranny of literalness" when reading a personnel document. In addition, the court expressed its reluctance to second-guess academic judgments about tenure decisions.[102]

> While the American Association of University Professors, representing one side of the inherent tension in such matters, contends that the "precise terms and conditions of every appointment should be stated in writing and be in the possession of the teacher before the appointment is consummated," stress on overly detailed written criteria can act as a straitjacket preventing consideration of sometimes critical but more subjective factors. Courts accordingly decline to impose either regime on an institution, or distort language used to force an institution into a more paperwork-based mode.[103] (citations omitted)

College and university administrators must be careful to avoid viewing the behavior of female or minority faculty members differently from that of male and nonminority faculty because of race or sex stereotypes. In *Pace College v. Commission on Human Rights of the City of New York,* a New York State court of appeals held that the university engaged in illegal discrimination when it terminated a female faculty member because she was "troublesome."[104] Valentine R. Winsey was an associate professor in Pace's new social science department. The department head told her that he did not like women around him because he could not use "four-letter" words in their presence. He also claimed that he could not pay her as much as a man because it would "demoralize" his department. Winsey encountered intradepartmental political problems because of recommendations made by an ad hoc curriculum committee, which she chaired. Historians in the department claimed Winsey "sold [them] down the river." Relations between Winsey and various university

---

[102]*Bresnick v. Manhattanville College,* 864 F.Supp. 327 (S.D.N.Y. 1994). The federal district court quoted several earlier cases that cautioned against the strict reading of a contract. For example, in *Guiseppi v. Walling,* 144 F.2d 608, 624, (2d Cir. 1944) *aff'd* 324 U.S. 244, 65 S.Ct. 605, 89 L. Ed. 921 (1945), the court said, "There is no surer way to misread any document than to read it literally."

[103]*Bresnick v. Manhattanville College,* 864 F.Supp. 327 (S.D.N.Y. 1994).

[104]The institution's name was changed from Pace College to Pace University.

administrators were also less than amicable. Subsequently, Winsey was denied a promotion to the rank of professor by the department peer review committee and, because the department head and dean regarded her as a troublemaker, they began to keep detailed records of their conversations with her. Winsey was later denied tenure and placed on a one-year terminal contract. The court found, however, that unlawful discrimination was the likely cause of her termination.

> Pace [College] asserts that it was just because Dr. Winsey was a "troublemaker" that she was terminated, with some reference to lack of publication and her not satisfying some of the minimal requirements in a faculty handbook which Dr. Winsey denied knowing about until after her failure to receive a promotion. Yet it is not controverted that what Dr. Winsey did in seeking promotion was not out of the ordinary course for faculty men. What became apparent is that she was a "troublesome" woman. What Dr. Winsey did to cause her termination would not have been considered "troublesome" if she had not been a woman. It often happens that those who are not supine and fight for their rights will be regarded as troublesome and those disturbed by the struggle would wish that the troublesome one "would just go away." To terminate Dr. Winsey's employment for this reason, if that were the reason, is to have unlawfully discriminated against her.[105]

Although this case involved the application of New York State law, the state court's ruling would appear to be applicable under federal law.[106]

---

[105]*Pace College v. Commission on Human Rights of the City of New York*, 19 FEP Cases 436 (1975).

[106]For example, an employer terminated a woman for "unladylike" behavior because she used profanity. A U.S. district court ruled that her termination was a violation of Title VII. See *EEOC v. FLC & Brothers Rebel, Inc.*, 44 FEP Cases 362 (1987).

7. THE BURDEN OF PROOF IN COLLEGE AND UNIVERSITY DISCRIMINATION CASES

W HEN A FACULTY MEMBER DECIDES to sue a college or university for wrongful discharge or discrimination, enough evidence must be compiled to convince a judge or jury that an illegal employment action has occurred. Such evidence might include the personnel folders of specific faculty members, statistics that illustrate patterns of discrimination, faculty handbooks, letters and memos, depositions and testimony from concerned parties, and copies of research articles and teaching evaluations. The gathering and analysis of such evidence can be a monumental task. At the outset, the institution is not required to defend or otherwise justify its decision to deny reappointment, promotion, or tenure to a faculty member. If the faculty member presents enough evidence to suggest the possibility of illegal discrimination, then the institution has the burden of showing that the promotion or tenure decision was made in good faith without a discriminatory animus. The plaintiff, however, has both the initial and the ultimate burden of proof.

Most cases of employment discrimination in colleges and universities involve disparate treatment rather than disparate impact. In a disparate treatment case, the plaintiff must present evidence of *intentional* discrimination by a peer review committee or academic administrators based on race, sex, age, or other impermissible grounds. Such evidence comes in a variety of forms. For example, a plaintiff may present a statistical analysis of institutional hiring, reappointment, promotion, or tenure patterns.[1] Qualitative compari-

[1]Evidence of disparate impact may be used to substantiate incidences of disparate treatment. See *Lieberman v. Gant*, 23 FEP Cases 511 (1980).

sons may be made between faculty members who received promotions or tenure and those who did not. Evidence may include documentation about the college or university's failure to follow a faculty or personnel manual when making performance evaluations or reappointment, promotion, and tenure decisions. Some plaintiffs have cited incidents of racial or sexual harassment, retaliation, unprofessional behavior by department chairs or deans, and hostile working conditions to bolster their claims of disparate treatment.[2]

McDonnell Douglas–Burdine Standards

The McDonnell Douglas–Burdine test is a three-stage procedure that is used to establish a case of disparate treatment.[3] In the first stage, the plaintiff must demonstrate that he or she is a member of a protected class. Under Title VII, every person can demonstrate the first requirement. The term "race" covers the prevalent situation in which blacks are victimized by whites, but it also applies to discrimination by blacks against whites or other racial groups.[4] Likewise, the

[2]See, for example, *Clark v. Claremont University Center and Graduate School*, 65 FEP Cases 919 (1992); *Jew v. University of Iowa*, 57 FEP Cases 647 (1990); *Jackson v. Harvard University*, 52 FEP Cases 981 (1990); *Chung v. Morehouse College*, 11 FEP Cases 1087 (1975); *Brown v. Trustees of Boston University*, 51 FEP Cases 827 (1989); *Goulianos v. Ramapo College*, 41 FEP Cases 334 (1986); *Farlow v. University of North Carolina*, 39 FEP Cases 1421 (1985); *EEOC v. Boston University*, 35 FEP Cases 711 (1984); *Craik v. The Minnesota State University Board, St. Cloud State University*, 34 FEP Cases 662, 677, and 681 (1984); *Zahorik v. Cornell University*, 34 FEP Cases 167 (1984); *Greer v. University of Arkansas Board of Trustees*, 33 FEP Cases 84 (1982); *Timper v. Board of Regents of the University of Wisconsin System*, 28 FEP Cases 695 (1981); and *Ishigami v. University of Hawaii*, 19 FEP Cases 1412 (1979).

[3]*McDonnell Douglas Corp. v. Green*, 5 FEP Cases 965 (1973), and *Texas Department of Community Affairs v. Burdine*, 25 FEP Cases 113 (1981). As a result of the numerous tenure denial cases brought under Title VII after the 1972 amendment, the McDonnell Douglas standard was altered somewhat to fit the academic setting. In *Smith v. University of North Carolina*, 23 FEP Cases 1739 (1980), the U.S. Court of Appeals (Fourth Circuit) modified the McDonnell Douglas–Burdine test and required that a plaintiff would establish a prima facie case if the following four steps were met: (1) the plaintiff belonged to a disadvantaged class (which includes women); (2) the plaintiff sought and was qualified for reappointment or promotion; (3) the plaintiff was not reappointed or promoted; and, (4) in the case of promotion, the employer had promoted other persons with similar qualifications at approximately the same time. See Christopher H. Kallaher, "*Namenwirth v. Board of Regents of the University of Wisconsin*: Proving Pretext in a Title VII Tenure Denial Case," *Wisconsin Law Review* (1987): 1043–44.

[4]See *Planells v. Howard University*, 32 FEP Cases 336 (1983), and *Craig v. Alabama State University*, 17 FEP Cases 558 (1978). Title VII also protects *subclasses* of persons who are victimized by discrimination. For example, an employer may not harbor prejudice for Asians, as a group, or females, as a group. The same employer, however, may discriminate against Asian women for reasons stemming from a particular set of stereotypes and assumptions not shared about either Asian men or white women. In *Lam v. University of Hawaii*, 66 FEP Cases 81 (1994), the Ninth Circuit stated: "When a plaintiff is claiming race *and* sex bias, it is necessary to determine whether the employer

term "sex" applies to the more common problem of males discriminating against females, but employment discrimination against males (based on their sex) is also a violation of Title VII.[5] Merely being the "first-to-fall victim" to a personnel policy is not evidence of illegal discrimination. In a previously discussed case, a female physical education instructor at Tufts University was denied tenure because of a new policy that made it very difficult to achieve tenure in the department. The court held that even though the new standards first worked to the disadvantage of a female, this by itself did not raise the specter of sex discrimination.[6]

In the second stage, the plaintiff must demonstrate that he or she was qualified for the job. The issue of qualifications is often vague and subjective in cases involving the reappointment, promotion, and tenure of college professors. The U.S. Court of Appeals (First Circuit) has stated that the plaintiff

> need only show that he was sufficiently qualified to be among those persons from whom a selection, to some extent discretionary, would be made. That is, he need show only that his qualifications were at least sufficient to place him in the middle group of tenure candidates as to whom both a decision granting tenure and a decision denying tenure could be justified as a reasonable exercise of discretion by the tenure-decision making body.[7]

Faculty might meet this burden by showing that their teaching, research, and service accomplishments compare favorably with those of tenured colleagues in their department. In addition, a favorable recommendation by a department peer review committee, a petition of support from students, or letters of recommendation from extramural scholars might help the faculty member demonstrate that he or she possesses "sufficient qualifications."[8]

A former faculty member (of Hispanic origin) at the John Jay

---

discriminates on the basis of that *combination* of factors, not just whether it discriminates against people of the same race or of the same sex" (emphasis in original).

[5]For a discussion of Title VII cases involving male plaintiffs, see James T. Poindexter, "Discrimination against Male Faculty in Higher Education: Will Title VII Become the 'Unfair Employment Act'?" *Labor Law Journal* 39 (Sept. 1988): 615–21.

[6]*Hooker v. Tufts University*, 37 FEP Cases 509 (1983).

[7]*Banerjee v. Board of Trustees of Smith College*, 25 FEP Cases 1074 (1981). Also see *Fields v. Clark University*, 59 FEP Cases 129 (1992).

[8]John Anthony Palombi, "The Ineffectiveness of Title VII in Tenure Denial Decisions," *DePaul Law Review* 36 (Winter 1987): 266–67.

College of Criminal Justice established a prima facie case by showing
that his department repeatedly recommended him for reappointment
and tenure. A U.S. district court held that the professor might have
been the victim of employment discrimination because he had twice
managed to overturn on appeals warrants decisions denying him
reappointment.[9] This degree of proof would appear to eliminate
faculty members whose qualifications are clearly inferior to those of
other recent candidates for reappointment, promotion, or tenure. In
relatively few academic cases, however, do the plaintiffs clearly fail to
meet minimal performance standards.[10] Furthermore, most colleges
and universities do not publish specific minimum standards for
teaching, research, and service. The courts also appear to require a
higher standard of proof for tenure or promotion cases than for
reappointment cases. Thus, Judge Henry J. Friendly in *Lieberman v.
Gant* noted that "a candidate for tenure does not make out the
elements needed for a *prima facie* case merely by showing qualifications for continuation as an untenured faculty member" (emphasis in
the original).[11]

In *Lynn v. Regents of the University of California*, the U.S. Court of
Appeals (Ninth Circuit) stated that objective qualifications (the plaintiff's level of education, years of experience, number of articles
published, and so on) are best treated during the early stages of the
McDonnell Douglas–Burdine test, whereas subjective criteria, along
with any supporting evidence, should be treated during the latter
stages of the process. To do otherwise would collapse the burden of
proof analysis into a single, initial step, thereby requiring that all
issues be resolved at once and defeating the underlying purpose of
the McDonnell Douglas–Burdine process.[12]

---

[9]*Torres v. City University of New York, John Jay College of Criminal Justice and Lynch*, 56
FEP Cases 1171 (1991).

[10]Faculty members who are hired before completing their doctoral dissertations and
who subsequently fail to complete requirements for the degree are frequently terminated after a stipulated period of time. Such individuals might be placed in the
category of failing to meet minimal performance standards. See *Ottaviani v. State
University of New York at New Paltz*, 50 FEP Cases 251 (1989). In addition, that an
institution is trying to upgrade the quality of its faculty has been regarded as a
legitimate, nondiscriminatory reason for terminating a professor who has not completed an advanced degree. See *Campbell v. Ramsey*, 484 F. Supp. 190 (E.D. Ark. 1980),
aff'd 631 F.2d 597.

[11]*Lieberman v. Gant*, 23 FEP Cases 508 (1980).

[12]*Lynn v. Regents of the University of California*, 28 FEP Cases 416 (1981). According to
the court: "However, in some instances a showing of specific or general discriminatory
conduct by a university through statistical or other evidence will be sufficient to raise
doubts as to whether objective criteria are applied in a non-discriminatory manner. In

The typical faculty member in a wrongful discharge or employment discrimination case presents both good and bad elements of job performance. Some faculty may have been productive researchers but poor teachers. Other faculty may have done an outstanding job with regard to professional and university service but have inadequate research records. Still others may have been strong on all major criteria but unable to work in harmony with colleagues. Given the subjective nature of performance appraisals in measuring faculty research, teaching, and service, it may be difficult for a faculty member to prove that he or she met some vaguely specified level of performance. In this respect, the U.S. Court of Appeals (Seventh Circuit) in a nonacademic case provides some insight:

> The plaintiff need not show perfect performance or even average performance to satisfy this element. He need only show that his performance was of sufficient quality to merit continued employment, thereby raising the inference that some other factor was involved in the decision to discharge him. . . .
>
> Satisfactory performance is an ordinary prerequisite of continued employment, just as job qualification is an ordinary prerequisite to hiring. However, the plaintiff need not, and indeed cannot, disprove as a cause of his discharge a source of dissatisfaction of which he is unaware. Accordingly, the employer's acceptance of his work without express reservation is sufficient to show that the plaintiff was performing satisfactorily for the purpose of shifting the burden of proof.[13]

The phrase "the employer's acceptance of his work without express reservation" poses a potential dilemma if applied to colleges and universities. Approximately two-thirds of the U.S. labor force are employed on an "at-will" basis. At-will employees can be terminated "on the spot" for almost any reason that does not violate a federal or state equal employment opportunity law. But most untenured faculty members have at least a one-year contract, which makes termination unlikely during the course of the academic year. An "express reservation" regarding the unacceptability of a faculty member's performance may not be made until it is time to renew the faculty member's contract or complete a tenure review. Thus, a faculty member may

---

those instances dismissal would not be proper, even though [the] plaintiff has failed to show he has met 'objective criteria.' "

[13]*Flowers v. Crouch-Walker Corp.*, 14 FEP Cases 1265 (1977).

contend that since the department head or dean did not express an immediate objection to the faculty member's job performance, the burden of proof for justifying a failure to reappoint, promote, or grant tenure automatically shifts to the institution.

Colleges and universities are free to establish high expectations of performance for their faculty and to refuse to reappoint, promote, or tenure those who fail to meet objective or subjective standards. It is important, however, to avoid any semblance of sexism, racism, or other illegal discriminatory animus when making employment decisions in academia. In *Price Waterhouse v. Hopkins*, the U.S. Supreme Court held that an employer could avoid liability for intentional discrimination in a "mixed-motive" case (a case with both legitimate and discriminatory elements) if the employer could demonstrate that the same action would have been taken in the absence of an illegal discriminatory motive.[14] Price Waterhouse bypassed Ann Hopkins for partnership even though her job performance was clearly exceptional. Some partners in the firm thought she should not be promoted because of her abrasive personality, use of profanity, and other "unladylike" characteristics.

The Civil Rights Act of 1991 reversed the Court's *Price Waterhouse* ruling by stipulating that any intentional discrimination is unlawful, even if the employer would have made the same adverse personnel decision in the absence of a discriminatory motive. Colleges and universities can refuse to reappoint, promote, or tenure faculty who exhibit personality characteristics that detract from their ability to work with others, but such actions cannot be taken with respect to stereotypes (such as a faculty member who is regarded as being too aggressive for a female) that affect a protected class. Evidence of a discriminatory animus through documented racist or sexist remarks may also create an inference of intentional discrimination.[15]

In the third stage of the McDonnell Douglas–Burdine test, the position for which the faculty member was rejected or not reappointed must remain open and the employer must continue to seek other applicants or candidates for promotion whose qualifications are either equivalent or inferior to the plaintiff's. This facet of the test

---

[14]*Price Waterhouse v. Hopkins*, 49 FEP Cases 954 (1989).

[15]See, for example, *Jew v. University of Iowa*, 57 FEP Cases 647 (1990); *Brown v. Trustees of Boston University*, 51 FEP Cases 815 (1989); and *Goulianos v. Ramapo College*, 41 FEP Cases 329 (1986).

may be satisfied by showing that tenured positions "were open at the time the plaintiff was denied tenure, in the sense that others were granted tenure in the department during a period relatively near to the time [the] plaintiff was denied tenure."[16] Kenneth J. Arenson, a white professor, employed at the Southern University Law Center (an institution in which a majority of faculty and students are black), was denied a tenure-track position allegedly because there was no vacancy. The U.S. Court of Appeals (Fifth Circuit) concluded that a reasonable jury could have determined that there was a vacancy but that it was denied to Arenson for a discriminatory purpose. Specifically, the university had terminated two faculty, thereby creating vacancies. Furthermore, the Law Center had offered a tenured position to a black woman who had less experience than Arenson. These actions, coupled with comments by the chair of the Law Center's promotion and tenure committee that the institution needed to maintain a black majority on its faculty, along with the university's failure to offer legitimate nondiscriminatory reasons for its decision, raised the inference of illegal race discrimination.[17] As noted earlier in the discussion of affirmative action programs, Title VII prohibits using race as a factor in an employment decision, even when a minority group that has historically suffered from discrimination is favored over a nonminority group that has not been victimized.

Promotion and tenure decisions are unique in that an unsuccessful candidate is not necessarily replaced immediately by a successful candidate.[18] In *Kunda v. Muhlenberg College*, a physical education instructor, Connie Rae Kunda, was denied promotion and tenure because she did not have a master's degree. Denying a promotion or tenure to a faculty member who fails to earn a postgraduate degree is legitimate and nondiscriminatory. The college had failed to counsel her, however, about the importance of obtaining a master's degree, whereas such counseling was provided to male faculty who were Kunda's contemporaries. According to the U.S. Court of Appeals (Third Circuit):

---

[16]*Banerjee v. Board of Trustees of Smith College*, 25 FEP Cases 1073 (1981).

[17]*Arenson v. Southern University Law Center*, 53 FEP Cases 1552 (1990). This case was appealed to the U.S. Supreme Court, but certiorari was denied. The case has been remanded back to the U.S. district court for retrial. See *Arenson v. Southern University Law Center*, 59 FEP Cases 1 (1992) and 66 FEP Cases 1520 (1995).

[18]*Roebuck v. Drexel University*, 47 FEP Cases 761 (1988).

The trial court [U.S. district court] found that "[d]efendants have given no convincing reason for their failure to inform Mrs. Kunda of the necessity of obtaining a masters [sic] degree," nor has appellant done so in this court. Thus, there was a failure on the part of Muhlenberg to articulate a legitimate basis for its failure to counsel Kunda comparably to males regarding the need for a master's degree. In view of the importance which the College itself placed on the possession of such a degree, notwithstanding the published standards referring to other criteria, the disparate treatment could reasonably have been considered substantial by the trial court. . . .

The trial court recognized the need to make findings on this issue, and determined that the disparate treatment with respect to counseling was not the result of mere inadvertence, but instead constituted purposeful discrimination on the basis of sex. Among the factors on which the trial court relied for this finding were the failure of Dean Secor and President Morey to tell Kunda that her failure to obtain a master's degree would be a barrier to her advancement, although she had sought them out concerning her future at Muhlenberg.[19]

Although a case of illegal disparate treatment requires the demonstration of intentional discrimination by the defendants, a faculty member does not have to present direct proof of a discriminatory motive to prevail in a Title VII suit.[20] Once a plaintiff has satisfied the McDonnell Douglas–Burdine criteria, a prima facie case is established and the burden of proof then shifts to the college or university to articulate a legitimate, nondiscriminatory reason for its personnel decision.[21] In essence, the college or university must show that its decision is based on a legitimate business consideration and not on an illegal one such as a faculty member's race, sex, or national origin.[22] Legitimate reasons might include an institution's financial problems; the elimination or scaling down of an academic program; a faculty member's inadequate research productivity, teaching effec-

[19]*Kunda v. Muhlenberg College*, 22 FEP Cases 72 (1980).

[20]*Fields v. Clark University*, 43 FEP Cases 1250 (1987).

[21]The requirements discussed in *McDonnell Douglas–Burdine* are not the only way of proving a prima facie case of discrimination. Case facts will vary, and the test established in *McDonnell Douglas–Burdine* is not necessarily applicable in every respect to differing factual contexts. Departures from the requirements are unusual and are warranted only when direct proof of discrimination is undisputed in the record. See *Taylor v. Southern University*, 30 FEP Cases 1343 (1983).

[22]*Furnco Construction Co. v. Waters*, 438 U.S. 567 (1978).

tiveness, or institutional and professional service; or a faculty member's inability to work in harmony with others.[23]

Timper v. Board of Regents of the University of Wisconsin System involved the denial of tenure to a female sociologist at the University of Wisconsin at Stout. The case provides an illustration of how the McDonnell Douglas–Burdine test is applied and how an institution may rebut accusations of illegal discrimination. Priscilla Timper began teaching in the social science department at the university during the 1972–73 academic year. Three years later, she was reviewed for tenure. A three-person review committee recommended Timper for tenure, as did the majority of tenured faculty in her department. The department head, however, recommended against tenure, citing the need for a person with a master's degree in social work as well as deficiencies in Timper's credentials. The dean and chancellor concurred with the department head's recommendation and Timper was terminated at the end of 1976. After a lengthy discussion of the problems of analyzing a tenure case under the McDonnell Douglas–Burdine standard, a U.S. district court held that Timper had established a prima facie case of sex discrimination. The university assumed the burden of proof and presented evidence "sufficient to raise a genuine issue of fact" regarding the reasons Timper was denied tenure. The burden of proof then shifted to Timper to show that the reasons advanced by the university were pretextual. She attempted to meet this burden by showing that each of its reasons was unworthy of credence. In addition, she attempted to show that the university had a poor record with respect to the employment and promotion of female faculty. She claimed that male faculty received more favorable treatment than female faculty with respect to tenure, and she accused the department head of being biased toward women.[24]

The court carefully evaluated all of the evidence submitted by Timper and concluded that the University of Wisconsin System met

---

[23]Colleges and universities are apparently held to the same level of proof as other organizations. In *Sweeney v. Board of Trustees of Keene State College*, 18 FEP Cases 520 (1978), the U.S. Supreme Court remanded the decision to the U.S. Court of Appeals because it found that the court appeared to impose a heavier burden on the employer than required by *McDonnell Douglas*. The lower court, on remand, again found that the college had discriminated against Sweeney.

[24]Thomas J. Flygare, "*TCDA v. Burdine:* The Decreasing Burden for Employers in Title VII Litigation," *Journal of College and University Law* 8 (1981–82): 527.

its burden to "articulate" by presenting evidence to support the denial of tenure to a female sociologist.

> Defendant's evidence was sufficient to raise a genuine issue of fact [as to] whether each of the following reasons was the reason for denial of tenure: (1) [Plaintiff] and the sociologists within the Department had identified the hiring of a sociologist/social worker, with the requisite credentials, as a critical programmatic need. (2) The credentials of other sociologists as well as social workers applying for a position with the Department at the time were more in keeping with its needs. (3) Granting plaintiff tenure would have meant that all of the sociologists and 15 of the 19 members of the Department would be tenured, leaving it little flexibility to recruit personnel in the future to respond to changing student needs.[25]

Although the burden of proof will shift to the college or university once a prima facie case has been established, both the original and the ultimate burden of proof remain with the faculty member. The institution normally does not have to go to great lengths to defend its reason for denying a promotion or tenure request as long as there is no evidence of a discriminatory animus: "Merely casting doubt on the employer's articulated reason does not suffice to meet the plaintiff's burden of demonstrating discriminatory intent for 'the defendant need not persuade the court that it was actually motivated by the proffered reasons in the first place'."[26]

The faculty member must prove that the college or university's reasons for denying a promotion or tenure were merely a pretext for illegal discrimination. If the plaintiff presents enough evidence for a court to find that the asserted reasons for the adverse employment decision were not the actual reasons, then it may infer that the college or university was motivated in its decision by race, sex, or other prohibited criterion. In *Brown v. Trustees of Boston University*, a federal district court ordered the university to reinstate English professor Julia Prewitt Brown and pay her damages for lost compensation and benefits as well as for emotional trauma.[27] In affirming the lower court's ruling, the U.S. Court of Appeals (First Circuit) stated:

[25]*Timper v. Board of Regents of the University of Wisconsin System*, 28 FEP Cases 698 (1981).

[26]Quoting *White v. Vathally*, 34 FEP Cases 1130 (1984), in *O'Connor v. Peru State College*, 39 FEP Cases 1240 (1985).

[27]"Federal Judge Orders Professor Reinstated at Boston University," *New York Times*, Nov. 9, 1987, pp. 22(N), A21(L).

An employee's right not to be denied tenure for discriminatory reasons prevents insulating the tenure process from any judicial review. As in other forms of employment, an inference of discrimination can be derived from a showing that a university's given reasons for denying tenure to the plaintiff were "obviously weak or implausible," or that the tenure standards for prevailing at the tenure decisions were "manifestly unequally applied." The essential words here are "obviously" and "manifestly." A court may not simply substitute its own views concerning the plaintiff's qualifications for those of the properly instituted authorities; the evidence must be of such strength and quality as to permit a reasonable finding that the denial of tenure was "obviously" or "manifestly" unsupported. In this case, Brown's burden was to show that the University *manifestly* applied an unequal standard to her tenure application.[28] (Emphasis in the original)

The plaintiff's burden of proving disparate treatment may be met "indirectly by showing that the employer's proffered explanation is unworthy of credence."[29] For example, in one case, the plaintiff succeeded in establishing that the defendant's reason for denying tenure was merely a pretext for discrimination on the basis of her sex. She demonstrated that: (1) "an atmosphere of exclusivity and [the] belittling of women existed" at the college; (2) women were not represented in equal numbers either on the faculty or in its higher ranks; (3) she and her only female colleague in the department were excluded from decision making and participation in department affairs; (4) the department director and several prominent senior faculty expressed the view that the plaintiff did not need to retain her job because she was married, and "other members of the faculty expressed exclusive or condescending views toward women"; and (5) male faculty members in the plaintiff's department showed little interest in her work and belittled its significance.[30]

A discriminatory animus on the part of a college or university may be demonstrated by submitting evidence of inconsistent judgments or past acts of discrimination.[31] In an age discrimination suit, a U.S.

---

[28]*Brown v. Trustees of Boston University* 51 FEP Cases 824 (1989). The court cited *Kumar v. Board of Trustees, University of Massachusetts*, 38 FEP Cases 1734 (1985).

[29]*Chipollini v. Spencer Gifts*, 43 FEP Cases 681, *cert. dismissed*, 198 S. Ct. 26 (1987).

[30]*Goulianos v. Ramapo College*, 41 FEP Cases 338 (1986).

[31]*Jepsen v. Florida Board of Regents*, 37 FEP Cases 327 (1985).

district court in New York held that a reasonable jury could conclude that a college's explanations for denying tenure were pretextual insofar as an ad hoc committee established by a faculty review board to assess the plaintiff's qualifications unanimously recommended him for tenure. The review board had concluded that the plaintiff's teaching was excellent and his scholarship was very good.[32]

In a case involving a female faculty member who was denied tenure at the University of California at Irvine, the U.S. Court of Appeals (Ninth Circuit) concluded that the university's negative attitude toward women's issues was "evidence of a discriminatory attitude toward women."[33] Furthermore, at least one court has noted that "evidence that an employer has failed to live up to an affirmative action plan is relevant to the question of discriminatory intent."[34]

One of the most flagrant and costly examples of intentional discrimination occurred in *Clark v. Claremont University Center*.[35] Reginald Clark, who held a doctorate in education from the University of Wisconsin at Madison, was hired in 1979 as an assistant professor in Claremont's education department. At that time, Clark was the only member of a minority group (he is black) out of the sixty-five to seventy faculty at Claremont. He was told by his department chair that his research focus on minority and multicultural issues was important to the institution.

Clark developed and taught several seminars in his area of expertise. He also wrote a 1,137-page technical report (funded by the Spencer Institute in Chicago) on family structure and the cognitive development of children, had scholarly articles accepted by academic journals, presented papers at scholarly meetings, and had a book published by the University of Chicago Press in 1983 on black families as educators.

In addition to his professional successes, however, Clark had several disturbing experiences during his time at Claremont. Several faculty offices in the education department, including Clark's, were vandalized, and a racial slur was spray-painted on Clark's office wall.

---

[32]*Guntur v. Union College*, 57 FEP Cases 926 (1991). A federal district court later held that Union College articulated a nondiscriminatory reason for its decision. *Guntur v. Union College*, 60 FEP Cases 163 (1992).

[33]*Lynn v. Regents of the University of California*, 28 FEP Cases 414 (1981).

[34]*Craik v. The Minnesota State University Board, St. Cloud State University*, 34 FEP Cases 654 (1984). Also see *Scelsa v. City University of New York*, 67 FEP Cases 41 (1992), and *Greer v. University of Arkansas Board of Trustees*, 33 FEP Cases 82 (1982).

[35]*Clark v. Claremont University Center and Graduate School*, 65 FEP Cases 919 (1992).

Several colleagues regarded him with suspicion, believing that he was linked somehow to the office ransacking, and some faculty allegedly made derogatory comments about him and other African Americans. Furthermore, the dean asked Clark to "push the affirmative action issue" at Claremont and told him to offer suggestions about ways to infuse multiracial content into the graduate programs. Yet when Clark offered ideas, the dean ignored them.

Despite his problems, Clark's prospects appeared to be good as the time for his tenure review drew near. His book had received favorable reviews, and he had published several journal articles. Five external scholars in Clark's field offered unanimous praise of his work and recommended that he be granted tenure. Of the fifty students who submitted critiques of his teaching effectiveness, thirty-eight were positive and twelve were negative. Members of the former group described Clark as an enthusiastic, creative, and energetic teacher who motivated and inspired students. The students who submitted negative comments described Clark as someone who had sudden mood swings, was rude and defensive, lost his temper, and had shouting matches with those who questioned or disagreed with his views.

On the day that the education department was to consider his request for tenure, Clark was viewing a tape in a department audiovisual room. Coincidentally, and apparently unknown to him, his tenure review was taking place in a room adjacent to the one in which he was working. He was distracted by loud voices next door and soon realized the nature of the meeting. Clark heard one professor remark that "us white people have rights, too." Another stated, "I don't know how I would feel working on a permanent base with a black man." The education faculty nevertheless voted five to three to grant Clark tenure. The Appointments, Promotions, and Tenure (APT) Committee, however, voted to deny tenure by an overwhelming majority.

Clark subsequently approached the president of Claremont to request "compensatory consideration" for his race, especially given that he would have been the first tenured minority faculty member in the school's history. He also told the president about the remarks he had overheard while working in the audiovisual room. The president concluded, however, that Clark's tenure review at the department level was not tainted by racial prejudice and that he did not meet Claremont's teaching and scholarship requirements. Thus, the president formally notified Clark that the APT Committee's denial of his tenure would stand.

Reginald Clark filed a race discrimination suit with the California Department of Fair Employment and Housing. The department issued a right-to-sue letter to him in 1985, and the case proceeded to state court. The first trial, in March 1989, ended in a mistrial because of juror attrition. The second trial, a year later, resulted in a $1.4 million judgment against Claremont for disparate treatment.[36]

The university appealed, and the California Court of Appeal (Second District) held that the verdict in the lower court was supported by sufficient evidence. The state appeals court held that the *McDonnell Douglas* burden of proof standard was appropriate for Clark's case. The court said that a plaintiff who is denied tenure need not prove intentional discrimination at each stage of the tenure review process. Even though a faculty member is supposed to have a "fresh" review at each stage of the tenure evaluation, it is permissible for a jury to conclude that a discriminatory evaluation at one level could influence the decision at another level. Thus, a racial animus at the department level (which the court regarded as the most significant step in the entire process) could have contaminated the decision of the APT Committee and president. The court also placed considerable weight on the racist remark of the faculty member ("us white people have rights, too"), even though this faculty member voted to grant tenure to Clark. The lukewarm nature of this faculty member's support could, according to the court, have been regarded by a jury as a subterfuge for discrimination.

The court also said that racial animosity toward Clark might be inferred from the following circumstances: (1) Claremont had never granted tenure to a minority faculty member; (2) external reviewers who were scholars in Clark's field had found his work to be of groundbreaking significance; (3) two other nonminority professors had received tenure even though their publication records were inferior to Clark's; (4) Claremont used unwritten, changing publication standards to justify its denial of tenure to Clark; (5) Clark was able to cast doubt on the credibility of the president's testimony by demonstrating an inconsistency between statements that he made during a deposition and statements that he made during the trial

---

[36]The jury awarded Clark $1 million plus $16,327 in punitive damages. The trial court awarded $416,633.13 for attorney's fees.

(regarding the racist remark of a faculty member); and (6) the president had been intensely criticized for alleged racial discrimination while working at another university (even though he had a record of civil rights activism and had not been accused of making racist remarks). In conclusion, the court stated:

> We must add we are not surprised by the jury's verdict. Many employment discrimination cases do not even survive to trial because evidence of the employer's proper motive is so difficult to obtain. This case is unusual, not because of Clark's claims, but because of Clark's strong evidence of improper motive. Our own computer-assisted research of tenure denial cases across the nation revealed none involving university professors who made such blatant remarks as in this case. We hold the jury's verdict is supported by substantial evidence.[37]

Most disparate treatment cases boil down to whether a faculty member would have been granted reappointment, promotion, or tenure *but for* his or her race, sex, national origin, or other protected classification.[38] A college or university is not likely to be judged guilty of illegal discrimination simply because it failed to make careful, well-reasoned personnel decisions or failed to follow prescribed procedures. The key to disparate treatment cases lies in the plaintiff's ability to provide a quantum of evidence that indicates an *intent* to discriminate by college or university officials for reasons that would be illegal under Title VII or other equal employment opportunity law. Such reasons might include holding black faculty members to higher standards for promotion than white faculty members, providing career counseling and timely performance appraisals to male faculty while failing to do so for similarly situated females, or claiming that a faculty member does not "fit in" because of his or her age, race, sex, religious beliefs, or national origin. In the absence of such proof, the plaintiff will fail to demonstrate disparate treatment.[39]

[37]*Clark v. Claremont University Center and Graduate School*, 65 FEP Cases 935 (1992).

[38]See, for example, *Roebuck v. Drexel University*, 47 FEP Cases 762–63 (1988).

[39]In 1983, the U.S. Supreme Court made an additional attempt to clarify its position regarding proof in disparate treatment cases. *Postal Service v. Aikens*, 108 S. Ct. 1478 (1983), focused on the McDonnell Douglas–Burdine test and established a three-stage process that is somewhat different from the one described above. In stage 1, the plaintiff must present sufficient evidence of discrimination to support a prima facie case, according to the elements set forth in *McDonnell Douglas–Burdine*. If a prima facie case is not established at stage 1, the employer's motion to dismiss the case will be granted. Stage 2 is reached if the court determines that the plaintiff has presented evidence of a prima facie case. At this stage, the employer must respond with evidence of a nondiscriminatory reason for the personnel decision against the plaintiff. Stage 3

A plaintiff cannot prove that the employer's reason for his discharge was pretextual merely by claiming that the employer's action was mistaken. The law is clear that an employer's reason for his action may be a good reason, a bad reason, a mistaken reason, or no reason at all, as long as the decision was not based on race or other unlawful discrimination criteria. An employer is not required to prove that its decision was correct; the tryer of fact need only determine that the defendant, in good faith, believed the plaintiff's performance to be unsatisfactory and that the asserted reason for the action was not a mere pretext for discrimination.[40]

The courts have made a distinction between merely articulating a legitimate, nondiscriminatory reason for a particular personnel decision and proving the absence of a discriminatory motive.[41] According to the U.S. Supreme Court, the employer's (defendant's) burden is satisfied under the McDonnell Douglas–Burdine standard if the employer explains what was done or produces evidence of legitimate, nondiscriminatory reasons for the personnel decision. The U.S. Court of Appeals (Second Circuit) stated:

> It is thus enough for the defendants in the second phase of the case to bring forth evidence that they acted on a neutral basis. They do not have the burden of establishing that their basis was sound; rather, the burden then falls on the plaintiff to demonstrate that it is pretextual. One way of doing this, of course, would be to show that the asserted neutral basis was so ridden

---

is known as the "pretext stage" because the plaintiff must either present additional evidence that rebuts the employer's proffered reasons for the decision or continue to rely on its original evidence of a discriminatory motive (presented in stage 1). At the end of stage 3, the court must weigh all evidence on record and decide which party's explanation of the employer's discriminatory intent is to be believed. See David P. Twomey, *Equal Employment Opportunity Law*, 2d ed. (Cincinnati: South-Western, 1990), pp. 50–51.

[40]Quoting *Bostic v. Wall*, 35 FEP Cases 1180 (1984), cited in *O'Connor v. Peru State College*, 39 FEP Cases 1240 (1985).

[41]There is a distinction between the burden of production and the burden of proof. The plaintiff must "prove"; the defendants need only "produce." In *Gutzwiller v. Fenik*, 42 FEP Cases 126 (1986), a U.S. district court noted: "Accordingly, the Court determines that [the] Plaintiff has not proved appropriate scholarship and that Defendants [University of Cincinnati] have produced a legitimate nondiscriminatory reason for the denial of tenure. The Court notes that support for [the] Defendants (sic) position may be found in the fact one member of the department who voted to deny tenure is a woman and that at the same time the department voted to grant tenure to another woman." Because the burden of *producing* is much lighter than the burden of *persuading*, most Title VII disparate treatment cases are decided on the pretext issue. See *Ford v. Nicks*, 47 FEP Cases 1537 (1988).

with error that the defendant could not honestly have relied upon it.[42]

For example, a college or university might use a nationally known scholar as an expert witness to demonstrate that a faculty member's research lacked quality or failed to make a significant contribution. The faculty member would then have to show that the institution's reason for denying him or her a promotion or tenure was a pretext to mask some form of illegal employment discrimination. A pretext cannot be inferred simply because there is disagreement among faculty and administrators regarding the merits of granting a promotion or tenure to a particular faculty member.[43] If the plaintiff is unable to prove that such a pretext exists, then the college or university is entitled to a dismissal of the case.

The burden of proof in disparate treatment cases shifts between the faculty member and the institution as the case progresses. Although the faculty member retains the ultimate burden of proving illegal discrimination, the sequence described here ensures that both sides have ample opportunity to present evidence and arguments to bolster their respective positions: "The 'shifting burdens' approach of *McDonnell Douglas* is not a prescription for refereeing carefully timed volleys of proof and counterproof, but rather 'merely a sensible, orderly way to evaluate the evidence in light of common experience as it bears on the critical question of discrimination.' "[44]

THE *HICKS* DECISION: PRETEXT AND CIRCUMSTANTIAL EVIDENCE OF DISCRIMINATION

Many promotion and tenure discrimination cases involve complaints of disparate treatment that are based on circumstantial evidence. In *St. Mary's Honor Center v. Hicks*, a nonacademic case, the U.S. Supreme Court was asked to answer the following question: in a disparate treatment case with circumstantial evidence, must a court rule in favor of a plaintiff once it determines that the employer's reasons for its actions lack credibility?[45] The Court answered no, and

[42]*Lieberman v. Gant*, 23 FEP Cases 509 (1980).

[43]*Kumar v. Board of Trustees, University of Massachusetts*, 38 FEP Cases 1745 (1985).

[44]Quoting *Furnco Construction Co. v. Waters*, 17 FEP Cases 1062 (1978), in *Craik v. The Minnesota State University Board, St. Cloud State University*, 34 FEP Cases 666 (1984).

[45]*St. Mary's Honor Center v. Hicks*, 62 FEP Cases 96 (1993). For discussions of *Hicks* in the academic context, see *Kobrin v. University of Minnesota*, 65 FEP Cases 1627 (1994), *Fisher v. Vassar College*, 64 FEP Cases 1372 (1994), and *Bina v. Providence College*, 66 FEP Cases 319 (1994).

ruled that a plaintiff in a Title VII case must go beyond showing that an employer's reasons for its personnel decision were pretextual. Rather, the plaintiff must prove that illegal bias was the real motive for the employer's decision. The justices disagreed with the Eighth Circuit's opinion, which stated that if the employer's reasons are found not to be credible, it is in no better position than had it remained silent and offered no justification for its actions. The Court reasoned that a plaintiff would be entitled to judgment as a matter of law only upon a finding that (1) he or she established a prima facie case of illegal discrimination by a preponderance of the evidence and (2) the defendant failed to present nondiscriminatory reasons for its personnel decision. When an employer produces evidence to justify its employment actions, the court must decide whether the plaintiff has proven intentional discrimination. Although a showing of pretext can form the basis for an inference of discrimination, the court must still examine all relevant evidence to determine whether the employer's motives were illegal.[46] The Court stopped short of saying that, as a matter of law, disbelief of the defendant's reasons *compels* judgment for the plaintiff.

The framework for drawing inferences of discrimination established under *McDonnell Douglas, Burdine,* and *Hicks* does not apply either to cases of disparate impact or to cases in which allegations of discrimination can be proven by direct (rather than circumstantial) evidence.[47] It should also be noted that the EEOC, in its investigations and hearings, is not overly concerned with the relative burdens of proof between plaintiffs and defendants. Instead, the EEOC focuses on gathering a wide array of evidence to determine whether discrimination has occurred. The burden of proof issues set forth in *McDonnell Douglas, Burdine,* and *Hicks* become relevant once a case proceeds to federal court.

Civil rights advocates are concerned that *Hicks* will given an edge to employers who fabricate nondiscriminatory reasons for a personnel action. It appears that the *Hicks* decision may place a greater

---

[46]In a dissenting opinion, Justice Paul Souter criticized the majority in *Hicks* by noting that "the [courts] still may proceed to roam the record, searching for some nondiscriminatory explanation that the defendant has not raised and that the plaintiff has had no opportunity to disprove. *St. Mary's Honor Center v. Hicks,* 62 FEP Cases 107 (1993).

[47]See EEOC, "EEOC: General Counsel's Memorandum on Supreme Court's *Hicks* Decision," March 8, 1994, and EEOC, "EEOC: Enforcement Guidance on *St. Mary's Honor Center v. Hicks,*" April 12, 1994.

burden on faculty to demonstrate disparate treatment. Some observers believe that the ruling establishes a "pretext-plus" requirement. Under pretext-plus, it appears a faculty member must (1) show that the college or university lied about the reasons for denying someone tenure *and* (2) provide direct evidence of illegal bias.[48] Given the subtle nature of employment discrimination, direct evidence may be difficult or impossible to obtain.

Management attorneys, however, are more likely to view the situation in *Hicks* as an anomaly.[49] According to Doug McDowell, general counsel for the Equal Employment Advisory Commission, the decision will have a limited impact on cases in which burden of proof is a key issue. He claims that most discrimination cases in which pretext is found are settled out of court.[50]

At the very least, the Supreme Court's decision in *Hicks* should remind colleges and universities to be even more thorough and meticulous in evaluating faculty performance and justifying personnel decisions. If an institution offers reasons for an adverse employment decision that are transparent or weak, the faculty member may

[48]"Direct evidence of discrimination is 'evidence which if believed proves the existence of a fact in issue without inference or presumption.' *Castle v. Sangamo Weston, Inc.*, 837 F.2d 1550, 1558 n.13 [46 FEP Cases 139] (11th Cir. 1988). Furthermore, '[o]nly the most blatant remarks, whose intent could be nothing other than to discriminate constitute evidence of discrimination.' *Carter v. Miami*, 870 F.2d 578, 581–82 [49 FEP Cases 1014] (11th Cir. 1989)." Cited in *Hassan v. Auburn University*, 64 FEP Cases 1386 (1993).

[49]Melvin Hicks, a black male, worked as a shift commander at the St. Mary's Honor Center, a halfway house. He was subjected to increasingly severe disciplinary actions for rules violations and for the manner in which he handled an inmate disturbance. Hicks was discharged after he threatened his supervisor during an argument. At trial, Hicks established a prima facie case of disparate treatment because (1) he is black, (2) he was qualified for the position of shift commander, (3) he was subjected to adverse employment actions, and (4) his position remained open after he was fired and was filled by a white male. The U.S. district court found that the reasons articulated by St. Mary's for Hicks's dismissal (the severity and frequency of his transgressions) were false; other co-workers were treated more leniently than Hicks, even though they had committed similar violations. The district court nonetheless held that Hicks was terminated for personal rather than racial reasons. The Eighth Circuit reversed and remanded, saying that Hicks was entitled to judgment as a matter of law once the employer's reasons were shown to lack credibility. The U.S. Supreme Court held that even though an employer's reasons may be pretextual, it does not necessarily mandate a finding for the plaintiff.

[50]BNA, "Legislation to Overturn, Debate Follows Hicks Decision," *Fair Employment Practices*, July 15, 1993, p. 81. At the time of this writing, a bill has been introduced in the House (HR 2787) to reverse the Supreme Court's ruling in *Hicks*. The proposed legislation would allow a Title VII plaintiff to prevail if he or she established a prima facie case of unlawful disparate treatment and the employer either fails to rebut the evidence or the plaintiff is able to show that the reasons set forth by the employer are untrue.

be able to disprove them in court. Once a faculty member convinces a court that the institution's proffered reasons for a negative promotion or tenure decision lack credibility, the plaintiff may gain a decided advantage in a jury trial. In some instances, one false reason may lead a judge or jury to suspect that the institution's other reasons are also false.[51] For these reasons, peer review committees and administrators should provide faculty with a complete and accurate account of the reasons for a promotion or the denial of tenure. Special attention should be paid to substantiating performance appraisals that have a critical or negative tone.[52]

CLASS ACTION AND DISPARATE IMPACT CLAIMS

Some employment discrimination cases involve class-action suits rather than suits filed by individuals.[53] Class-action suits are usually intertwined with disparate impact cases in which a group of individuals have been affected by certain personnel policies. The major point of contention in a class-action suit usually is the definition of the class, a concern that has important ramifications for the degree of liability that a college or university may encounter.[54] Faculty in a class action must prove that (1) there was a systemwide (e.g., across a department, school, or university) pattern or practice of disparate treatment or (2) facially neutral policies affected one or more protected groups unfavorably.[55]

Class-action claims must meet several prerequisites. First, the number of persons in the class must be so numerous that filing individual claims is impracticable. Second, there must be questions of law or fact that are common to the class. Third, the claims or defenses of the faculty members and the college or university must be typical of the claims and defenses of the class. Fourth, the representative parties

---

[51]For an analysis of the factors that attorneys should consider in litigating disparate treatment cases in light of *Hicks*, see EEOC, "EEOC: General Counsel's Memorandum on Supreme Court's *Hicks* Decision," Aug. 3, 1993, pt. IV.

[52]BNA, "The *Hicks* Decision and Its Effect on Employment Bias Litigation," *Fair Employment Practices*, March 14, 1994, p. 27.

[53]For a discussion of two class-action suits in academia, see "The Feminist Implosion," which discusses *Mecklenberg v. Montana State University*, and "Rah Rah Rajender—Rah for the U of M," which discusses *Rajender v. University of Minnesota*, in George R. LaNoue and Barbara A. Lee, *Academics in Court: The Consequences of Faculty Discrimination Litigation* (Ann Arbor: University of Michigan Press, 1987), pp. 145–219.

[54]For a discussion of class-action issues as they pertain to faculty members, see *Cooper v. University of Texas at Dallas*, 22 FEP Cases 1064 (1979), and *Scott v. University of Delaware*, 19 FEP Cases 1730 (1979).

[55]*International Brotherhood of Teamsters v. United States*, 14 FEP Cases 1514 (1977).

(legal counsel) must be willing to protect fairly and adequately the interests of the class.[56]

Statistical analyses are almost always used in class-action claims to help prove or disprove discrimination. That is, the plaintiffs "must do more than establish the occurrence of isolated or sporadic acts of discriminatory behavior."[57] Instead, they must prove by a preponderance of the evidence that their employer's standard personnel policies resulted in widespread discrimination. The college or university can rebut a prima facie showing of discrimination by discrediting the statistical analyses or otherwise demonstrating the inaccuracy or insignificance of the plaintiffs' proof. If the college or university is unable to rebut successfully the evidence of discrimination, explain it away, or cite a lawful reason for the personnel policy in question, then the court can conclude that the alleged violation occurred. A class-action suit does not bar an individual faculty member from pursuing a claim of disparate treatment against a college or university.[58]

USE OF FACULTY-VERSUS-FACULTY COMPARISONS

Legal counsel representing faculty have frequently used comparisons and statistics to prove disparate treatment or disparate impact. Comparisons are made to demonstrate that a faculty member who was denied a promotion or tenure possessed qualifications that were not significantly different from those of faculty who received more favorable treatment.[59] A faculty member may take two approaches

[56]Barbara Lindemann Schlei and Paul Grossman, *Employment Discrimination Law* (Washington, D.C.: BNA, 1976), pp. 1085–86. See *Mecklenberg v. Montana State University*, 13 FEP Cases 462 (1976); *Melani v. Board of Education*, 17 FEP Cases 1618 (1976); *Sanday v. Carnegie Mellon University*, 17 FEP Cases 562 (1976); *Solin v. State University of New York*, 416 F. Supp. (S.D.N.Y. 1976); *Townsel v. University of Alabama*, 80 F.R.D. 741 (N.D. Ala. 1978); and *Molthan v. Temple University*, 39 FEP Cases 816 (1985).

[57]*Chang v. University of Rhode Island*, 40 FEP Cases 22 (1985).

[58]See *Chang v. University of Rhode Island*, 40 FEP Cases 23 (1985); *International Brotherhood of Teamsters v. United States*, 14 FEP Cases 1514 (1977); and *Craik v. The Minnesota State University Board, St. Cloud State University*, 34 FEP Cases 649 (1984).

[59]See *Fields v. Clark University*, 59 FEP Cases 129 (1992); *Villanueva v. Wellesley College*, 55 FEP Cases 1063 (1991); *Bennun v. Rutgers, the State University of New Jersey*, 56 FEP Cases 746 (1991); *Jackson v. Harvard University*, 52 FEP Cases 979 (1990); *Lever v. Northwestern University*, 55 FEP Cases 1141 (1990); *Timper v. Board of Regents of the University of Wisconsin System* 28 FEP Cases 698 (1981); *Kutska v. California State College*, 15 FEP Cases 1033 (1976); *EEOC v. Franklin and Marshall College*, 39 FEP Cases 216 (1985); *Brown v. Trustees of Boston University*, 51 FEP Cases 824 (1989); *Dixon v. Rutgers, the State University of New Jersey*, 52 FEP Cases 1623 (1988); *Farlow v. University of North Carolina*, 39 FEP Cases 1421 (1985); *Namenwirth v. Board of Regents of the University of Wisconsin System*, 38 FEP Cases 1159 (1985); *Chang v. University of Rhode Island*, 40 FEP Cases 3 (1985); *Penk v. Oregon State Board of Higher Education*, 48 FEP Cases 1705 (1984);

when making such comparisons. First, the faculty member may claim that his or her credentials are at least as good as those possessed by faculty who have already been promoted or tenured. Second, the faculty member may contend that his or her position was filled by a person who was less qualified.[60] Criteria that are used in these comparisons include (1) the number of years since the faculty member was awarded a terminal degree; (2) the quality of the institution from which he or she received the degree; (3) the academic specialties of faculty in the comparable group; (4) differences in the quantity and quality of the publications between faculty members who received tenure and those who did not; (5) the teaching abilities of the plaintiff and faculty in the comparable group; (6) career interruptions or other extenuating circumstances affecting the plaintiff's career; and (7) differences in administrative responsibilities and committee work between the plaintiff and faculty in the comparable group.[61]

Comparing the relative qualifications and merit of professional and academic employees is difficult, but it may be necessary to prove a discriminatory animus.[62] The courts appear to view comparative analyses with some skepticism for two reasons. First, they want to give colleges and universities as much discretion as possible in their reappointment, promotion, and tenure decisions. In *Lieberman v. Gant*, for example, the female faculty member presented as evidence seventeen folders outlining the relative qualifications of male faculty members who had received tenure or been promoted to the rank of full professor. The U.S. Court of Appeals (Second Circuit) held, however, that such evidence did not help the plaintiff establish a prima facie case under the McDonnell Douglas–Burdine standards.

Briseno v. Central Technical Community College Area, 37 FEP Cases 59 (1984); *Langland v. Vanderbilt University*, 36 FEP Cases 213 (1984); *Craik v. The Minnesota State University Board, St. Cloud State University*, 34 FEP Cases 679 (1984); *Ritter v. Mount St. Mary's College*, 33 FEP Cases 1862 (1981); *Planells v. Howard University*, 32 FEP Cases 340 (1983); *Meehan v. New England School of Law*, 27 FEP Cases 1124 (1981); *Lieberman v. Gant*, 23 FEP Cases 510 (1980); *Powell v. Syracuse University*, 17 FEP Cases 1322 (1978); *Cap v. Lehigh University*, 19 FEP Cases 1125 (1978); *Northern Illinois University v. Fair Employment Practices Commission of the State of Illinois*, 37 FEP Cases 1047 (1978); *Presseisen v. Swarthmore College*, 15 FEP Cases 1481 (1977); *Perham v. Ladd*, 20 FEP Cases 128 (1977); and *Huang v. College of the Holy Cross*, 15 FEP Cases 706 (1977).

[60]Nearly all cases used the first approach. It is not uncommon for a faculty member who is denied tenure after six years of post-Ph.D. employment to be replaced by one with little or no post-Ph.D. experience.

[61]*Presseisen v. Swarthmore College*, 15 FEP Cases 1481 (1977).

[62]*Namenwirth v. Board of Regents of the University of Wisconsin System*, 38 FEP Cases 1159 (1985).

The comparative evidence offered in this case is a far cry from the comparative evidence to which the court referred in Mc-Donnell Douglas. Title VII does not require that the candidate whom a court considers most qualified for a particular position be awarded that position; it requires only that the decision among candidates not be discriminatory. When a decision to hire, promote, or grant tenure to one person rather than another is reasonably attributable to an honest, even though partially subjective evaluation of their qualifications, no inference of discrimination can be drawn. Indeed, to infer discrimination from a comparison among candidates is to risk a serious infringement of first amendment values. A university's prerogative "to determine for itself on academic grounds who may teach" is an important part of our long tradition of academic freedom.[63]

To admit comparative evidence, the court must be satisfied that the evidence is so compelling as to permit a reasonable finding going beyond honest differences of opinion or judgment among professionals.

Second, comparative evidence is often an "apples-and-oranges" proposition. It is rare for two faculty members to have identical teaching, research, and service responsibilities, and it is equally rare for them to exhibit comparable levels of performance in each of these areas. Colleges and universities often encourage diversity among faculty and may use a compensatory approach to evaluate candidates for reappointment, promotion, and tenure.[64] For example, an outstanding teacher with a mediocre research record might be granted tenure while a more productive researcher whose teaching is only satisfactory might be denied tenure. Furthermore, personnel decisions (especially tenure decisions) are based not only on a faculty member's past performance but also on his or her potential to continue contributing to the institution and academic discipline.[65]

---

[63]*Lieberman v. Gant*, 23 FEP Cases 510 (1980), and citing *Sweezy v. New Hampshire*, 354 U.S. 234, 263 (1957).

[64]The term "compensatory," as used here, refers to the fact that faculty members are usually required to demonstrate at least a satisfactory level of competence in all areas of evaluation (research, teaching, and service) but may be required to be rated at least very good in teaching *or* research. At some institutions, a rating of very good in research would be a necessary but not sufficient condition for a promotion or tenure. Under a compensatory model, an excellent rating in research might offset satisfactory ratings in both teaching and service.

[65]*Namenwirth v. Board of Regents of the University of Wisconsin System*, 38 FEP Cases 1160 (1985). A dilemma faced by peer review committees, department heads, deans, and other academic administrators is the faculty member who, after being promoted

In *Langland v. Vanderbilt University*, the plaintiff (Elizabeth Langland) attempted to prove sex discrimination by using the files of nine faculty members from a sample of forty that had been reviewed by the dean for promotion or tenure.[66] With some files, Langland tried to show that the dean would have found her worthy of tenure had she been given credit for the same achievements that the men were. With other files, she tried to show that the dean could not have found certain males qualified for tenure had he held them to the same standard that he applied to her. Langland also introduced the files of two female candidates for tenure as corroborative evidence that women were held to a higher standard than men. Nevertheless, the court noted that these comparisons "were the least convincing part of her case." The court stated that the dean offered legitimate academic reasons, none of which were based on sex discrimination, to justify his promotion and tenure decisions. These reasons included departmental needs as well as differences in the scholarly and teaching competencies among the faculty being compared. Furthermore, the court recognized that promotion and tenure standards may vary from one department to another within the same institution: "It is perfectly legitimate for one department to have different or even higher standards for tenure than another so long as those standards are neither higher than the contractual terms of employment nor discriminatory in origin or application."[67] If other courts adopt a similar position, it will tend to restrict meaningful comparisons to those that are intradepartmental and will make it more difficult for faculty members to establish a prima facie case or to reveal a discriminatory animus on the part of an academic institution.

Even when legitimate comparisons can be made among faculty members, a plaintiff who compares favorably on several dimensions with other faculty who have received more favorable treatment will not necessarily demonstrate illegal employment discrimination. *Smith v. University of North Carolina* involved a charge of sex discrimination by Mary Carroll Smith, a religion professor whose academic specialty was Sanskrit and Indian studies. She was denied reappointment in the second year of her three-year contract because of inadequacies in

---

or tenured, ceases to work hard and declines in effectiveness as a teacher and scholar. A question that is not addressed in the cases analyzed is the extent to which subjective predictions can be made about the future behavior of a faculty member.

[66]*Langland v. Vanderbilt University*, 36 FEP Cases 212, 213 (1984).

[67]*Langland v. Vanderbilt University*, 36 FEP Cases 215 (1984).

her scholarship and teaching. Although Smith was deemed to be technically competent in Sanskrit, her peer review committee thought her work was too narrow in focus and that she did not have the ability to integrate her scholarly expertise with other facets of religious studies. There was also concern that Smith would not contribute to the department's research needs or academic growth. As part of her defense, she attempted to compare her academic accomplishments with those of faculty who had been promoted or granted tenure. On this point, the court noted:

> Smith also compares her academic performance and achievements with other faculty members who were reappointed or promoted. Conducting a point by point analysis, she is able to develop arguments of superiority as to particularized attributes. What she ignores by this approach, besides the inevitable element of subjectivity involved, is the department's predominant reason for its decision: Smith was a specialist unable to transfer her knowledge to the generalized study of religion. There was no evidence to indicate that the professors to whom she sought to compare herself were deficient in that ability. Thus, Smith was unable to prove that the University's justification was mere pretext.[68]

To establish illegal discrimination, it is not enough to compare the qualifications of an individual plaintiff who was denied tenure with those who attained it. The plaintiff must also compare those who were rejected for tenure with those who received favorable recommendations. In criticizing the inadequacy of one comparative analysis, a U.S. district court noted:

> Those for whom tenure had been eschewed were, in reality, not a part of the examination. Almost by definition, despite its sophisticated trappings, the analysis did *not* study whether women deserving tenure were denied it due to their sex; it did not—and could not—analyze whether women were disproportionately denied tenure. It is a sheep in wolf's clothing.[69] (Emphasis in the original)

A court may also be reluctant to permit comparisons that involve decisions made at different times. A U.S. district court held that a

---

[68]*Smith v. University of North Carolina*, 23 FEP Cases 1756 (1980).
[69]*Chang v. University of Rhode Island*, 40 FEP Cases 84 (1985).

female associate professor of music who was denied promotion to
the rank of professor could not compare her qualifications with two
men, in part because they were promoted two and three years
respectively before her application for promotion was denied. During
that time the university had upgraded its standards for promotion.

> The promotion of two male faculty members . . . in 1977–78 . . .
> and . . . in 1978–79, does not support a finding of sexual
> discrimination, although neither men (sic) possessed a doctorate
> degree or any publications in refereed journals. Both men were
> members of the School of Business, and both were promoted
> before the upgrading of standards for promotion at the Univer-
> sity. These factors make comparisons to [the] plaintiff
> impossible.[70]

A similar line of reasoning was used by the U.S. Court of Appeals
(First Circuit) in 1991 in the case of a Wellesley College professor who
was rejected for tenure in the college's Spanish department. The
professor compared his qualifications for tenure with those of two
faculty members who had received tenure six and eight years earlier.
The First Circuit stated that "comparisons over such a length of time
are simply not probative, especially where, as here, the structure of
the relevant department had changed quite dramatically during the
intervening years."[71]

Not all comparison efforts are doomed to failure. Cynthia Fisher, a
fifty-three-year-old biology professor, was denied tenure by Vassar
College. She and her counsel did a superb job of comparing her
credentials with recently tenured biology faculty to demonstrate a
pretext for both sex discrimination against married women and age
discrimination. Fisher was able to demonstrate that the peer review
committee and the Vassar administration stacked the deck against
her by applying inconsistent standards, demeaning her scholarly and
teaching accomplishments, and looking hard for reasons to reject her
tenure bid. The court found that she compared favorably with four
assistant professors (three men and one unmarried woman) who
were tenured either shortly before or shortly after her tenure was
denied.

Fisher used the following criteria for comparison: (1) the number

---

[70]*Farlow v. University of North Carolina*, 39 FEP Cases 1421 (1985).
[71]*Villanueva v. Wellesley College*, 55 FEP Cases 1063 (1991).

of first-authored papers, (2) the frequency of citations in the *Science Citation Index*, (3) the fact that her research was performed under more difficult circumstances than her colleagues' research, (4) the impact of her research based on the evaluations of outside experts, (5) the amount of funded research she conducted, (6) productivity during her sabbatical leave, (7) student teaching evaluations and teaching load, (8) service activities, (9) leadership within the department, and (10) the fact that she was approximately nine years older than the other biology faculty. Relying on a direct comparison of Fisher's credentials with those of recently tenured biology faculty, the court found that Vassar's reasons for denying her tenure were pretextual, were clearly made in bad faith, and were part of a pattern and practice of discrimination against married women. The court also distinguished this case from the situation in *Lieberman*.

> While the court in *Lieberman* recognized that "academic freedom does not include 'the freedom to discriminate,' "[72] the court, nevertheless, observed that Congress could not have intended that "courts would sit as 'Super-Tenure' Review Committees." *Lieberman*, 630 F.2d at 67 (citations omitted).
>
> *Lieberman*, however, concerned the comparison of files for the purpose of determining qualification. To that extent, *Lieberman* can be distinguished from the case at hand because plaintiff here, in addition to assessing qualifications, uses comparative evidence to show that the tenure process is a front for intentional discrimination.
>
> Moreover, in *Gibson v. American Broadcasting Cos., Inc.*, 892 F.2d 11289 [54 FEP Cases 1435] (2d Cir. 1989), the Second Circuit limited the holding in *Lieberman* to the facts of that case. While acknowledging that the university may be a special setting, the *Gibson* court noted that the tenure files in *Lieberman* were incomplete so as not to permit accurate comparison. *Gibson*, 892 F.2d at 1133. Additionally, the court in *Lieberman* merely held that the district court's exclusion of comparative evidence was not an abuse of discretion.[73]

The court also noted that all the other biology faculty were at least nine years younger than Fisher. The statistical disparity between Fisher's age and the age of the other biology faculty was used as basis for "an inference of age discrimination."[74] In addressing the subjec-

---

[72]*Lieberman v. Gant*, 23 FEP Cases 510 (1980), quoting *Powell v. Syracuse University*, 17 FEP Cases 1316 (1979).

[73]*Fisher v. Vassar College*, 64 FEP Cases 1371 (1994).

[74]*Fisher v. Vassar College*, 64 FEP Cases 1369 (1994).

tive weighting scheme used in Fisher's tenure decision, the court noted:

> Another indication of the pretextual nature of defendant's claim that plaintiff's denial was the outcome of the ordinary tenure process is the arbitrary nature of defendant's "standards" for review. Even if [the] defendant had listed the specifics of each of the tenure categories, defendant's witnesses admitted at trial that there was no scale by which to weigh the various categories. As a result, in any given case a candidate's teaching performance could be considered as a very important qualification in some cases and only a moderately important qualification in other cases. More to the point, the "standards" could be used as a mask to disguise discriminatory intent by allowing evaluators to arbitrarily place importance on the categories in which a less favored candidate is weak and place no importance on the categories in which a less favored candidate is strong.[75]

USE OF STATISTICAL ANALYSES

Statistical analyses have been used in numerous cases to demonstrate patterns of discrimination in faculty recruitment, hiring, promotions, tenure, and compensation.[76] The use of statistical proof in discrimination cases has been approved by the U.S. Supreme Court in *International Brotherhood of Teamsters v. United States* and *Hazelwood School District v. United States*.[77] The major objective of most statistical

---

[75]*Fisher v. Vassar College*, 64 FEP Cases 1376 (1994).

[76]See *Scelsa v. City University of New York*, 67 FEP Cases 41 (1992); *Ottaviani v. State University of New York at New Paltz*, 50 FEP Cases 251 (1989); *Dugan v. Ball State University*, 43 FEP Cases 833 (1987); *Monroe-Lord v. Hytche*, 59 FEP Cases 1703 (1987); *Merrill v. Southern Methodist University*, 432 FEP Cases 1050 (1986); *Chang v. University of Rhode Island*, 40 FEP Cases 3 (1985); *Penk v. Oregon State Board of Higher Education*, 48 FEP Cases 1705 (1984); *Craik v. The Minnesota State University Board, St. Cloud State University*, 34 FEP Cases 649 (1984); *Zahorik v. Cornell University*, 34 FEP Cases 171 (1984); *Coser v. Moore*, 36 FEP Cases 60 (1983); *Planells v. Howard University*, 32 FEP Cases 336 (1983); *Carpenter v. Board of Regents of the University of Wisconsin System*, 30 FEP Cases 1409 (1983); *Lynn v. Regents of the University of California*, 28 FEP Cases 413 (1981); *Wilkins v. University of Houston*, 26 FEP Cases 1248 (1981); *Banerjee v. Board of Trustees of Smith College*, 25 FEP Cases 1073 (1981); *Carton v. Trustees of Tufts College*, 25 FEP Cases 1123 (1981); *Cooper v. University of Texas at Dallas*, 22 FEP Cases 1067 (1979); *Ishigami v. University of Hawaii*, 19 FEP Cases 1412 (1979); *Smith College v. Massachusetts Commission against Discrimination*, 20 FEP Cases 1658 (1978); *Craig v. Alabama State University*, 17 FEP Cases 561 (1978); *Presseisen v. Swarthmore College*, 15 FEP Cases 1471 (1977); *Perham v. Ladd*, 20 FEP Cases 128 (1977); and *Berry v. University of Texas*, 38 FEP Cases 894 (1977).

[77]*International Brotherhood of Teamsters v. United States*, 14 FEP Cases 1514 (1977), and *Hazelwood School District v. United States*, 15 FEP Cases 1 (1977).

arguments and comparisons is to show that a plaintiff (or class of plaintiffs) would have received favorable treatment had it not been for his or her race, sex, national origin, or other protected classification. In nearly all cases in which statistics were employed, the plaintiff's counsel presented the statistical evidence and the college or university then attempted to refute it. Experts on mathematics and statistics were often called either to present or rebut the statistical evidence.

Statistical analyses often form the backbone of class-action or disparate impact cases. In some cases, a variety of statistics are used to help establish a prima facie case of a pattern or practice of illegal discrimination.[78] In disparate treatment cases, statistics are frequently used in conjunction with other evidence. In *Lamphere v. Brown University*, the U.S. Court of Appeals (First Circuit) summarized their value: "Statistics concerning the general atmosphere of discrimination, although not conclusive, are usually relevant to show that the same employer discriminated against an individual plaintiff."[79] The primary advantage of statistical proof is that it highlights trends in selection, promotion, and tenure decisions in a precise and succinct fashion. Statistics also provide a method for determining the likelihood that promotion and tenure decisions were made for random or discriminatory reasons.[80]

The statistical evidence and arguments in the cases analyzed here ranged from simple presentations of frequencies and percentages to complex multiple regression analyses. Attempts were often made to show that members of one race or sex were promoted or tenured more frequently than those of the other sex or another race. In other instances, more rigorous statistical tests such as regression analysis were used in an attempt to isolate discriminatory personnel actions. Plaintiffs who used regression analysis often went to great lengths to control for variables such as the type of degree held; years since the terminal degree was awarded; length of service in a tenure-track position; and the specific teaching, research, and administrative duties of the faculty members under scrutiny.

A faculty member can make inroads into establishing a prima facie case of discrimination by showing that individuals in a protected

---

[78]*Presseisen v. Swarthmore College*, 15 FEP Cases 1472 (1977).

[79]*Lamphere v. Brown University*, 29 FEP Cases 701 (1982).

[80]For an excellent discussion of the use of statistical analysis in discrimination cases, see David C. Baldus and James W. L. Cole, *Statistical Proof of Discrimination* (New York: McGraw-Hill, 1980).

group received favorable reappointment, promotion, or tenure decisions at a significantly lower rate than members of other groups.[81] As
noted above, a prima facie case only temporarily shifts the burden of
proof to the college or university to offer a nondiscriminatory motive
for its personnel actions. Once statistical evidence has been presented, the college or university usually attempts to attack the pro-
priety of the analysis. Both sides may go to great lengths and
considerable expense to present or rebut the evidence.

ATTACKS ON STATISTICAL EVIDENCE

An analysis of employment discrimination cases in academia suggests that using statistics to prove disparate treatment or impact in
employment is quite difficult. As a result, the majority of attempts
have failed. According to David C. Baldus and James W. L. Cole,
attacks on the reliability of statistical proof usually focus on one or
more of five issues.[82]

1. *Selection and use of unreliable, irrelevant, and incomprehensible measures.* Subjective criteria used by peer review committees and other
college officials often defy quantification. Suppose a faculty member
who receives tenure has published six journal articles, whereas a
faculty member at the same institution who was denied tenure has
published nine. On the surface, there appears to be a statistical
disparity. Publishing six articles in top-tier journals, however, would
usually be regarded as more meritorious than publishing nine articles
in less prestigious publications. Thus, statisticians or legal counsel
might argue that the number of journal articles a faculty member has
published is an unreliable or irrelevant measure unless something is
known about the quality of the articles. For example, in *Merrill v.
Southern Methodist University* (SMU), a female faculty member asserted that she published as frequently as her male colleagues. The
court noted, however, that there were qualitative differences between

---

[81]The EEOC's *Uniform Guidelines on Employee Selection Procedures* have adopted a rule
of thumb known as the "4/5ths" or "80 percent" rule for detecting disparate impact. If
the minority selection rate is less than 80 percent of the nonminority selection rate,
then a potential disparate impact problem exists. Thus, if a college tenures 60 percent
of its male faculty, no suspicion of disparate impact is likely as long as the institution
grants tenure to at least 48 percent (60% × 80%) of its eligible female faculty. This rule
is not a legal definition of discrimination. Rather, it is a practical device to attract the
attention of enforcement agencies such as the EEOC with respect to serious discrep-
ancies in promotion rates (or other employment decisions such as hiring). See *Uniform
Guidelines* (1978), 29 *Code of Federal Regulation*, pt. 1607.

[82]Baldus and Cole, *Statistical Proof of Discrimination*, pp. 6–7.

her publications and those of the men: "Academic scholarship is not measured by volume alone but by the comprehensiveness and direction of the research. Moreover, much of Merrill's work was printed in journals with little or no recognition in the academic community."[83] Many characteristics of an effective college professor, such as collegiality, enthusiasm for the work, and other elements of good citizenship, likewise defy quantification and comparison using standard statistical tests.

The manner and level at which the data are collected (often referred to as "sampling") and measured is also highly relevant. Data that are collected centrally at the university level may be viewed by the courts as irrelevant when the major impetus for reappointment, promotion, and tenure decisions exists at the department or college level. The U.S. Court of Appeals (Second Circuit) made such an observation in *Zahorik v. Cornell University*:

> Plaintiffs' proffer of statistical data adds nothing to their claim of discriminatory treatment. The weakness of the data is self-evident. It has been deliberately culled from a broader sample and includes "estimates" as to when particular decisions were made. Moreover, tenure decisions at Cornell are not made by a single authority but are highly decentralized. Gross statistics are thus meaningless absent a departmental breakdown. Finally, even if statistics reliably demonstrating that 65% of male candidates during an appropriate period were granted tenure as against only 42% of female candidates was sufficient by itself to permit a finding of discrimination against some women at Cornell—a proposition which the caselaw does not support—such data would not be sufficient to prove that the particular plaintiffs were among the women who were not treated neutrally. More particularized evidence relating to the individual plaintiffs is necessary to show discriminatory treatment.[84]

2. Confusion between relevant and irrelevant data. It is well established that reappointment, promotion, and tenure decisions are based largely on merit, as measured by a faculty member's research, teaching, and service record. Quantitative measures that assess merit are likely to be regarded by the courts as relevant, whereas measures that have little or no bearing on meritorious performance are likely to

---

[83]*Merrill v. SMU*, 42 FEP Cases 1049 (1986).
[84]*Zahorik v. Cornell University*, 34 FEP Cases 172 (1984).

be regarded as irrelevant. For example, a plaintiff might compare his or her length of service to an institution (or the time that has elapsed since receiving a terminal degree) with faculty who have received favorable promotion or tenure decisions. Length of service is not necessarily a good proxy for quality of service, however, and might be regarded as irrelevant by the courts. As *Coser v. Moore* illustrates, even when variables such as length of service are accorded weight, problems arise if the plaintiff makes unrealistic assumptions about the nature of the data:

> Plaintiffs' statistics . . . do not account for the length of time faculty had been within each rank, and they assume, unrealistically, that every faculty member is eligible for promotion in any given year. The impact of this misplaced assumption is exaggerated by the fact that women faculty were hired in increasing numbers as the years passed, so that on the average, and at any given time, the percentage of women who would normally become eligible for promotion would be less than the percentage of women in the work force. The same fundamental defect applies to [the] plaintiffs' analyses of the number of years to first promotion and the numbers and percentages of faculty receiving second promotions.[85]

If regression analysis is to be used in proving discrimination, the selection of dependent and independent variables is critical.[86] Part of *Craik v. The Minnesota State University Board* involved alleged salary discrimination against female faculty. Although salary discrimination in academia is not the focus here, the court's comments about the selection of independent variables is of critical concern:

> Choosing the proper independent variables is therefore critical to the success of a regression model. It is important to note that the choice of variables should be the result of a theoretical determination, made before the data are examined, of what factors are likely to be relevant; the proper variables cannot be identified statistically, because statistically correlated relation-

---

[85]*Coser v. Moore*, 36 FEP Cases 70 (1983).

[86]In employment discrimination cases involving institutions of higher learning, the dependent variable might be academic rank, tenure status, or salary. Independent variables are those factors that "explain" variance or change in the dependent variable, such as the number of publications credited to a faculty member, years of institutional service, and scores from evaluations of teaching effectiveness. The dependent and independent variables that are selected for analysis are known collectively as the statistical model or regression model.

ships may be accidental, lacking practical significance. Indeed, the results of models constructed by trial and error in an effort to discover statistically significant relationships are suspect, because this method increases the likelihood of stumbling on coincidental correlations. . . .

Despite their air of mathematical precision . . . the calculations are only as strong as the model itself. The model may be subject to attack because of omission of relevant independent variables, multicollinearity, or on other grounds. The fiercest disputes in cases of this kind therefore typically concern the design of the regression model. Because the choice of proper variables is not an issue on which statisticians have particular expertise, many of these disputes are no more arcane than everyday disputes about relevancy.[87]

Institutions have succeeded in rebutting adverse statistical evidence by showing that the statistics were not put into their proper perspective or that they revealed only part of an otherwise positive picture. The analysis in *Craik* indicates that the courts are often wise to plaintiffs and counsel who pick statistics that support a particular viewpoint or who "torture the data until it confesses."[88] Colleges and universities have used the following statistics to challenge a plaintiff's statistical evidence:[89] (1) the percentage of female professors at the institution versus the national average,[90] (2) the number of graduate assistants per student female faculty are provided versus the number male professors have,[91] (3) the number of women granted tenure out of the number of women considered compared with these statistics for men,[92] and (4) the percentage of female applicants granted tenure compared with those in the "tenure stream."[93]

---

[87]*Craik v. The Minnesota State University Board, St. Cloud State University*, 34 FEP Cases 685–86 (1984). Multicollinearity occurs when independent variables are correlated such that their separate effects cannot be distinguished. For example, age and education are typically correlated and cannot be separated. If two predictors or variables are highly correlated, their regression coefficients become so unstable that we cannot rely on estimates of them. A procedure known as factor analysis may be used as a preliminary measure before regression analysis to reduce the problem of intercorrelated independent variables. See William G. Zikmund, *Business Research Methods* (Chicago: Dryden Press, 1984), p. 532.

[88]Such practices are condemned by reputable researchers in the social sciences.

[89]Cases are cited in Stuart H. Bompey and Barry N. Saltman, "The Role of Statistics in Employment Discrimination Litigation—A University Perspective," *Journal of College and University Law* 9 (1982–83): 277.

[90]*Keyes v. Lenoir Rhyne College*, 522 F.2d 579 (4th Cir.), *cert. denied*, 434 U.S. 904 (1977).

[91]*Cussler v. University of Maryland*, 15 FEP cases 1299 (1977).

[92]*Cap v. Lehigh University*, 19 FEP Cases 1119 (1978).

[93]*Johnson v. University of Pittsburgh*, 15 FEP Cases 1516 (1977).

3. *Comparison of noncomparables.* When faculty attempt to demonstrate a discriminatory animus by a college or university, some
compare faculty in one department who were granted a promotion
or tenure with those in another department who were not. Because
many academic units are small and only one or two candidates seek
a promotion or tenure during an academic year, plaintiffs are often
hard-pressed to find faculty with whom to make meaningful comparisons. Ideally, comparisons should be made with persons in the same
(or similar) departments on the same campus or within the same
university system.[94]

Distinctions also need to be made between terminal degrees. In a
large university a Ph.D. is the terminal degree in the mathematics
department; the J.D. or L.L.M is usually regarded as the terminal
degree in the law school; a master of fine arts degree (M.F.A.) might
be the terminal degree in the theater department; and the M.D. or
Ph.D. is likely to be regarded as the proper terminal degree in the
school of medicine. Terminal degrees cannot necessarily be lumped
together in a single statistical category. When qualitative differences
among degrees are ignored, the courts are likely to disregard the
comparison. In addition, departments within the same institution
frequently use significantly different procedures and standards when
deciding personnel matters, making statistical comparisons difficult.
Attempts to make statistical comparisons that ignore these differences
are often unsuccessful.[95]

As noted earlier, some plaintiffs and their legal counsel use sophisticated statistical tests such as multiple regression. Professional statisticians who are retained as advisers or expert witnesses may help the
plaintiff construct a model that incorporates a series of independent
variables such as years of service, number of publications, and
terminal degree. The variations that occur in an independent variable
are alleged to have an effect on a dependent variable such as salary,
academic rank, or tenure status.[96] When the dependent or indepen-

---

[94]*Dugan v. Ball State University,* 43 FEP Cases 837 (1987).

[95]*See Penk v. Oregon State Board of Higher Education,* 48 FEP Cases 1867 (1984). See also
Banerjee v. Board of Trustees of Smith College, 25 FEP Cases 1077 (1981), in which the
plaintiff's statistical evidence was discounted by the U.S. Court of Appeals (First
Circuit). Percentages of tenured and nontenured faculty by minority status were
presented, but "the evidence was far from compelling. Plaintiff skirts entirely the
statistics for the actual tenure decisions."

[96]For example, a statistical analysis might show that there is a relationship between
the number of publications by faculty and the likelihood of achieving tenure. The
strength of an independent variable's correlation to a dependent variable is revealed
by its coefficient of regression formula. The weaker the relationship, the closer the

dent variables are not subject to exacting data collection and measurement, however, problems arise.

In *Craik v. The Minnesota State University Board*, the plaintiffs examined the proportions of male and female professors within each rank and then performed a multiple regression analysis to test whether female faculty at St. Cloud State University were discriminatorily assigned to lower ranks than similarly situated male faculty. An examination of the distribution of faculty members between 1974 and 1979 revealed that a higher proportion of women served as instructors (rank IV), whereas a smaller proportion served as full professors (rank I). Nonetheless, the court did not find that the male-female distribution by academic rank was indicative of sex discrimination:

> These statistics alone do not necessarily justify a conclusion that women have been discriminatorily relegated to the lower ranks, however, because (1) they are "snapshots" of the faculty in given years and therefore, given the low turnover rate of academics, include many faculty members hired in the past when the criteria for hiring and promotion may have been different and when the applicant pool of women may have been smaller; and because (2) they do not consider whether the women and men in the snapshot had similar qualifications. It would be wrong to conclude that discrimination exists if men dominate the upper ranks only because they earlier dominated the applicant pool and meanwhile have progressed through the ranks, and if the women on the faculty have been treated similarly to similarly situated men.[97]

The multiple regression model used in this case included the dependent variable of faculty rank and the independent variables

---

coefficient of a particular variable will be to zero. If the multiple regression formula fits all of the data exactly, the coefficient of a variable totally unrelated to the dependent variable would be zero, an event that almost never occurs. But because the formula is calculated from sample data rather than from data for an entire population (e.g., all faculty members nationwide), and because some marginally relevant independent variables may be omitted, the regression formula is subject to a margin of error. In addition, an independent variable that is actually unrelated to the dependent variable may yield a coefficient that is slightly different from zero. To determine the degree of confidence that can be placed in the relationship between independent and dependent variables, it is necessary to test statistically whether the coefficient is significantly different from zero. Errors in a regression coefficient may result from the margin of error in the regression function itself, imprecise measures of dependent and independent variables, poor selection of independent variables, or the inclusion of redundant variables (which measure the same thing).

[97]*Craik v. The Minnesota State University Board, St. Cloud State University*, 34 FEP Cases 683 (1984).

sex, highest degree, years of experience, and years since the highest degree was awarded. The statistical expert who performed the study claimed that between 2.5 and 2.9 women out of every 10 were ranked one step lower than men with similar qualifications. The Minnesota State University Board successfully attacked the analysis on three fronts: (1) the data included comparisons beyond the scope of the class (e.g., administrators were included in the sample), (2) the analysis failed to include certain relevant independent variables (subcategories of the master's of arts degree), and (3) the analysis improperly included discrete variables (four different academic ranks) although the statistical procedure was based on continuous variables.[98] The latter attack was most damaging because it pointed out that erroneous assumptions were made about the "distance" between ranks. As the court noted, "It is possible that the rank of instructor is so much lower than the others that the proper values to be assigned to the four ranks were one, two, three, and ten" (rather than one, two, three, and four). The third criticism of the analysis also dealt with the fact that criteria such as length of service or degree are not equally important at different ranks.[99]

> It is possible, for example, that experience is an insignificant variable at the instructor level, but overshadows the other variables in importance at the [full] professor level. In fact, it is rather unlikely that the relative importance of degree, experience, and time from degree is the same for each rank, because under the published criteria in effect since 1972, . . . the same degree is required for ranks I and II, and no experience is required for rank IV [instructor]. These requirements suggest that experience, which is unimportant for rank IV, may be determinative for distinctions between ranks I and II. Combining the analysis of the four ranks in one equation imposes a questionable uniformity on the criteria, and may produce misleading results.[100]

[98]A continuous variable is one that can theoretically assume any value between two given values (e.g., the length of service of a faculty member can be stated in years, months, days, hours, minutes, seconds, and fractions of a second). A discrete variable is one that is not continuous (e.g., tenure status can be either "tenured" or "not tenured"; academic rank can be assistant professor, associate professor, and so on).

[99]*Craik v. The Minnesota State University Board, St. Cloud State University,* 34 FEP Cases 687 (1984). Similar criticisms were levied against the regression analysis that was used to show that there was sex discrimination by academic rank in the Oregon state university system. See *Penk v. Oregon State Board of Higher Education,* 48 FEP Cases 1867 (1984).

[100]*Craik v. The Minnesota State University Board, St. Cloud State University,* 34 FEP Cases 687 (1984).

4. *Gaps between the assumptions and requirements of a statistical procedure and the characteristics of the data analyzed.* The use of a statistical procedure is based on a particular set of mathematical assumptions. Sophisticated statistical methods such as regression analysis often assume that the dependent and independent variables conform to a normal distribution. Most statistical tests also make assumptions about the sample size and nature of the data. When the mathematical assumptions underlying the statistical tests are modified or ignored, the credibility of the entire analysis is destroyed.

Plaintiffs and legal counsel who use statistical tests to prove discrimination in academia often find it impossible to produce an adequately large and relatively homogeneous sample of faculty, some of whom have received a favorable promotion or tenure decision and others of whom have not. When the sample is small, any statistical test, especially a more sophisticated one, is vulnerable to successful rebuttal. This dilemma was illustrated in *Carton v. Trustees of Tufts College* when a female faculty member attempted to use simple statistics to prove sex discrimination.

> The statistical evidence which was offered by the plaintiff and received in evidence did not establish sexual discrimination against her. To put it otherwise, after a study of these statistics, I cannot confidently derive any reliable reference from them. The smallness of the numbers available for study diminishes their importance. The Department of Education, it is true, has not had a tenured woman since before World War II, but it has only four tenured members. In the decade prior to 1979, there appears to have been no statistically significant difference between the rate at which Tufts granted tenure to males and the rate at which it granted tenure to females. Indeed, when non-lateral entry tenure cases are taken into consideration, the percentage difference between males and females becomes an advantage in favor of women. In the faculty of Arts and Sciences the hiring of women by the university for full-time positions has exceeded the percentage of women in the available pool. It is noteworthy also, when one considers statistics, that [the] plaintiff chose to be compared to Drs. Yaeger, Becker, and Lin. The first two were denied tenure for lack of scholarly credit. Dr. Lin had done scholarly research, although its quality was doubtful. Only Dr. Lin achieved tenure. There were discrepancies, but underlying explanations for these discrepancies would have to be ignored. Plaintiff claimed that women were relegated to part-time status.

In many instances the women requested part-time status for
family reasons, or wanted to pursue other work which would be
inconsistent with a full-time position. With respect to the departure of women from Tufts, there were non-sex-related factors
which apparently were not explored. Women might have left to
bear children, or to follow their spouses to other geographic
locations. At any rate I do not find that the difference is statistically significant.[101]

The use of statistical analyses often leads to the argument that a
discriminatory animus must exist simply because no alternative explanation can be found. That is, the residual portion of the statistical
model is interpreted as illegal discrimination. Such reasoning not
only is statistically unsound but also is not likely to pass muster in
the courts.[102] Even when a large sample is used and the dependent
and independent variables are carefully selected and measured, the
"unexplained" variance in the dependent variable cannot be attrib-
uted to illegal discrimination. Thus, in *Cooper v. University of Texas at
Dallas*, the district court noted that a statistical test "merely rejects
the null hypothesis—that only random chance is operating. It does
not necessarily establish the counter hypothesis—in this case that
[the university] discriminates."[103]

5. *Disregard for the possible effects of chance.* Statistical tests of significance are used to determine whether the frequency or percentage of
adverse reappointment, promotion, or tenure decisions against a
specified group such as women is caused by random events (chance)
or factors other than chance.[104] For example, if 61 percent of the male

---

[101]*Carton v. Trustees of Tufts College*, 25 FEP Cases 1123–24 (1981). Also see *Smith v.
University of North Carolina*, 23 FEP Cases 1757 (1980). Footnote 23 of *Smith* reads:
"While we are mindful that Smith was the first and only [female] fulltime professor
that the Department had employed, we, in assessing the significance of that fact, must
also bear in mind that the Department had but 10 full-time faculty members and, on a
nationwide basis during the early 1970s, only 5–8% of the Ph.D.'s in religion were
women. Therefore, applying a strict statistical analysis, a Department the size of the
one at the University would not be expected to have more than one female fulltime
professor of religion in 1974."

[102]Cornell University astronomer Carl Sagan observed that although space explora-
tion has increased our knowledge of the universe, much remains to be learned. He
cautioned, "Just because we can't identify a light doesn't make it a space ship." In
George T. Milkovich and Jerry M. Newman, *Compensation*, 3d ed. (Homewood, Ill.:
Irwin, 1990), p. 471. The same logic holds true when analyzing statistical data in an
attempt to uncover illegal discrimination.

[103]*Cooper v. University of Texas at Dallas*, 22 FEP Cases 1069 (1979), aff'd 648 F.2d 1039
(5th Cir. 1981).

[104]"The basis of statistical analysis is that all relevant factors being equal, representation of majority and minority groups will remain proportional throughout. Thus, if we

faculty members at an institution are granted tenure as opposed to 49 percent of the female faculty, is the disparity the result of chance or are other factors operating to create the gap? The courts have been highly reluctant to infer a discriminatory motive on the part of colleges and universities even when valid statistical tests demonstrate that differences in the reappointment, promotion, and tenure rates for members of a specific race or sex are based on factors other than chance.

To the extent that the statistical evidence at bar comprises simple compilations of raw data, it is easy to understand and to manage. Analytical statistics, which in this litigation took the form of regression and multivariate analyses of the raw numbers, are of a genre as to which caution is most advisable. Cf. *International Brotherhood of Teamsters*, 431 U.S. at 340. These analyses, treading the trail blazed by the court in *Castaneda v. Partida*, 430 U.S. 482, 496 n. 17 (1977) and *Hazelwood School District v. United States*, 433 U.S. 299, 309 n. 14, 15 FEP Cases 1 (1977), calculate the fluctuation of a sample from some expected value (the standard deviation). The Court in *Castaneda* and in *Hazelwood* had indicated that a finding of two or three standard deviations would lead a protypical social scientist to conclude that random variation did not explain an observed disparity. But, though the parties to these cases treat the standard deviation with a deference rarely seen since the heyday of the Oracle of Delphi, even a finding of two or more standard deviations does not prove the existence of discrimination; rather, a spread of that magnitude means only that chance can likely be excluded as an explanation for the result. Nor does the converse—a standard deviation of less than two or three—necessarily exclude discrimination as a possible cause.[105]

---

have 800 smooth surfaced and indistinguishable red stones and 200 similarly indistinguishable blue stones in a barrel, mixed evenly, we would expect a color-blind filtering process removing 100 stones to result in 80 red stones and 20 blue stones. A grossly disproportionate result might lead us to infer that the filtering process is less than color blind. However, in the academic context, a decision regarding tenure, for example, manifestly does not involve indistinguishable stones or even interchangeable unskilled or semi-skilled workers. On the contrary, each candidate for tenure presents the university with a multi-faceted particle, significant not only in its own right but also as it relates to the thousands of other facets in the complex balance of university learning. Accordingly, statistical analysis may be inapplicable in such an environment unless the statistical model takes into account the special circumstances and requirements of academic life. Even then, the decision remains at its core an individual one." Bompey and Saltman, "Role of Statistics in Employment Discrimination Litigation," p. 273.

[105]*Chang v. University of Rhode Island*, 40 FEP Cases 24 (1985). In *Cooper v. University of*

If the statistical test indicates that factors beyond random chance are at work in an employment discrimination case, then the establishment of a prima facie case is likely and the college or university must provide evidence of legal, nondiscriminatory factors to justify its adverse personnel decision. To establish a prima facie case, the U.S. Supreme Court has stated that the difference between the expected value and the observed number should exceed two or three standard deviations. For example, the expected percentage of tenured female faculty in a sociology department, based on the percentage of female Ph.D.s in sociology in the United States, must be significantly higher than the actual (observed) number of tenured female Ph.D.s in the department. The Court has not stated, however, the critical level of significance required to establish a prima facie case. Rather, the Court has stated that "gross disparities" must be shown.[106]

COURTS' VIEW OF STATISTICAL ANALYSES

The courts have had few qualms about allowing statistical evidence to be used in academic cases. In fact, reliance on statistical proof at the prima facie stage has been regarded as sound policy, especially in promotion and tenure evaluations in which the criteria used are highly subjective.[107] Although statistical data do not provide direct evidence of discrimination in individual promotion and tenure decisions, they may provide circumstantial evidence. Moreover, by allowing statistical evidence, the courts avoid dealing directly with the merits of a college or university's promotion or tenure decision and thus can "steer a careful course between excessive intervention in the affairs of the university and the unwarranted tolerance of unlawful behavior."[108] But despite the courts' generally receptive attitude toward statistical analyses, they have often viewed the use of such analyses with skepticism and even amusement:

> In closing, we add a note both rueful and cautionary. The bar is reminded that sound statistical analysis is a task both complex

---

Texas at Dallas, 22 FEP Cases 1069 (1979), it was noted that "it has become a convention in social science to accept as statistically significant values which have a probability of occurring by chance 5% of the time or less." The Supreme Court, however, has not stated whether a .05 level of statistical significance is sufficient to establish a prima facie case. See *Hazelwood School District v. United States,* 15 FEP Cases 1 (1977).

[106]*Hazelwood School District v. United States,* 15 FEP Cases 1 (1977).

[107]*Lynn v. Regents of the University of California,* 28 FEP Cases 414 (1981).

[108]*Powell v. Syracuse University,* 17 FEP Cases 1316 (1978).

and arduous. Indeed, obtaining sound results by these means, results that can withstand informed testing and sifting both as to method and result, is a mission of comparable difficulty to arriving at a correct diagnosis of disease.

We are no more statisticians than we are physicians, and counsel who expect of us informed and consistent treatment of such proofs are well advised to proceed as do those who advance knotty medical problems for resolution. Our innate captivity in such matters extends to "the inexorable zero" and perhaps, unevenly, somewhat beyond; but the day is long past—past at least since the Supreme Court's sophisticated analysis in *Castaneda v. Partida*, 430 U.S. 482, 97 S. Ct. 1272, 51 L.Ed.2d 498 (1977)—when we proceed with any confidence toward broad conclusions from crude and incomplete statistics. That everyone who has eaten bread has died may tell us something about bread, but not very much.[109]

The most effective approach to using statistics in proving employment discrimination in an academic setting appears to be twofold. First, a simple statistical calculation of, for example, percentages or frequencies may be more persuasive than "high-powered" procedures such as multiple and multivariate regressions. Second, uncorroborated raw data and statistical tests rarely provide adequate proof of illegal discrimination. As one experienced attorney has suggested, statistical evidence should be fortified with qualitative or anecdotal evidence of illegal discrimination.

> What I am concerned about is that the court is likely to be baffled by the numbers as well as by the obfuscations offered by the university. Judges seem to be perfectly willing to accept almost any explanation that allows them to avoid involving themselves in the sacred academic process. This is why it is essential that, in addition to the statistics, we present cases of individuals who actually have experienced discrimination so that the court can understand how these practices operate and how they affect living, breathing human beings. Numbers are not enough.

> I used a statistical witness in one case, and the judge, a very literate man, said, "I refuse to rely on the *regressive* analysis that was presented by plaintiff's expert." The judge was so literate that I am convinced the word regressive was deliberately chosen.

[109]*Wilkins v. University of Houston*, 26 FEP Cases 1248–1249 (1981).

> We cannot rely on statistics alone. We must rely on the kinds of testimony that will give the court an understanding of how the system really works, that is, how the committees work, how there are departments that still say, "We don't want women," and how the committees work when there is fighting over promotions or tenure.[110] (Emphasis in the original)

Two cases, *Planells v. Howard University* and *Craig v. Alabama State University*, illustrate this point. Both involved charges of race discrimination filed by white faculty members who were employed at institutions whose faculty and student bodies had traditionally been predominantly black. Using simple statistics supplemented by anecdotal evidence of overt illegal discrimination, the plaintiffs showed that white faculty were treated less favorably than blacks.[111]

During Antonio Planell's four-year stay at Howard, between 1976 and 1980, the Department of Romance Languages terminated five of eight white faculty but none of its ten black faculty; and of twenty-one hires, only three were white. Thus, the number of white faculty declined from twelve to eight, whereas the number of black faculty increased from fourteen to twenty-four during the four-year period. A similar set of statistics was used to demonstrate that it was much more difficult for white faculty at Alabama State University to climb the academic ladder than it was for black faculty. The plaintiffs in both these cases supplemented their statistical data with ample evidence of acts of overt discrimination.[112]

---

[110]Judith P. Vladeck, "Litigation: Strategy of Last Resort," in Jennie Farley, ed., *Sex Discrimination in Higher Education: Strategies for Equality* (Ithaca, N.Y.: New York State School of Industrial and Labor Relations, Cornell University, 1981), p. 11.

[111]*Planells v. Howard University*, 32 FEP Cases 343 (1983), and *Craig v. Alabama State University*, 17 FEP Cases 558 (1978).

[112]The changes in the number of black and white faculty in the Department of Romance Languages at Howard during the relevant time frame were taken directly from the case. Since the numbers do not explain fully the changing racial composition of the department faculty, other aspects of personnel flow within the department may have been omitted from the case discussion. In a footnote, the U.S. district court made the following comment about Howard's attempt to justify discriminating against white faculty members: "We believe that Howard University's novel defense to this Title VII action violates the very spirit of racial equality which has animated the civil rights movement since the historic Supreme Court decision in Brown v. Board of Education, 347 U.S. 483 (1954). Defendant's suggestion that black institutions are free to give preference to blacks in faculty recruitment and promotion marks it, in this Court's view, as an apostate to the cause of racial equality. Ironically, many eminent leaders in the civil rights movement of the past half-century emanated from the halls of the Howard University, which now asks this court to abandon the 'colorblind' policies for which those leaders fought." *Planells v. Howard University*, 32 FEP Cases 345 (1983). Also see *Villanueva v. Wellesley College*, 55 FEP Cases 1063 (1991), and *Bachman v. Board of Trustees of University of District of Columbia*, 777 F. Supp. 990 (D.D.C. 1991).

It appears that comparative and statistical evidence, while given seemingly unequivocal approval in *McDonnell Douglas*, *Burdine*, and *Postal Service v. Aikens*, is still routinely misunderstood in Title VII litigation. Judges have suggested that making direct comparisons of faculty members' qualifications should be avoided because of the courts' fears of going beyond their expertise and encroaching on the autonomy of academic institutions. Instead, plaintiffs should emphasize procedural irregularities, such as differences in the advice and counseling given to untenured male and female faculty members, as was done by Connie Rae Kunda in her successful suit against Muhlenberg College.[113] Plaintiffs must exercise great care in gathering and analyzing statistical evidence while avoiding the five pitfalls discussed earlier. As much data as possible should be gathered regarding the department in which the discrimination allegedly occurred as well as the institution as a whole. Applicant-flow data and data from the relevant labor pool should be analyzed by someone with statistical expertise.[114] Unlike a "snapshot" of an institution's faculty composition at one point in time, personnel-flow data provides a more complete and reliable portrait of recruitment, selection, reappointment, promotion, and tenure decisions. Snapshots of a department's faculty may reveal more about an institution's past employment practices but often provides little insight into a college's current promotion and tenure practices.[115]

In summarizing burden of proof issues in Title VII cases in academia, several points have emerged. First, it is not difficult for a faculty member to establish a prima facie case against a college or university. The faculty member in a disparate treatment case need only demonstrate that he or she has the minimum requisite qualifications for promotion or tenure. A reading of the cases indicates that, in the absence of specific criteria for tenure, the courts have established a low threshold for meeting this initial burden. In disparate impact suits, the plaintiff must show that members of a specific race, sex,

[113]*Brown v. Trustees of Boston University*, 51 FEP Cases 815 (1989), *cert. denied*, 110 S. Ct. 3217 (1990), represents one of the few cases in which a court (U.S. Court of Appeals, First Circuit) addressed the plaintiff's qualifications rather than the procedural irregularities surrounding the promotion and tenure process.

[114]These suggestions are based on the observations and recommendations in Kallaher, "*Namenwirth v. Board of Regents of the University of Wisconsin System*," pp. 1058–59.

[115]See Donald W. Jarrell, *Human Resource Planning: A Business Planning Approach* (Englewood Cliffs, N.J.: Prentice-Hall, 1993), pp. 256–80.

age group, or other protected category have been promoted or tenured at a significantly lower rate than members of other groups.

Second, the establishment of a prima facie case requires the college or university to set forth a nondiscriminatory reason for denying the faculty member a promotion or tenure. Almost any nondiscriminatory reason is acceptable, regardless of its soundness from an academic or personnel management standpoint. The institution's reason must be of sufficient rationality, however, to permit the EEOC or courts to infer that the adverse personnel decision was not based on illegal employment discrimination.

Third, the faculty member must show that the college or university's stated reason for denying him or her a promotion or tenure was a pretext designed to cover up an illegal discriminatory motive. It is at this stage that comparative evidence, statistical analyses, and anecdotal accounts are presented by the plaintiff's counsel. It is also at this stage that most faculty lose their cases.

8. THE CONFIDENTIALITY OF THE PEER REVIEW PROCESS

C OURTS HAVE LONG HONORED the fundamental principle that the right to full and fair litigation depends on a party's ability to procure pertinent evidence.[1] Faculty who feel that they have been wrongly denied a promotion or tenure have, in a number of cases, demanded access to confidential files and other documents. The issue of discovery in academic cases usually deals with the plaintiff's ability to collect evidence that is germane to his or her case but in the sole possession of the institution. Two discovery-related questions have arisen in wrongful discharge and discrimination cases in academia. First, does a college or university have to relinquish to the EEOC or courts information pertaining to the reappointment, promotion, or tenure recommendations of peer review committees, or is such information protected by a qualified privilege?[2] Second, if peer review or other information must be provided to the EEOC or courts, to what extent can the identities of peer review committee members or others be sanitized or redacted (edited)?[3]

[1]*United States v. Bryan*, 339 U.S. 323 (1950), which stated that "the public . . . has a right to every man's evidence," quoted in Jayna Jacobson Partain, "A Qualified Academic Freedom Privilege in Employment Litigation: Protecting Higher Education or Shielding Discrimination?" *Vanderbilt Law Review* 40 (1987): 1398.

[2]See 29 *CFR*, pt. 1601 (1991), "EEOC: Title VII and ADA Procedural Regulations," sec. 1601.16, Access to Production of Evidence; Testimony of Witnesses; Procedure and Authority: "(a) To effectuate the purposes of Title VII and the ADA [Americans with Disabilities Act], any member of the Commission [EEOC] shall have the authority to sign and issue a subpoena requiring . . . (1) the attendance of testimony and witnesses; (2) the production of evidence including, but not limited to books, records, correspondence, or documents, in the possession or under control of the person subpoenaed; and (3) access to evidence for the purposes of examination and the right to copy."

[3]"You're weighing two good principles against each other—the right to privacy and the right to know. You want to protect the review process, and at the same time you

The confidential materials sought by a plaintiff may include evaluations written by peer review committee members at his or her institution, letters of assessment written by professors in his or her field at other colleges or universities, and notes or minutes from promotion and tenure committee deliberations.[4] The plaintiff's ability to acquire sufficient evidence of disparate treatment or impact may be crucial in demonstrating a discriminatory animus by a peer review committee or college official. University officials or legal counsel may claim, however, that certain information is protected by a qualified privilege and is not subject to disclosure. Legal counsel for colleges and universities have challenged subpoenas requesting peer review and other documents on a number of grounds,[5] including the irrelevancy of the information sought,[6] overbreadth of the subpoena's scope,[7] lack of probable cause for the subpoena, in violation of the Fourth Amendment of the Constitution,[8] confidentiality of the communications,[9] and rights associated with First Amendment guarantees under the Constitution.[10]

A qualified privilege is normally granted in certain professional and personal relationships to protect the confidentiality of communications. Relationships such as attorney-client,[11] priest-penitent,[12] husband-wife,[13] and newspaper reporter–informant[14] have traditionally enjoyed a qualified privilege status. A common-law precedent that recognizes a qualified privilege is generally based on the public's

---

don't want to allow unfair discrimination." L. Francis, Associate Secretary for the American Association of University Professors, "Academic Freedom vs. Affirmative Action: Ga. Professor Jailed in Tenure Dispute," *Chronicle of Higher Education*, Sept. 2, 1980, p. 10, quoted in Charles J. Stevens, "Preventing Unnecessary Intrusions on University Autonomy: A Proposed Academic Freedom Privilege," *California Law Review* 69 (1981): 1539.

[4]Mary DeLano, "Discovery in University Employment Discrimination Suits: Should Peer Review Materials Be Privileged?" *Journal of College and University Law* 14 (Summer 1987): 121.

[5]Frank M. Baglione, "Title VII and the Tenure Decision: The Need for a Qualified Academic Freedom Privilege Protecting Confidential Peer Review Materials in University Employment Discrimination Cases," *Suffolk University Law Review* 21 (1987): 704.

[6]*EEOC v. University of New Mexico*, 504 F.2d 1296, 1301 (1974).

[7]*EEOC v. University of Notre Dame du Lac*, 32 FEP Cases 1057 (1983).

[8]*EEOC v. University of New Mexico*, 504 F.2d 1296, 1301 (1974).

[9]*McKillop v. Regents of the University of California*, 386 F. Supp. 1270 (N.D. Cal. 1975).

[10]*EEOC v. Franklin and Marshall College*, 39 FEP Cases 217 (1985). The above cases are cited in Baglione, "Title VII and the Tenure Decision," pp. 703–4.

[11]See *Fisher v. United States*, 425 U.S. 391 (1976).

[12]See *Mullen v. United States*, 263 F.2d 275 (1958).

[13]See *Blau v. United States*, 340 U.S. 332 (1951).

[14]See *Baker v. F&F Investment*, 470 F.2d 778 (1972), *cert. denied*, 411 U.S. 966 (1973).

interest in candid communications that are kept free from fear of disclosure during litigation.[15] Furthermore, the relationship must be one that society values and desires to protect; the benefits of maintaining confidentiality and preserving the relationship must outweigh society's need to compel disclosure of sensitive information.[16] For example, an attorney representing a person who is charged with a serious crime cannot reveal the contents of private conferences with the client to judges, law enforcement officers, or other interested parties. If attorney-client communications were not privileged, it would be difficult for legal counsel to gather information that could be critical to the client's defense. For years, however, the courts remained divided on the extent to which colleges and universities were entitled to a qualified privilege for tenure review materials. In *Gray v. Board of Higher Education, City of New York,* for instance, a U.S. district court stated, "A qualified right to confidentiality in academia does not fall readily into one of the traditionally recognized privileges against disclosure."[17]

Colleges and universities have fought vigorously to protect the contents of personnel files and the deliberations of peer review committees. Compelling the disclosure of promotion and tenure deliberations is thought by some to pose a threat to academic freedom by discouraging open and frank discussion of a faculty member's qualifications and accomplishments, thereby creating a "chilling effect" on the entire peer review process. Supporters of a qualified privilege for tenure review documents claim, however, that when assurances of confidentiality are eliminated, peer review committees and administrators may be reluctant to provide candid assessments of a faculty member's work. There is speculation that the value and integrity of the entire promotion and tenure system may erode as the

---

[15]Partain, "A Qualified Academic Freedom Privilege," p. 1414.

[16]See Lynda E. Frost, "Shifting Meanings of Academic Freedom: An Analysis of *University of Pennsylvania v. EEOC,*" *Journal of College and University Law* 17 (1991): 344. "Wigmore describes four basic conditions necessary to establish privilege: (1) The communications must originate in a *confidence* that they will not be disclosed. (2) This element of *confidentiality* must be *essential* to the full and satisfactory maintenance of the relation between the parties. (3) The *relation* must be one which in the opinion of the community ought to be sedulously *fostered.* (4) The *injury* that would inure to the relation by the disclosure of the communications must be *greater than the benefit* thereby gained for the correct disposal of the litigation." (Emphasis in original)

[17]*Gray v. Board of Higher Education, City of New York,* 30 FEP Cases 297 (1982). The quote is from the district court's decision in this case. *Gray v. Board of Education,* 27 FEP Cases 256 (1981).

candor surrounding the process diminishes. Department heads, deans, provosts, presidents, and university governing boards may begin to place less weight on formal recommendations and resort to a less formal system that depends primarily on oral and undocumented evaluations. An informal system might offer fewer procedural safeguards and less accuracy and fairness for the faculty member. Furthermore, written evaluations of faculty performance by peer review committees could become bland and noncommittal, providing little guidance for department heads, deans, and others involved in promotion and tenure decisions. There is also the fear that forced disclosure of negative comments about a colleague's worth might create strained relations among faculty.[18]

In the past, a qualified privilege protecting the promotion and tenure deliberations of peer review committees and university administrators received mixed support from the courts. Recently, however, the federal courts have significantly eroded this right. With greater frequency, both faculty members and EEOC investigators seeking evidence to support charges of discrimination in promotion and tenure decisions have demanded and received access to confidential peer review materials.[19]

Those who oppose the protection of promotion and tenure documents through a qualified privilege believe that the chances of proving a valid claim of discrimination are low if the plaintiff, the EEOC, or the courts are denied access to relevant facts surrounding the case.[20] Evidence of discrimination is often subtle and difficult to detect. It is rare for a faculty member to be subjected to flagrant discrimination; rather, discrimination is usually based on circumstantial evidence that must be culled from personnel records and the testimony of peer review committee members, administrators, and the plaintiff's colleagues. Foreclosing an EEOC investigation by denying access to peer review materials would have the effect of removing the agency from Title VII cases involving colleges and universities and make it difficult for the plaintiff to uncover evidence for use in a subsequent private action under Title VII.[21]

[18]Stevens, "Preventing Unnecessary Intrusions," pp. 1551–52.

[19]Baglione, "Title VII and the Tenure Decision," pp. 692–93.

[20]David McMillin, "*University of Pennsylvania v. EEOC* and *Dixon v. Rutgers:* Two Supreme Courts Speak on the Academic Freedom Privilege," *Rutgers Law Review* 42 (Summer 1990): 1089.

[21]Ieuan G. Mahony, "Title VII and Academic Freedom: The Authority of the EEOC to Investigate College Faculty Tenure Decisions," *Boston College Law Review* 28 (May 1987): 560–61.

Some have argued that if there were less confidentiality and greater openness surrounding promotion and tenure deliberations, academic freedom would actually be enhanced rather than diminished. A review process that is protected by a qualified privilege may discourage open debate because relevant information and the free exchange of opinions are restricted to the small group of scholars who sit on the peer review committees.[22] Thus, opponents of a qualified privilege might argue that it is contrary to the ideal of academic freedom because it permits committees, without fear of exposure, to deny tenure to persons who espouse unpopular or unconventional views.[23] Others claim, however, that if peer review materials and other documents were not confidential, decision makers might be more thorough in their deliberations. In *Paul v. Leland Stanford University*, a federal district court made the following observation:

> The court also feels constrained to note that there is some support for the view that it is not always *necessary* to protect even the *identity* of peer reviewers. Cf. *EEOC v. Franklin and Marshall College* 775 F.2d 110, 39 FEP Cases 211 (3d Cir. 1985); *In re Dinnan*, 661 F.2d 426, 27 FEP Cases 288 (5th Cir. 1981). It can be non-laughably argued that reviewers who know that their identity might be disclosed will neither refuse to comment nor retreat into useless abstractions or disingenuous flattery, but instead, will articulate their opinions, and describe the bases for them with greater precision and better developed logic. Judges, like professors making tenure decisions, regularly are called upon to make difficult decisions. The legal system has accepted the notion that the quality of those difficult decisions will be better if judges are compelled to disclose the bases on which they rule. Judges' decisions virtually always disappoint someone, and judges who hold elective office may well have more reason to be concerned about the consequences of causing people disappointment than do tenured faculty, especially when those faculty work at some institution other than the one where the candidate is being considered for promotion. The point made forcefully by the 5th Circuit in *In re Dinnan* . . . is that it is not clear that an assured cloak of secrecy improves the quality of decision-making or is an essential prerequisite to acquiring thoughtful evaluations

---

[22]Frost, "Shifting Meanings of Academic Freedom," p. 349.

[23]Comment, "Drawing the Line on Academic Freedom: Rejecting an Academic Peer-Review Privilege for Tenure Committee Deliberations," *Washington University Law Quarterly* 64 (1986): 1272–73.

of the qualifications of young academics. These considerations lead this court to ascribe somewhat less weight than it otherwise might to the interest the University says would be damaged if plaintiff had access to the substance of the evaluations in her tenure review file.[24] (Emphasis in the original)

DISCOVERY RULES

Confidential communications that arise in various professional and personal relationships are not necessarily privileged communications.[25] Since the EEOC and federal courts are engaged in a search for the truth surrounding a charge of employment discrimination, granting colleges and universities a qualified privilege to protect peer review files must be done after the interests of the plaintiff and the institution have been carefully analyzed. The Federal Rules of Evidence require that any proposed evidentiary privilege be analyzed in terms of four sources: federal statutes, U.S. Supreme Court rules, common-law principles, and constitutional principles. No federal statute deals explicitly with the right of institutions of higher learning to use a qualified privilege to protect promotion and tenure files or related information. The constitutional basis for extending this privilege is based primarily on the previously discussed issue of academic freedom. Common-law principles and a recent U.S. Supreme Court decision have significantly diluted this privilege, however, for institutions of higher learning.

Federal Rule of Evidence 501 allows faculty members and college or university administrators who are defending their institution against charges of discrimination to work within the liberal discovery rules of the federal courts. These rules direct a party to obtain information regarding any matter that is not protected by a qualified privilege if such information is relevant to the pending suit. A court may grant a protective order prohibiting the discovery of relevant, nonprivileged material, however, when it is necessary to protect a party from the annoyance, embarrassment, undue burden, or expense associated with unreasonable requests for information.[26] A court may also require a litigant to exhaust all possible alternative means for obtaining the desired material before requiring a party to

---

[24]*Paul v. Leland Stanford University*, 46 FEP Cases 1351–52 (1986).

[25]James H. Brooks, "Confidentiality of Tenure Review and Discovery of Peer Review Materials," *Brigham Young University Law Review* (1988): 708.

[26]Partain, "A Qualified Academic Freedom Privilege," p. 1404.

disclose confidential information. Before compelling an institution to reveal the contents of promotion and tenure files, a court must weigh two competing interests: (1) the social benefits of discovery as a means of eradicating employment discrimination and (2) the private interests of the college or university to preserve academic freedom and avoid unnecessary intrusions on the work of peer review committees and administrators. Thus, Federal Rule 501 instructs courts to resolve claims of privilege on a case-by-case basis.[27]

Common-law rules may also be used to compel discovery of information germane to a wrongful discharge or employment discrimination case. When an institution claims a common-law academic privilege, a court must first examine the interests of the plaintiff. There is a strong common-law tradition that favors the free accessibility of evidence. Further, Congress's 1972 extension of Title VII to colleges and universities and recent court decisions support a faculty member's right to confidential promotion and tenure files. Thus, a university's qualified privilege to protect such files is overridden in a discrimination suit if the faculty member can demonstrate a need for information that is both relevant and critical to his or her case. Furthermore, the faculty member must not be able to obtain the information through alternative channels.

History of Qualified Privilege in Academia

Some courts have traditionally protected the qualified privilege of reappointment, promotion, and tenure documents and proceedings, whereas others have required colleges and universities to relinquish confidential information. For example, a strong social interest in protecting academic freedom and the integrity of the peer review process was acknowledged by the Second and Seventh Circuits of the U.S. Court of Appeals in granting a qualified privilege to LaGuardia Community College and the University of Notre Dame. In contrast, the Third and Fifth Circuits denied the privilege and, instead, gave greater weight to the full disclosure of confidential materials during the course of employment discrimination litigation against Franklin and Marshall College and the University of Georgia.[28]

---

[27]McMillin, "*University of Pennsylvania v. EEOC* and *Dixon v. Rutgers*," p. 1092.
[28]Baglione, "Title VII and the Tenure Decision," pp. 693–94.

Cases Supporting a Balanced Approach to Protection

Colleges and universities have been successful in preserving the confidentiality of tenure documents in several cases. In *McKillop v. Regents of the University of California*, a federal district court issued a strong statement supporting the confidentiality of peer review because of the need to preserve academic excellence and because the plaintiff had other means of discovery at her disposal.[29] Similarly, in another case, *Keyes v. Lenoir Rhyne College*, the U.S. Court of Appeals (Fourth Circuit) decided that the plaintiff was not entitled to access to peer review documents because (1) she had failed to establish a prima facie case of discrimination and (2) the college did not use the peer review committee's evaluations to defend itself against the discrimination charges.[30]

The Second Circuit, in *Gray v. Board of Higher Education, City of New York*, held that the votes of individual members of a tenure review committee would be protected from discovery if the unsuccessful candidate received a meaningful explanation of the committee's decision.[31] In this case, S. Simpson Gray, a professor at LaGuardia Community College, sought to discover the votes of two faculty members who served on the collegewide promotion and budget committee, which rejected his application for promotion. Both the U.S. district court and the Second Circuit adopted a "balancing approach" to the issue of qualified privilege.

> Rather than adopting a rule of absolute disclosure, in reckless disregard of the need for confidentiality, or adopting a rule of complete privilege that would frustrate reasonable challenges to the fairness of hiring decisions, our decision today holds that absent a statement of reasons, the balance tips toward discovery and away from recognition of privilege. A policy requiring disclosure of votes in the absence of stated reasons when they have been requested permits a plaintiff a fair opportunity to uncover evidence necessary to establishing a prima facie case of discrimi-

[29]*McKillop v. Regents of the University of California*, 386 F. Supp. 1270 (N.D. Cal. 1975).

[30]*Keyes v. Lenoir Rhyne College*, 552 F.2d 579, *cert. denied*, 434 U.S. 904 (1977). In *Jepsen v. Florida Board of Regents*, 21 FEP Cases 1695 (1980), however, the U.S. Court of Appeals (Fifth Circuit) held that faculty evaluations used to deny someone tenure had to be released because the university used these documents to defend itself against a charge of discrimination.

[31]*Gray v. Board of Higher Education, City of New York*, 30 FEP Cases 297 (1982). See Mary DeLano, "Discovery in University Employment Discrimination Suits: Should Peer Review Materials Be Privileged?" *Journal of College and University Law* 14 (1987): 142–44.

nation. But unlike a rule of complete disclosure, the discovery permitted in this case will not chill peer review decisions. Future decisions supported by a detailed statement of reasons given to the faculty member on request will be shielded from routine discovery.[32]

The Second Circuit was strongly influenced by a brief filed by the American Association of University Professors. The brief stated that "if an unsuccessful candidate for reappointment or tenure receives a meaningful written statement of reasons from the peer review committee and is afforded proper intramural grievance procedures," disclosure of individual votes should be protected by a qualified privilege.[33] The court did not establish criteria, however, by which an explanation for the denial of tenure would be measured and deemed either adequate or inadequate. Nor did the court explain who would be responsible for assessing the adequacy of such an explanation. If a plaintiff were made to accept a peer review committee's reasons for denial of tenure without the assurance that the statement were adequate, the college or university would be able to hide all but the most overt forms of discrimination.[34] Gray, in essence, recognized a qualified privilege, although the court did not find the privilege applicable to the case before it.[35]

One reason that has been cited for not disclosing the votes or deliberations of peer review committees is a concern for faculty harmony. The Second Circuit addressed this issue in *Gray:*

> The risk that revelation of committee votes will lead to faculty disharmony is also reduced or eliminated by the qualified privilege established here. Where the faculty member has been denied tenure by the committee, whatever "harmony" may have existed between that applicant and the rest of the faculty is already largely lost, and unless the applicant is reinstated, no harm would follow the loss of harmony. If the complaint is that disappointed tenure applicants will not get along harmoniously with the faculty members who discriminated against them when these applicants are later reinstated because they prove that the reasons for not hiring were pretexts for racial discrimination,

[32]*Gray v. Board of Higher Education, City of New York,* 30 FEP Cases 302 (1982).
[33]*Gray v. Board of Higher Education, City of New York,* 30 FEP Cases 301 (1982).
[34]See DeLano, "Discovery in University Employment Discrimination Suits," pp. 143–44.
[35]McMillin, "*University of Pennsylvania v. EEOC* and *Dixon v. Rutgers,*" p. 1128.

then we find the interest in collegial goodwill in that context to be easily outweighed.[36]

In *EEOC v. University of Notre Dame du Lac,* the Seventh Circuit recognized a qualified academic freedom privilege that permitted the institution to remove all identifying features (name, address, institutional affiliation, and so on) of the reporting scholars who contributed to the evaluation of a professor.[37] Oscar T. Brookins, a former Notre Dame faculty member in the Department of Economics, filed race discrimination charges against the university under Title VII. As part of its investigation, the EEOC issued a subpoena that required the university to produce a detailed description of its promotion and tenure process as well as the files of Brookins and several other faculty members in his department. The Notre Dame administration objected on the grounds that the personnel files contained peer review evaluations "which were made with the assurance and expectations that the evaluations would remain confidential and therefore the evaluations were protected by qualified academic privilege." The university also contended that it should be permitted to delete the names and identifying information of all academicians who were associated with the peer evaluations and require the EEOC to execute a nondisclosure agreement as a condition for the release of the confidential material. The U.S. district court declined to protect the information in question, but the U.S. Court of Appeals (Seventh Circuit) reversed. The circuit court noted that the district court ignored the chilling effect on academic personnel decisions that could occur if peer review materials were allowed to be disclosed to the EEOC.[38] The Seventh Circuit thus created a qualified privilege for colleges and universities under Federal Rule of Evidence 501 by allowing the university to produce the peer review files in redacted form. By protecting the confidentiality of peer review materials, the court felt that both First Amendment academic freedom interests and academic excellence interests would be supported. Redacted information would be available to the party seeking discovery only if a "substantial showing" of a "particularized need" could be demonstrated.[39] The "substantial showing" would involve balancing the

---

[36]*Gray v. Board of Higher Education, City of New York,* 30 FEP Cases 302 (1982).

[37]*EEOC v. University of Notre Dame du Lac,* 32 FEP Cases 1057 (1983). The issue in this case was whether to protect the identities of the persons associated with the evaluation of Brookins's credentials rather than whether peer review documents were protected by a qualified privilege.

[38]Brooks, "Confidentiality of Tenure Review," pp. 719–21.

[39]McMillin, "*University of Pennsylvania v. EEOC* and *Dixon v. Rutgers,*" pp. 1100–1102.

interests of the EEOC against "the adverse effect such disclosure would have on the policies underlying the privilege." In addition, the court declared that it would not condone exploratory searches of peer review information.[40]

In *Zaustinsky v. The University of California,* a federal district court required the plaintiff to establish a prima facie case of discrimination before compelling the university to release confidential peer review information. Once the plaintiff established a prima facie case, the courts would examine the contents of the peer review files to determine whether the university's reasons for an adverse personnel decision were a pretext for illegal discrimination.[41] The *Zaustinsky* court concluded, in deciding that materials submitted in confidence for use in a tenure decision should be protected from disclosure by a qualified privilege, that "confidentiality is a prerequisite to the effectiveness of a peer evaluation system of faculty selection and promotion." In announcing this conclusion, however, the court did not distinguish between disclosing the *identities* of the faculty members who submitted tenure evaluations and the *substance* of such evaluations. It is quite possible that a plaintiff could determine the identity of an evaluator simply by reading the evaluation. This problem is most likely to arise in departments with a small number of tenured faculty.

At Stanford University (*Paul v. Leland Stanford University*), a Japanese faculty member was denied tenure and sought to discover the contents of her tenure review file. A federal district court said that she was entitled to discovery because of the likelihood that she could present evidence sufficient to create an inference of impermissible discrimination. The suspected discriminatory animus was based on derogatory comments about women—particularly Japanese women— allegedly made by both a former department head and male faculty in the Department of Religious Studies. The court stated that justifying the release of tenure review documents required the consideration of two factors. The first factor was the magnitude of harm that would be caused by disclosure. When the magnitude of harm to the institution was great, the plaintiff would be required to show considerable justification for access to the documents. The court added that

---

[40]Edward L. McCord, "Out of Balance: The Disruptive Consequences of *EEOC v. Franklin & Marshall College*," *University of Pittsburgh Law Review* 50 (1988): 341.

[41]*Zaustinsky v. The University of California,* 30 FEP Cases 1535 (1983).

doubts about the magnitude of potential harm should be resolved in favor of the party seeking disclosure. The second factor the court had to consider was what the plaintiff hoped to achieve by gaining access to the tenure review materials. The federal district court considered that the plaintiff's qualifications for tenure were minimal and that Stanford was regarded as one of the finest universities in the world, so that its faculty were required to meet exceedingly high standards for promotion or tenure. The court also discussed subjective aspects of promotion and tenure decisions. The court in *Paul* seems to indicate that even when peer review information is obtained, it may not provide a great deal of insight into the nuances of a tenure decision because of the subjectivity and wide range of discretion that must be given to peer review committees. In an effort to seek an equitable solution to the discovery issue, the court appointed a special master who was acceptable to both parties and who possessed "substantial experience in related academic matters" to prepare a full summary of the materials in the plaintiff's file and release only those summaries to the plaintiff.[42]

In *Jackson v. Harvard University*, the U.S. district court ruled that Harvard administrators were not required to reveal the identities of the faculty and peer review committee members who voted to deny tenure to a female professor in the Graduate School of Business Administration. The court did require, however, that material from the tenure files of male colleagues (whose identities were not revealed) in the plaintiff's department be produced to determine whether a prima facie case could be established. Harvard had failed to comply with internal university procedures on the destruction of documents and had prematurely destroyed the files of some male faculty who had received tenure. Further, the university was tardy in producing evidence related to tenure votes on the plaintiff. The plaintiff contended that Harvard's misconduct should have encouraged the federal district court to act more decisively under federal rules of evidence in producing confidential files. A U.S. district court disagreed, and the U.S. Court of Appeals (First Circuit) affirmed the lower court's decision.[43]

---

[42]*Paul v. Leland Stanford University*, 46 FEP Cases 1350 (1986).
[43]*Jackson v. Harvard University*, 52 FEP Cases 979 (1990).

CASES REJECTING THE QUALIFIED PRIVILEGE PROTECTION

One of the most controversial and widely publicized suits dealing with sex discrimination in academia occurred at the University of Georgia during 1980 and 1981. Maija Blaubergs alleged that she had been unlawfully denied promotion to the rank of associate professor and her employment unconstitutionally terminated.[44] During the course of discovery, a deposition was taken from James A. Dinnan that pertained to his service on the College of Education Promotion Review Committee. When asked how he voted on Blaubergs's application for promotion, however, Dinnan refused to answer. After a motion was filed to compel discovery, the U.S. Court of Appeals (Fifth Circuit) ordered Dinnan to testify; he again refused to answer questions regarding his vote. Dinnan was held in contempt of court, fined $100 for every day he defied the court order, and sentenced to ninety days in prison. Dinnan contended that he had the privilege not to testify because of the shelter provided by academic freedom. Although the Fifth Circuit conceded that academic freedom has long been viewed by the U.S. Supreme Court as a special concern, it held that there was no common-law privilege that protected Dinnan's secret-ballot vote. The court also felt that the disclosure of Dinnan's vote would neither inhibit tenure decisions nor encourage retaliation by dissatisfied parties.

> In the instant case, society has no strong interest in encouraging timid faculty members to serve on tenure committees. Additionally, this court is unconvinced that an applicant who is denied tenure can retaliate against tenured faculty members. Therefore, the reasoning that protects political and labor election ballots from discovery is inapplicable here. . . . We fail to see how, if a tenure committee is acting in good faith, our decision today will adversely affect its decision-making process. Indeed, this opinion should work to reinforce responsible decision-making in tenure questions as it sends out a clear signal to would-be wrongdoers that they may not hide behind "academic freedom" to avoid responsibility for their actions.

No one compelled Professor Dinnan to take part in the tenure decision process. Persons occupying positions of responsibility, like Dinnan, often must make difficult decisions. The conse-

---

[44]*Blaubergs v. Board of Regents of the University of Georgia*, 27 FEP Cases 287 (1980), and *In re Dinnan*, 27 FEP Cases 288 (1981).

quence of such responsibility is that occasionally the decision-maker will be called upon to explain its actions. In such a case, he must have the courage to stand up and publicly account for his decision. If that means that a few weak-willed individuals will be deterred from serving in positions of public trust, so be it; society is better off without their services. If the decision-maker has acted for legitimate reasons, he has nothing to fear. We find nothing heroic or noble about the appellant's position; we see only an attempt to avoid responsibility for his actions. If appellant was unwilling to accept responsibility for his actions, he should never have taken part in the tenure decision-making process. However, once he accepted such a role of public trust, he subjected himself to explaining to the public, and any affected individual his decisions and the reasons behind them.[45]

EEOC v. Franklin and Marshall College involved the college's French department, which had denied tenure to Gerard Montbertrand primarily because of deficiencies in his scholarship.[46] Montbertrand petitioned for a reconsideration of the decision in light of additional information he and others submitted. When the decision to deny tenure was reaffirmed, Montbertrand petitioned the college's grievance committee for a review, alleging denial of academic freedom and denial of due process. The grievance committee found no merit to these claims. Montbertrand then filed Title VII charges with the EEOC, claiming illegal discrimination by Franklin and Marshall College because of his French national origin. In the course of its investigation, the EEOC issued a subpoena that required the college to provide detailed information on each individual who was either granted or denied tenure between November 1977 and June 1981.[47] Franklin and Marshall officials refused to provide the files sought by the EEOC, and a district court later compelled the college to relinquish the information in accordance with the subpoena.[48] The college

---

[45]*In re Dinnan*, 27 FEP Cases 293 (1981). Also see Carolyn Bolarsky, "Tenure in Academe: Secret Ballots and Civil Rights," *Spokeswoman*, Dec. 1980, pp. 8–9, and John H. Bunzel, "The Case of the Jailed Georgia Professor: Let's Cut through the Intellectual Smog," *Chronicle of Higher Education*, Jan. 12, 1981, p. 96.

[46]*EEOC v. Franklin and Marshall College*, 39 FEP Cases 211 (1985).

[47]The subpoena requested tenure recommendation forms; summaries of student evaluations; enrollment data; annual and governance evaluation forms; publication information and evaluations by outside experts; letters of reference information regarding academic advising; all notes, letters, memoranda, or other documents considered during each tenure case, including curricula vitae; recommendations of the professional standards committee in each tenure case; and actions taken by the president in each tenure case.

[48]Franklin and Marshall College, a small liberal arts college located in Lancaster,

administration and amici curiae contended that "the quality of a college, and in a broader sense, academic freedom, which has a constitutional dimension is inextricably intertwined with a confidential peer review process." For this reason, legal counsel for Franklin and Marshall College argued that "disclosure of peer review material should be compelled only when facts and circumstances give rise to a sufficient inference that some impermissible consideration played a role in the tenure decision." The college urged the court to adopt a qualified academic privilege, which would have prevented disclosure of the confidential peer review materials absent a showing or an inference of illegal discrimination. Citing Congress's 1972 amendment of Title VII to include institutions of higher learning, and the lack of evidence that Congress intended for colleges and universities to receive a qualified privilege, the Third Circuit sustained the district court's ruling that Franklin and Marshall should provide the documents requested by the EEOC. In finding that the EEOC's requests were "relevant and not overbroad," the court cited the U.S. Supreme Court's decision in *EEOC v. Shell Oil Co.*, which rejected the proposition that a district court must find the charge of discrimination to be well founded, verifiable, or based on a reasonable suspicion before enforcing an EEOC subpoena.[49]

Clearly an alleged perpetrator of discrimination cannot be allowed to pick and choose the evidence which may be necessary for an agency investigation. There may be evidence of discriminatory intent *and* of pretext in the confidential notes and memorandum which the appellant seeks to protect. Likewise, confidential material pertaining to other candidates for tenure in a similar time frame may demonstrate that persons with lesser qualifications were granted tenure or that some pattern of discrimination appears. . . .

Relative qualifications of those who teach in academic institutions are not amenable to objective comparison in charts. Instead, the peer review material itself must be investigated to determine whether the evaluations are based on discrimination and whether they are reflected in the tenure decision.[50] (Emphasis in the original)

Pennsylvania, was joined by several other area colleges (Allegheny College, Bucknell University, Chatham College, Haverford College, Lafayette College, and Lehigh University) in an amici curiae brief.

[49]*EEOC v. Shell Oil Co.*, 34 FEP Cases 709 (1984), cited in *EEOC v. Franklin and Marshall College*, 39 FEP Cases 216 (1985).

[50]*EEOC v. Franklin and Marshall College*, 39 FEP Cases 217 (1985). Also see Debra E. Blum, "Supreme Court Rejects Privacy Claim for Tenure Files, Says University Must

The rights of faculty to obtain essential information in an effort to establish discrimination claims was also recognized in *Rollins v. Farris*.[51] The U.S. district court in *Rollins* regarded the discovery of such information as a "necessary infringement on the confidential peer review process."[52]

SUPREME COURT RULING ON QUALIFIED PRIVILEGE: UNIVERSITY OF PENNSYLVANIA V. EEOC

Although the U.S. Supreme Court refused to grant certiorari in *EEOC v. Franklin and Marshall College*, it decided to do so in a tenure denial case at the University of Pennsylvania.[53] In essence, the Court agreed to consider whether confidential peer review documents should be protected from discovery by the EEOC in employment discrimination litigation. The Court ruled that such documents were not protected by a common-law evidentiary privilege or a First Amendment academic freedom privilege.[54]

In 1985, Associate Professor Rosalie Tung was denied tenure at the University of Pennsylvania's Wharton School (the university's business school). She subsequently filed sex discrimination charges against the university, claiming that her department head had sexually harassed her. After she insisted that their relationship remain professional, she claimed that he submitted a negative letter to the university's personnel committee, which possessed the final authority on tenure decisions. Tung also claimed that her qualifications were "equal to or better than" those of the five male faculty members who received more favorable treatment. She also noted that a majority of the faculty in her department had recommended her for tenure and that she had not been given a reason for being denied tenure by university officials. Tung later learned that the personnel committee had attempted to justify its decision against her by claiming that the Wharton School was not interested in "China-related research."

The EEOC investigated Tung's charges and requested a variety of information from the university. When the university refused to provide certain information, the EEOC's acting district director issued

Disclose Information in Bias Case," *Chronicle of Higher Education*, Jan. 17, 1990, pp. A1, A17.

[51]*Rollins v. Farris*, 39 FEP Cases 1102 (1985).
[52]See *Orbovich v. Macalester College*, 47 FEP Cases 265 (1988).
[53]*University of Pennsylvania v. EEOC*, 51 FEP Cases 1118 (1990).
[54]See Frost, "Shifting Meanings of Academic Freedom," p. 330.

a subpoena seeking, among other things, Tung's tenure file and the files of five male faculty members who were identified in the charge. The university refused to produce several documents from these files and subsequently applied to the EEOC for a modification of the subpoena to exclude what it termed "confidential peer review information." Specifically, the university wanted to exclude (1) confidential letters written by Tung's evaluators; (2) the department head's letter of evaluation; (3) documents reflecting the internal deliberations of faculty committees considering applications for tenure, including the department evaluation report summarizing the deliberations relating to Tung's application for tenure; and (4) comparable portions of the files of the five male faculty members. The university urged the EEOC to "adopt a balancing approach reflecting the constitutional and societal interests inherent in the peer review process" and to resort to "all feasible methods to minimize the intrusive effects of its investigations."

The EEOC denied the University of Pennsylvania's request to withhold the documents and concluded that they were needed to determine the merits of Tung's charges. The commission also rejected the university's proposed "balancing test" because "such an approach . . . would impair the Commission's ability to fully investigate this charge of discrimination."[55] In so ruling, the EEOC noted:

> There has not been enough data supplied in order for the Commission to determine whether there is reasonable cause to believe that the allegations of sex, race, and national origin discrimination is (sic) true. . . . The Commission would fall short of its obligation . . . if it stopped its investigation once [the university] has . . . provided reasons for its employment decisions without verifying whether that reason is a pretext for discrimination.[56]

When the University of Pennsylvania continued to withhold the tenure review materials, the EEOC then applied to a U.S. district court for enforcement of its subpoena. The court entered the enforcement order. Relying on its earlier opinion in *EEOC v. Franklin and Marshall College*, the U.S. Court of Appeals (Third Circuit) rejected the university's claim that First Amendment principles of academic

---

[55]*University of Pennsylvania v. EEOC*, 51 FEP Cases 1120 (1990).
[56]*University of Pennsylvania v. EEOC*, 51 FEP Cases 1120 (1990).

freedom required the recognition of a qualified privilege or the adoption of a balancing approach. The university contended that the EEOC should be required to demonstrate a particularized need beyond a showing of relevance before obtaining the peer review materials in question.[57]

Because of the conflicting federal court decisions regarding the qualified privilege of tenure review materials, the U.S. Supreme Court granted certiorari regarding the disclosure question (but not as to whether the university actually discriminated against Tung in violation of Title VII). The Court specifically mentioned the conflict created by the Seventh Circuit's decision in *EEOC v. University of Notre Dame du Lac*.

In unanimously denying a qualified privilege protecting the tenure review documents, the Court addressed a number of issues. First, it said that, although Congress meant for Federal Rule of Evidence 501 to be applied on a case-by-case basis, "we are disinclined to exercise this authority expansively." The Court also said that it was especially reluctant to recognize a qualified privilege in an area in which Congress had not provided the privilege itself. The Court noted that, by extending Title VII to institutions of higher learning in 1972 and by providing the EEOC with broad subpoena powers, Congress did not see fit to create a special privilege for peer review documents.[58]

Second, the Court addressed the scope of the EEOC's authority to obtain documentation relevant to charges of employment discrimination. The university contended that "relevance," by itself, was not sufficient. The legal counsel for the university thought that the EEOC did not have an unqualified right to acquire such evidence. The Court noted, however, that Title VII provides procedural safeguards and criminal sanctions that protect the confidentiality of the information obtained by the EEOC during the investigation of a charge of employment discrimination. The Court was unwilling to strike a balance to safeguard confidentiality that was different from that intended by Congress.

> We readily agree with petitioner [University of Pennsylvania] that universities and colleges play significant roles in American society. Nor need we question, at this point, petitioner's assertion that confidentiality is important to the proper functioning of the

[57]*University of Pennsylvania v. EEOC*, 51 FEP Cases 1120 (1990).
[58]*University of Pennsylvania v. EEOC*, 51 FEP Cases 1121 (1990).

peer review process under which many academic institutions operate. The costs that ensue from disclosure, however, constitute only one side of the balance. As Congress has recognized, the costs associated with racial and sexual discrimination in institutions of higher learning are very substantial. Few would deny that ferreting out this kind of invidious discrimination is a great if not compelling governmental interest. Often, as even petitioner seems to admit . . . disclosure of peer review materials will be necessary in order for the Commission to determine whether illegal discrimination has taken place. Indeed, if there is a "smoking gun" to be found that demonstrates discrimination in tenure decisions, it is likely to be tucked away in peer review files.[59]

The Court was afraid that granting a qualified privilege to the University of Pennsylvania would trigger a wave of similar suits by publishers, writers, musicians, and lawyers who have a significant interest in furthering free speech and learning in society. The Court claimed that the withholding of peer review documents by a college or university unless the EEOC could demonstrate a showing beyond relevance "would place a substantial litigation-producing obstacle in the way of the Commission's effort to investigate and remedy alleged discrimination."[60]

The U.S. Supreme Court next addressed the issue of academic freedom and its relation to a qualified privilege. The University of Pennsylvania contended that it asserted its right of academic freedom by using the tenure process to select faculty and shape the institution's identity. Furthermore, the university maintained that the peer review process is the most important element in the effective operation of the tenure system, and a properly functioning tenure process requires candid, detailed, and confidential peer reviews. Based on these premises, the university claimed that the "mere relevance" standard would undermine the existing process of awarding tenure and infringe on the First Amendment right of academic freedom. The university pointed to the previously discussed chilling effect on candid peer review evaluations, the erosion of tenure standards, the divisiveness and tension among faculty who are forced to reveal their tenure votes, and the deleterious effects on American colleges and

[59]*University of Pennsylvania v. EEOC*, 51 FEP Cases 1122 (1990).
[60]*University of Pennsylvania v. EEOC*, 51 FEP Cases 1123 (1990).

universities. The Court's response was that the fears expressed by institutions over revealing the content of tenure review files were unfounded.

> In our view, petitioner's reliance on the so-called academic freedom cases is somewhat misplaced. In those cases [the] government was attempting to control or direct the *content* of the speech engaged in by the university or those affiliated with it. In *Sweezy*, for example, the Court invalidated the conviction of a person found in contempt for refusing to answer questions about the content of a lecture he had delivered at a state university. Similarly in *Keyishian*, the Court invalidated a network of state laws that required public employees, including teachers at state universities, to make certifications with respect to their membership in the Communist party. When in those cases, the Court spoke of "academic freedom" and the right to determine on "academic grounds who may teach" the Court was speaking in reaction to content-based regulation. . . .
>
> Also, the cases upon which petitioner places emphasis involved *direct* infringements on the asserted right to "determine for itself on academic grounds who may teach." In *Keyishian*, for example, [the] government was attempting to *substitute* its teachings employment criteria for those already in place at the academic institutions, directly and completely usurping the discretion of each institution. In contrast, the EEOC subpoena at issue here affects no such usurpation. The Commission is not providing criteria that petitioner *must* use in selecting teachers. Nor is it preventing the University from using criteria it may wish to use, except those—including race, sex, and national origin—that are proscribed under Title VII.[61] (Emphasis in the original)

The Supreme Court continued by noting that it had no intention of encroaching on the autonomy of colleges and universities insofar as the selection of promotion and tenure criteria was concerned. Furthermore, it contended that the University of Pennsylvania's First Amendment infringement on academic freedom was "extremely attenuated" and distant from the asserted right. In essence, the Court stated that the university was actually attempting to expand, not just protect, the right of academic freedom by restricting EEOC access to peer review materials.[62]

---

[61]*University of Pennsylvania v. EEOC*, 51 FEP Cases 1124 (1990).

[62]The Court discussed the imposition of taxes or other government regulation on institutions of higher learning and academic freedom. "But many laws make the

In addressing the contention that the absence of a qualified privilege would have a chilling effect on the peer review process, the Court noted that

> We are not so ready as petitioner seems to be to assume the worst about those in the academic community. Although it is possible that some evaluators may become less candid as the possibility of disclosure increases, others may simply ground their evaluations in specific examples and illustrations in order to deflect potential claims of bias or unfairness. Not all academics will hesitate to stand up and be counted when they evaluate peers.[63]

University of Pennsylvania v. EEOC removed a great deal of uncertainty regarding the ability (or inability) to invoke a qualified privilege to protect peer review materials and other sensitive personnel documents. Although this case dealt with the EEOC's ability to procure tenure review materials, there is little reason to believe that the outcome would have been different had the suit involved a private plaintiff.[64]

The U.S. Supreme Court declined to determine whether it is permissible to redact peer review documents before they are submitted to the EEOC.[65] If colleges and universities are allowed a wide latitude in not disclosing the identities or editing evaluations provided by peer review committee members or extramural reviewers, then a limited de facto qualified privilege may still exist.[66]

---

exercise of First Amendment rights more difficult. For example, a university cannot claim a First Amendment violation simply because it may be subject to taxation or other government regulation, even though such regulation might deprive the university of revenue it needs to bid for professors who are contemplating working for other academic institutions or in industry. We doubt that the peer review process is any more essential in effectuating the right to determine 'who may teach' than is the availability of money." *University of Pennsylvania v. EEOC*, 51 FEP Cases 1125 (1990).

[63]*University of Pennsylvania v. EEOC*, 51 FEP Cases 1125 (1990).

[64]McMillin, *"University of Pennsylvania v. EEOC and Dixon v. Rutgers,"* p. 1127.

[65]Frost, "Shifting Meanings of Academic Freedom," p. 349.

[66]On June 26, 1992, the University of Pennsylvania and Rosalie Tung entered into a settlement agreement, resolving charges of employment discrimination. The mutual settlement was made without any findings or admissions of fault or liability. As part of the settlement, the parties agreed to the following statement: "In 1985, Rosalie Tung, then an Associate Professor, was denied tenure by the Wharton School, University of Pennsylvania. After considering her complaint, a faculty grievance panel concluded that certain procedural irregularities had occurred. The Panel further concluded that these irregularities, although not individually significant, when taken collectively resulted in a flawed review of Dr. Tung's qualifications. The University administration accepted this conclusion and agreed that the review process did not result in an adequate review of Professor Tung's performance, qualifications, and credentials." "Statement," *Academy of Management News* 22 (Oct. 1992): 25.

State Public Disclosure Laws and Confidential Promotion and Tenure Documents

Some states have enacted "sunshine laws" that permit access to public documents, data, and meetings. For example, state-assisted colleges and universities are occasionally required to provide information on the salaries of college professors and administrators to interested parties. Other states may allow public access to collective bargaining negotiation sessions or other meetings. Although sunshine laws may exempt certain types of records or meetings, such as those pertaining to confidential law enforcement investigations, the courts are still resolving whether promotion and tenure files fall within the public domain.

In 1994, the Supreme Court of Ohio reviewed the case of *State ex. rel. James v. Ohio State University*, brought by William Calvin James, an assistant professor in the Department of Geological Sciences at Ohio State University. James sought access to and copies of records contained in promotion and tenure files in various departments at Ohio State. The dean of the College of Mathematics and Physical Sciences offered James access to his own file but refused to give him access to the promotion and tenure files of other faculty. The dean also refused to provide James with a copy of the department chairperson's evaluation letter or any information that might reveal the identities of persons who evaluated James's work.

Counsel for Ohio State contended that (1) these records were exempt under the Ohio Public Records Act and (2) the disclosure of the evaluators' identities would infringe substantially on the university's constitutionally protected right to academic freedom. The court rejected both arguments. First, the Ohio Supreme Court said that promotion and tenure records could not be regarded as "confidential law enforcement investigatory records," which were exempted under the Ohio Public Records Act. To the contrary, the university's promotion and tenure guidelines stated specifically that letters of evaluation were subject to disclosure under the act. Ohio State faculty and administrators were cautioned both in the promotion and tenure guidelines and by the university's senior vice president for academic affairs to inform prospective external evaluators of this fact. Second, the Ohio Supreme Court rejected the university's academic freedom argument. In doing so, it cited and quoted the U.S. Supreme Court's ruling in *University of Pennsylvania v. EEOC*. The Ohio Court also said that "it seems the antithesis of academic freedom to maintain secret files upon which promotion and tenure decisions are made, unavailable even to the person who is subject to the evaluation."[67]

Persons involved in promotion and tenure evaluations should understand the applicable state laws and court decisions that regulate access to personnel files and committee deliberations. External reviewers also need to be apprised of the extent to which their comments on a candidate for promotion or tenure may be disclosed to others.

Recent legal developments may discourage peer review committees, department heads, and deans from keeping detailed records of committee deliberations. Some external reviewers, fearing disclosure of their identities, may refuse to write letters of evaluation for a candidate for promotion or tenure. Others may be willing to write evaluations only if the candidate's credentials are strong; they may decline to comment on candidates whose research and publication records are marginal. Still others may write evaluations that are either superficial or less than candid.

The Ohio Supreme Court noted in State ex. rel. James that "academic scholars routinely critique each other's work in public forums such as conferences, journal articles, and book reviews." This comment overlooks three important points. First, the identities of persons who review papers submitted to academic and professional journals are usually not revealed, even if the article is accepted for publication. Second, critiques of papers and books at academic conferences or in published reviews are typically tactful, especially if the reviewer and author work in the same professional circles.[68] Third, and most important, the critique of a single book or article rarely has the same career implications for a faculty member as a letter from an external reviewer that is used in his or her promotion or tenure evaluation.

Cases similar to State ex. rel. James v. Ohio State University will undoubtedly arise elsewhere. State courts will have to examine the language of their respective public disclosure laws to determine whether the contents of promotion and tenure documents as well as the identities of evaluators must be revealed. As was the case in Ohio, state courts may also look to University of Pennsylvania v. EEOC for guidance.

---

[67]State ex. rel. James v. Ohio State University, 70 Ohio St. 3d 168 (1994). See Douglas Lederman, "Will Unlocking the Files Disrupt the Process?" Chronicle of Higher Education, April 14, 1995: A18–A19.

[68]There are, of course, some academics who are willing to provide open, candid, and even ruthless criticism of the work of others. These individuals are, however, in the minority.

9. Remedies for Employment Discrimination in Academia

A LTHOUGH THE VAST MAJORITY of discrimination cases in academia have been decided in favor of the college or university, instances in which faculty prevailed raise some interesting issues regarding remedies. In fashioning a remedy in an employment discrimination suit, the EEOC and courts must consider two issues. First, they need to discourage discriminatory behavior by peer review committees, department heads, deans, and other college officials. As noted earlier, the adverse publicity surrounding an employment discrimination suit may be a sufficient deterrent. The provision in the Civil Rights Act of 1991 that allows for punitive damages may also discourage further discrimination. Second, the victim of discrimination must receive sufficient relief from or compensation for the discriminatory acts. There are seven categories of relief under state and federal equal employment opportunity laws: (1) preliminary relief, (2) affirmative relief, (3) back pay, (4) front pay, (5) compensatory damages, (6) punitive damages, and (7) attorney's fees.

PRELIMINARY AND AFFIRMATIVE RELIEF

Preliminary relief involves the use of an injunction to prevent a college or university from engaging in employment discrimination while a complaint is being resolved by the EEOC or courts. Preliminary relief is usually granted in exceptional circumstances when irreparable harm is likely to occur to the plaintiff. For example, an injunction might be issued to prevent an institution from terminating a faculty member pending the outcome of a grievance hearing or trial.

Affirmative relief is the most controversial remedy for discrimination suits arising in colleges and universities;[1] it may involve such actions as reinstating a faculty member to his or her job or ordering an institution to promote or grant tenure to a faculty member. Such actions are often enforced through court-approved agreements known as consent decrees.

The aim of the remedies in Title VII cases is "to make persons whole for injuries suffered on account of unlawful employment discrimination."[2] Congress has vested broad discretion to the federal courts in fashioning these remedies. As noted earlier, affirmative remedies include back pay, reinstatement, and promotions. The awarding of tenure, however, is undertaken only under unusual circumstances. In *Brown v. Trustees of Boston University*, the U.S. Court of Appeals (First Circuit) stated:

> Courts have quite rarely awarded tenure as a remedy for unlawful discrimination, and those that have, have done so under circumstances distinguishable from those here. The University argues that tenure is a significantly more intrusive remedy than remedies ordinarily awarded in Title VII cases, such as reinstatement or seniority, because a judicial tenure award mandates a lifetime relationship between the University and the professor. The University further contends that due to the intrusiveness of tenure awards and the First Amendment interest in academic freedom, a court should not award tenure unless there is no dispute as to a professor's qualifications. Thus, the University concludes, the district court should not have awarded tenure to Brown, because there existed a dispute as to her qualifications.
>
> We agree that courts should be "extremely wary of intruding into the world of university tenure decisions. . . ." However, once a university has been found to have impermissibly discriminated in making a tenure decision, as here, the University's prerogative to make tenure decisions must be subordinated to the goals embodied in Title VII. The Supreme Court has ruled that the remedial provision of Title VII . . . requires courts to fashion the most complete relief possible for victims of discriminatory employment decisions.[3]

---

[1]See "Tenure and Partnership as Title VII Remedies," *Harvard Law Review* 94 (1980): 457–76.

[2]*Albemarle Paper Co. v. Moody*, 10 FEP Cases 1181 (1975).

[3]*Brown v. Trustees of Boston University*, 51 FEP Cases 836 (1989). Citations omitted.

Boston University contended that the awarding of tenure under such circumstances infringes on the university's First Amendment academic freedom right to determine who may teach. The university also argued that the special needs of academic institutions dictated a less restrictive remedy than the imposition of tenure, although it did not suggest an appropriate remedy.[4] The court observed, however, that "Brown's near unanimous endorsement by colleagues within and without her department suggest strongly that there are no issues of collegiality or the like which might make the granting of tenure inappropriate."[5]

In *Ford v. Nicks*, a U.S. district court ordered Middle Tennessee State University (MTSU) to grant tenure and back pay to Lani Ford, a faculty member in MTSU's Department of Youth Education. The district court stated that it was "mindful of the undesirability of overturning the judgment of professional educators with respect to decisions made by them in hiring other professionals" but that comparative and circumstantial evidence demonstrated that Ford was a victim of sex discrimination. Noting that it was following the path between excessive intervention in the affairs of the university and an unwarranted tolerance of unlawful behavior, the federal district court granted the aforementioned relief.[6] The U.S. Court of Appeals (Sixth Circuit) affirmed the federal district court's findings with regard to the finding of sex discrimination and reinstatement, but said that it abused its discretion in ordering Ford reinstated with tenure. Prior to 1976, state college and university faculty in Tennessee were granted tenure automatically upon completion of their probationary period. After 1976, state law required that tenure be granted to a faculty member only "upon positive approval by the board [of regents]." Since Lani Ford's probationary period would have ended in 1976, the Sixth Circuit ruled that her tenure was subject to board approval. "It seems clear that Mrs. Ford would not have attained tenure automatically, and we are not prepared to say that the Board of Regents would have given its 'positive approval' to tenure for her. For us to make that sort of assumption would entangle us in a matter 'best left to academic professionals.' "[7]

---

[4]Some amici suggested that Brown be reinstated with a three-year probationary period before a tenure decision was made. The Court regarded such a remedy as impractical and claimed that it fell short of the "make-whole" remedies of Title VII.

[5]*Brown v. Trustees of Boston University*, 51 FEP Cases 837 (1989).

[6]*Ford v. Nicks*, 47 FEP Cases 1539 (1988). See also *New York Institute of Technology v. State Division of Human Rights*, 35 FEP Cases 1123 (1976).

[7]*Ford v. Nicks*, 48 FEP Cases 1667 (1989).

Nearly a decade before *Brown* and *Ford*, the U.S. Court of Appeals upheld a conditional tenure award in *Kunda v. Muhlenberg College*. In this case, the court ordered that Kunda be granted tenure if she obtained a master's degree within two academic years. The Third Circuit affirmed the lower court's remedy. Unlike the decision in *Brown*, the court did not grant an outright tenure award to Kunda but instead attempted to place her in the position that she should have been "but for" the unlawful discrimination (failing to advise her that she needed a master's degree to get tenure while making this requirement clear to her male colleagues).[8]

In a case mentioned earlier, *Bennun v. Rutgers*, an extensive analysis of the comparative qualifications of two candidates for promotion to the rank of professor, one successful and one unsuccessful, led a U.S. district court to award back pay and a retroactive promotion to Alfred Bennun, an Argentine-born faculty member. Bennun had a strong research record and had already been awarded tenure at Rutgers. This case suggests, therefore, that the ramifications for the university are less severe in a promotion-only case of this type. The long-term financial implications are more severe in cases in which a court orders an institution to grant tenure.[9] But when denial of a promotion is linked to sexual harassment or other unprofessional conduct, not only is the court likely to order the institution to promote the plaintiff but the faculty members who are involved are likely to confront considerable adverse publicity.[10]

Opponents of court-awarded tenure argue that monetary awards should adequately compensate a faculty member who has been subjected to illegal employment discrimination. Some also contend that forcing a college or university to reemploy a faculty member who has been terminated leads to interpersonal conflicts among the faculty. Monetary awards represent inadequate compensation, however, for the loss of the intrinsic rewards associated with an academic position. Many university professors enjoy a variety of such rewards, including a pleasant work environment, the challenge of research and publishing, and the pleasure of teaching bright and inquisitive students. Denial of tenure may preclude the faculty member from

[8]*Kunda v. Muhlenberg College*, 22 FEP Cases 74 (1980). Also see *Fields v. Clark University*, 40 FEP Cases 670 (1986).

[9]*Bennun v. Rutgers, The State University of New Jersey*, 56 FEP Cases 746 (1991). See also *Flanders v. William Paterson College*, 34 FEP Cases 1456 (1976).

[10]See *Jew v. University of Iowa*, 57 FEP Cases 647 (1990).

obtaining a comparable position elsewhere, especially if labor market conditions are unfavorable or the faculty member's skills have become overly specialized. Supporters of court-awarded tenure might also argue that back pay and compensatory and punitive damages pose no significant deterrent to administrators at large institutions. Thus, financially strong colleges and universities may be able to "buy the right to discriminate" if remedies for civil rights violations are restricted to monetary awards.[11]

ECONOMIC REMEDIES

One common economic remedy, back pay, compensates a faculty member for wages lost as the result of a discriminatory termination, promotion, or tenure decision. For example, a female assistant professor who is denied a promotion to the rank of associate professor because of sex discrimination may receive back pay to compensate her for the loss of wages during the time that her promotion was delayed. Usually, the faculty member will receive the amount he or she would have earned (plus a reasonable bonus for interest), less any income received from outside sources, while the discrimination suit is pending. The back pay may be terminated once the faculty member finds substantially equivalent employment or is reinstated.

Front pay compensates victims of discrimination for the loss of future salary. For example, a faculty member who is denied a promotion because of illegal racial discrimination may receive front pay to compensate him for loss of future income in the event that a tenured position in his department is no longer available. Front pay may be used in lieu of affirmative relief such as reinstatement if discord, tension, or antagonism will prevent effective job performance by the plaintiff.[12] In such cases, a court may award front pay until the plaintiff secures substantially equivalent employment elsewhere.[13]

Before the passage of the Civil Rights Act of 1991, remedies were based primarily on the "make-whole" concept. Under this concept, a victim of discrimination was entitled to remedies that would restore him or her to the economic position that would have existed had the

---

[11]"Tenure and Partnership as Title VII Remedies," pp. 475–76.

[12]See, for example, *Briseno v. Central Technical Community College Area*, 37 FEP Cases 60 (1984).

[13]See EEOC, "EEOC: Policy Statement on Front Pay as a Remedy under ADEA," in BNA, *Fair Employment Practices Manual* (Washington, D.C.: BNA, 1988), sec., 405.

discrimination not occurred. The Civil Rights Act of 1991, however, provides for compensatory and punitive damages for victims of sex, national origin, religious, or disability discrimination.

Compensatory damages under the Civil Rights Act of 1991 are awarded for "future pecuniary losses, emotional pain, suffering, inconvenience, mental anguish, loss of enjoyment of life, and other nonpecuniary losses." Given the trauma experienced by faculty who immerse themselves in lengthy employment discrimination proceedings, compensatory damages could pose a significant threat to institutions of higher learning.

Punitive damages are designed to discourage legal employment discrimination, regardless of the economic or emotional damages suffered by a faculty member. Such damages are limited and are based on a sliding scale that is linked to the number of persons employed by the faculty member's college or university. Institutions with five hundred or more employees have a maximum punitive damage liability of $300,000 under the Civil Rights Act of 1991. Punitive damages are not awarded for liability arising out of disparate impact cases.

Attorney's fees for reasonable legal costs may be assessed under Title VII against a college or university that has been found guilty of employment discrimination. If the institution prevails, however, it will be awarded attorney's fees only if the plaintiff's suit was frivolous, unreasonable, and without foundation. According to the Wisconsin Supreme Court, a faculty member who uses the services of an attorney during an internal grievance hearing may not necessarily be entitled to a reimbursement of legal fees. A University of Wisconsin professor filed a complaint with an internal grievance committee charging that her contract was not renewed because of sex discrimination. The university committee, which was established under state law, found no evidence of discrimination. It decided, however, that the professor had not been given fair consideration. Members of the committee recommended that she be given another chance to obtain tenure and be reimbursed for 50 percent of her attorney's fees. When the university chancellor refused to pay her fees, she filed suit claiming that she was entitled to the fees as a prevailing party under Title VII. The Wisconsin court ruled that the attorney's fees provision applies only to state or local administrative proceedings, which complainants must use before filing court action. The court reasoned that if fees were allowed for optional internal proceedings, employers would be discouraged from implementing grievance mechanisms.[14] It remains to be seen whether other state or federal courts will follow the logic of the Wisconsin Supreme Court on the issue of legal fees incurred during internal hearings.

One of the most significant judgments against a university by a state court was the $1.4 million award to the faculty plaintiff at Claremont University who was victimized by racial discrimination in a tenure decision.[15] A federal court awarded a similar amount in *Rajender v. University of Minnesota* to Shyamala Rajender, who was denied a tenure-track position in the University of Minnesota's renowned chemistry department in 1973. She filed a suit under the post–Civil War Civil Rights Acts, federal executive orders mandating affirmative action, and Title VII. Rajender's suit was certified as a class action representing all past, present, and future nonstudent female employees.[16] The final consent decree, which was signed in August 1980, awarded her $100,000, imposed a quota for the hiring of women in the department, and required that three special masters be appointed to resolve all past or future sex discrimination grievances against the university. These masters were empowered to award cash damages and faculty positions, including positions with tenure, and to oversee hiring at the University of Minnesota until 1989. Rajender's attorneys were awarded approximately $2 million in legal fees.[17]

The U.S. Court of Appeals (Eleventh Circuit) recognized the impact of decades of sex discrimination against a female faculty member when it fashioned a remedy in *Jepsen v. Florida Board of Regents*. Even though pre-1972 discrimination is not actionable under Title VII, Laura Jepsen contended that Florida State University's earlier failure to promote her had a discriminatory effect on her current rank and

[14]*Duello v. University of Wisconsin Board of Regents*, Wis. Sup. Ct., No. 91-1047 (1993). Discussed in BNA, "Title VII Attorney's Fees," *Fair Employment Practices*, June 17, 1993, p. 95.

[15]*Clark v. Claremont University Center and Graduate School*, 65 FEP Cases 919 (1992).

[16]The group of employees numbered approximately thirteen hundred.

[17]*Rajender v. University of Minnesota*, 24 FEP Cases 1045 (1978), as discussed in Jennie Farley, *Academic Women and Employment Discrimination: A Critical Annotated Bibliography* (Ithaca, N.Y.: New York State School of Industrial and Labor Relations, Cornell University, 1982), p. 20, and George R. LaNoue and Barbara A. Lee, *Academics in Court: The Consequences of Faculty Discrimination Litigation* (Ann Arbor: University of Michigan Press, 1987), pp. 42–43, 177–219. Also see Debra E. Blum, "10 Years Later, Questions Still Abound over Minnesota Sex-Bias Statement," *Chronicle of Higher Education*, June 13, 1990, pp. A13–A15.

salary. The trial court could not find sufficient comparative data to conclude that Jepsen would have been promoted from the rank of associate to the rank of full professor in the absence of illegal discrimination. The court concluded, however, that if she deserved a promotion to associate professor in 1971, "she undoubtedly merited it in the 1950s." Based on that conclusion, the court formulated a remedy designed to compensate her for the effects of discrimination on her salary since 1972. The salaries of male faculty who were hired close to the same time as Jepsen was and who were promoted to associate professor at approximately the same time as she should have been promoted were averaged to arrive at an adjusted salary. The university was ordered to pay her this amount and to adjust her retirement benefits accordingly.[18]

The courts expect victims of discrimination to minimize their economic losses by seeking comparable employment elsewhere. In *Ford v. Nicks*, the U.S. Court of Appeals (Sixth Circuit) ruled that Lani Ford failed to mitigate her damages after she was terminated at Middle Tennessee State University. Ford testified during her sex discrimination trial that she and her husband were willing to relocate, and court records disclosed that they had applied for positions in California, New Mexico, Georgia, and North Carolina. Tennessee Technological University, which is located approximately 70 miles from where the Fords lived (Murfreesboro, Tennessee), offered Ford a job similar to the one that she had held at Middle Tennessee State. She rejected the job offer and, according to the court, "failed to exercise reasonable diligence in applying for other substantially equivalent positions that were available."[19] "Mrs. Ford simply left the labor market for entry level professors of education in 1974 and made no further effort to obtain work in that field, apart from the prosecution of this lawsuit. She was perfectly free to make this choice, of course, but under [Title VII] she was not free to impose the costs of this decision on her former employer. We believe that the district court's findings to the contrary are clearly erroneous."[20]

Although a court may limit the monetary awards to which a professor is entitled if he or she fails to mitigate damages by seeking employment elsewhere, at least one state court has considered the

---

[18]*Jepsen v. Florida Board of Regents*, 37 FEP Cases 328 (1985).
[19]*Ford v. Nicks*, 48 FEP Cases 1665 (1989).
[20]*Ford v. Nicks*, 48 FEP Cases 1666 (1989).

difficulties of finding another job for professionals who have been discharged under questionable circumstances. In *Frye v. Memphis State University*, a tenured professor of industrial organizational psychology was accused of theft and fraud and subjected to an ethics committee investigation. He was wrongfully discharged and reinstated nine years later. A lower Tennessee court limited damages to one year following the wrongful termination because the plaintiff failed to seek comparable employment. The Tennessee Supreme Court held, however, that he did not fail to exercise reasonable diligence in reducing the economic damages to himself. According to the court, the plaintiff was "a tenured professor, a highly protected employment status under the law, whose specialty was such that his professional reputation was perhaps his most valued asset." The court found that the media coverage and extensive adverse publicity surrounding his termination made it difficult, if not impossible, for him to find a job commensurate with his professional background. It also noted that he had established a consulting business in the Memphis area, which would have been adversely affected had he been forced to move elsewhere.[21]

Some out-of-court settlements can also be expensive. The University of Colorado agreed to settle with an associate professor of psychology who alleged that the university discriminated against women in hiring and granting tenure. The professor is to receive $30,000 a year for life, tax free, in exchange for her resignation and the withdrawal of her sex discrimination lawsuit. She accused the university's psychology department of sabotaging her career and · waging a "vicious, unrelenting, retaliatory harassment" campaign designed to force her from her job on the Boulder campus.[22]

Another university (not identified) agreed to pay $2.2 million to settle a discrimination claim that was precipitated by an Office of Federal Contract Compliance Programs audit. Although the claim involved a number of sex discrimination issues, part of the settlement required the university to extend the probationary period for untenured faculty so that they could meet family obligations.[23]

---

[21]*Frye v. Memphis State University*, 806 S.W.2d 170 (Tenn. 1991), cited and discussed in Fernand N. Dutile, "Higher Education and the Courts: 1991 in Review," *Journal of College and University Law* 19 (1992): 154–55.

[22]See "Faculty Notes," *Chronicle of Higher Education*, Oct. 19, 1994, p. A32. As part of the agreement, the University of Colorado admitted no wrongdoing, and the faculty member is prohibited from ever seeking future employment at the university.

[23]BNA, "In Brief," *Fair Employment Practices*, Aug. 12, 1993, p. 95.

10. Preventing Employment Discrimination Suits

F EW WRONGFUL DISCHARGE AND CIVIL RIGHTS suits in institutions of higher learning involve flagrant acts of employment discrimination. Nevertheless, white male faculty and college officials seriously influence reappointment, promotion, and tenure decisions. The opportunity for subtle and covert forms of employment discrimination continue to exist, especially in institutions where personnel policies are vague or procedural controls are lax.

Discrimination may be precipitated by several factors. Some peer review committee members and college administrators believe that women, because of demands imposed by family obligations, are not capable of holding faculty positions. In addition, male faculty may believe that women whose husbands are well-paid professionals should not take faculty positions because they rightfully belong to men whose spouses are not employed.[1] Faculty may feel that affirmative action programs have forced colleges and universities to employ "undeserving" minorities; peer review committees and administrators may be quick to purge their institutions of these individuals, believing that they do not have the talent and work ethic to warrant tenure.

Some peer review committees and administrators have a cavalier attitude toward personnel procedures, mentoring programs, and formal performance appraisals. They regard such "administrivia" as impositions that detract from scholarly endeavors. Unfortunately, a

---

[1]See Stephen E. Baldwin, "Subconscious Sex Bias and Labor Market Reality," *Labor Law Journal* 30 (July 1979): 439–40.

disdain for personnel policies and procedures may cost an institution a considerable amount of money and bad publicity in the wake of a discrimination suit. The cases in which faculty have prevailed against an institution of higher learning have usually involved substantial amounts of circumstantial evidence that provided proof of disparate treatment or disparate impact based on race, sex, national origin, age, or other proscribed reasons. The vast majority of cases could have been prevented or resolved without resort to extensive litigation had the college or university adhered to reasonable personnel and human resource management policies. When an institution loses an employment discrimination case, it may revamp its personnel policies or install tighter controls, which typically make department heads and deans more accountable for their actions. When the institution prevails, however, administrators may make the mistake of assuming that existing personnel practices are acceptable. Such an assumption may lead to similar problems in the future.

Preventing or dealing with wrongful discharge or employment discrimination suits precipitated by the promotion and tenure process is more than a matter of taking proper legal precautions. Rather, the personnel and human resource management policy should create an organizational culture that supports equal employment opportunity, equitable employment decisions, and the opportunity for faculty members to fulfill their potential as teachers and scholars. The development of reasonable criteria for promotion and tenure that are applied fairly represents a major step toward eradicating employment discrimination in colleges and universities. Recruitment and selection, training and development, performance appraisal, and grievance programs can also be effective in reducing the chances of discrimination suits. U.S. colleges and universities should strongly consider following the lead of such major corporations as IBM, Kodak, Avon, Shell Oil, and Boise Cascade in implementing diversity management programs that foster recognition and respect for individual and cultural differences.

RECRUITMENT AND SELECTION OF FACULTY

The process of recruiting and hiring faculty represents the first stage at which the potential for employment discrimination problems can be reduced. Colleges and universities must cast a wide net in their search for faculty to ensure that female and minority candidates are not overlooked. Institutions that recruit junior faculty primarily through a network of colleagues at a few select institutions are restricting their applicant pool and may exclude qualified female and minority applicants.

Departments and colleges within institutions of higher learning should tailor their recruitment and selection processes to institutional needs. Position announcements placed by colleges and universities typically focus on teaching needs, whereas the fate of the faculty member at promotion and tenure time is more likely to depend primarily on his or her research and publications. If an institution has specific teaching and research needs, they should be clarified during the hiring process so that a faculty member is not later deemed unacceptable for promotion or tenure because his or her teaching interest or research agenda was unsuitable. This problem arose in *University of Pennsylvania v. EEOC*, in which the plaintiff, Rosalie Tung, was terminated, in part, because the university allegedly had no interest in "China-related" research.[2] Although a college or university has a legal right to terminate a faculty member whose research and teaching interests are incongruous with institutional needs, such a decision may spark a wrongful discharge suit, especially if the faculty member believes that he or she was misled during the hiring process or the "official" reason for denying a promotion or tenure was a pretext for illegal discrimination.

Discussions during job interviews should cover both the good and bad aspects of the position, the working environment, and the institution. Job previews that provide such uncensored views were originally designed to help reduce employee turnover. Research has not been conclusive on whether this tactic does, in fact, reduce turnover.[3] Such an approach should help avoid potential misunderstandings, however, that could later lead to a wrongful discharge or employment discrimination suit.

Academic departments in universities typically have a job candidate meet with some of the faculty individually, either at a convention or during an on-campus visit. During these interviews, the candidate frequently begins to learn about the department's expectations regarding teaching, research, and service.[4] Faculty who conduct such

---

[2] *University of Pennsylvania v. EEOC*, 51 FEP Cases 1119 (1990).

[3] Robert L. Dipboye, *Selection Interviews: Process Perspectives* (Cincinnati: South-Western, 1992), pp. 237–38.

[4] Dipboye, *Selection Interviews*, p. 238.

interviews should be careful to avoid remarks that could indicate a discriminatory animus. Likewise, recruitment and selection committees, department heads, and deans should avoid painting a glowing but unrealistic picture of a job during an interview with a candidate. There may be a great temptation to promise reduced teaching loads, ample resources for research and writing, or other amenities, especially when the labor market is competitive or the institution is making a concerted effort to hire females and minorities. A faculty member who is denied a promotion or tenure may claim that the institution reneged on promises of resources and support. Furthermore, when a faculty member later discovers that the job is not as good as advertised, he or she may feel misled, bitter, and ready to file employment discrimination charges.

The job interview should focus exclusively on the candidate's qualifications and job-related issues. Although there are no illegal interview questions per se under federal law, questions that focus on a candidate's personal life, religious preferences, ancestry, age, or marital status are of dubious value.[5] Most questions of a personal nature are directed at female job applicants and focus on child-care arrangements, the career aspirations of the candidate's spouse, or the likelihood that the candidate will need a maternity or parental leave. Since these questions are usually not directed at male faculty candidates and are of questionable relationship to the job, they should be avoided. They may be used as circumstantial evidence against an institution in an employment discrimination suit.[6]

Finally, an institution should carefully monitor its recruitment and selection trends. If there is reason to believe that female and minority candidates are not adequately represented in the interviewing and hiring process, then a closer examination of recruitment advertisements, the interviewing process, and the criteria used to hire faculty may be warranted.

---

[5]The New York State Division of Human Rights has issued a guide that delineates legal and illegal inquiries under section 296 of the New York Human Rights Law. See BNA, "New York: Pre-Employment Inquiry Guide," in *Fair Employment Practices Manual* (Washington, D.C.: BNA, 1992), sec. 456. Extreme care should be taken when making pre-employment inquiries regarding a faculty candidate's age or the presence of physical or mental disabilities. In the absence of business necessity, such inquiries are likely to violate the ADEA and the ADA.

[6]Some faculty positions, such as those in university agriculture extension divisions, require frequent travel and work at night or on weekends. It is legitimate to ask an applicant for such positions whether he or she would be able to work irregular hours.

Establishing Promotion and Tenure Standards

The *criteria* for promotion or tenure are those that an institution regards as important (e.g., research grants, publications in refereed journals, teaching innovations), whereas the *standards* for promotion or tenure are the degree to which such criteria must be fulfilled (e.g., amount of grant monies received, number of articles in top-tier journals, types of teaching innovations). Promotion and tenure criteria and standards are established on a decentralized basis at most colleges and universities. As discussed earlier in chapter 6, although criteria may be consistent within an institution (i.e., all departments value articles published in refereed journals), it is not unusual for standards to vary across campus. A stellar research and publication record may be required for tenure in one department or college, whereas faculty in another department at the same institution may achieve tenure with relatively inferior accomplishments. Regardless of the standards, it is important that they be reasonable, reflect institutional needs, and be applied fairly and consistently.

Criteria and standards for promotion and tenure are not usually set by one individual. Rather, they may evolve as a result of collaboration by senior faculty, department heads, and deans. In some institutions, junior faculty have input into promotion and tenure standards, but this input is likely to be limited. Large private universities that pay close attention to institutional prestige and rankings are likely to emphasize research productivity in promotion and tenure decisions. State universities may also have a strong research mission but reward faculty who engage in extension and service activities that meet the needs of the state's citizens. Smaller, regional colleges and universities may place primary emphasis on teaching quality and addressing the needs of undergraduate students.

The criteria and standards for promotion and tenure should be specific enough to provide guidance to faculty members, yet flexible enough to enable peer review committees, department heads, deans, and others to consider the faculty member's total accomplishments. Having a flexible set of standards will also enable university officials to assemble a competent group of senior, tenured faculty who have diverse teaching, research, and service orientations. Academic units in which faculty perform diverse roles may use a dual tenure track system. Some medical school faculty, for example, are predominantly clinicians, whereas others are predominantly researchers. Faculty in schools of journalism may engage in either traditional research and writing, or creative visual communications and photojournalism projects. Diverse academic units such as these may use broad promotion and tenure criteria, or faculty may be expected to choose between a "traditional" or "nontraditional" tenure track. When dual systems are used, faculty may be required to select a track early in their careers. Dual-track promotion and tenure criteria should be discussed with faculty candidates during the interviewing process as well as during the early stages of a faculty member's career.

Written reappointment, promotion, and tenure guidelines should be available for all faculty members. Performance standards for research productivity should address such issues as the acceptability of specific journals or other publication outlets, whether a distinction is made between textbooks and scholarly books, the importance of funded research, and the extent to which research in progress is considered in promotion and tenure decisions.

Faculty should know the weight attached to student evaluations (which should be carefully designed to ensure reliability and validity), pedagogical innovations, and other facets of teaching. Likewise, service activities that are regarded as acceptable should be enumerated in the written guidelines for promotion and tenure.

Reappointment, promotion, and tenure criteria and standards should be based on a careful assessment of an institution's mission and resources. Administrators who harbor high expectations for faculty yet are unable to provide the reduced teaching loads and resources necessary to meet these expectations are being unrealistic. The department head who expects faculty to teach twelve hours (four courses) per semester, serve on several department or college committees, and publish three top-tier journal articles a year does not have an adequate grasp of the realities of the academic world. Performance standards such as these are almost certain to generate personnel problems.

Proper communication and the consistent application of performance standards are critical to preventing or minimizing the damage caused by wrongful discharge or employment discrimination suits. Information regarding changes in criteria or standards should be disseminated to all faculty members. College and university officials must carefully monitor the reappointment, promotion, and tenure process to ensure that illegal discrimination does not affect the decisions of peer review committees, department heads, and deans. Inconsistencies in recent recommendations within a department or college, vague or unclear explanations regarding unfavorable recommendations, and abrupt changes in standards should be viewed with suspicion by deans and other college officials.

ORIENTATION AND CAREER DEVELOPMENT

Colleges and universities have traditionally provided little orientation for new faculty other than a basic introduction to personnel policies and institutional procedures. The time-honored assumption that junior faculty, by virtue of their graduate school experience, already know how to teach and engage in scholarly activities may no longer be true. Except for the required three to twelve hours of scheduled class time per week, faculty members have few constraints on their time. Some junior faculty may have difficulty dealing with the unstructured work environment and unsurpassed freedom that are found in institutions of higher learning. Furthermore, a competitive publishing environment, the increased emphasis on research grants, and the complex political nature of colleges and universities may make it increasingly more difficult for newly minted Ph.D.s to step into faculty positions and perform effectively. In some cases, new faculty may need considerable help in developing their teaching competencies and research programs.

The first step in the socialization process is to ensure that new faculty members have a clear understanding of the institution's research, teaching, and service expectations. Department heads should meet with each new faculty member and carefully explain criteria for reappointment, promotion, and tenure. As noted earlier, such criteria should also be clearly specified in a department or college faculty handbook. New faculty may underestimate the time, effort, and expertise required to publish in leading academic journals. They may also have an unrealistic idea of the demands of teaching a full schedule of classes or the amount of time that can be consumed by some committee assignments. For these reasons, the careful orientation of new faculty is of critical importance.

MENTORSHIP PROGRAMS

Mentorship programs can provide a useful means of establishing proper expectations and a professional orientation for junior faculty.[7]

---

[7]For an excellent discussion of mentorship programs in academia, see Mary P. Rowe, "Building Mentorship Frameworks as Part of an Effective Equal Opportunity Ecology," in Jennie Farley, ed., *Sex Discrimination in Higher Education: Strategies for Equality* (Ithaca,

Under a mentorship program, a new faculty member is placed under the tutelage of a senior faculty member who understands the institution's culture and expectations. The mentor is available to offer advice, discuss the faculty member's performance, and collaborate on teaching and research projects. Ideally, a mentor-protégé relationship is approached with the idea that each newly hired faculty member has the potential to become tenured if the institution does an adequate job of faculty development. Through a process of mutual collaboration, the mentor and protégé work together so that the junior faculty member develops the research record, teaching competencies, and professional reputation that will result in a favorable tenure decision. Thus, mentors enhance faculty development as well as serve as a source of control for faculty who are not meeting institutional standards. Mentor relationships may also evolve informally as senior and junior faculty migrate to one another because of mutual scholarly interests or friendships.

Senior faculty may be reluctant to become involved in mentoring relationships for several reasons. First, effective mentoring can consume a lot of time from a senior faculty member's already busy schedule. Second, some faculty believe that there is neither a reason nor an incentive to establish the relationship. Less sympathetic faculty may believe that junior faculty should have to endure the same "sink-or-swim" academic environment that they faced during the early years of their careers. Third, senior faculty may perceive a conflict of interest with regard to the relationship. Some male faculty may be reluctant to become involved as mentors with female faculty for fear that their relationship will be misunderstood. The fears associated with accusations of sexual harassment and romantic liaisons of questionable professional integrity are well founded. In addition, senior faculty who serve on peer review committees may be hesitant to establish close relationships with junior faculty for fear that their personal feelings will affect their ability to make an objective judgment on a protégé's qualifications for promotion or tenure.

If a university department elects to have a mentorship program, it is important that it be made available to all junior faculty, not just females or minorities. To do otherwise is to invite charges of discrimination by nonminority men.

N.Y.: New York State School of Industrial and Labor Relations, Cornell University, 1981), pp. 23–33.

Department heads may have a difficult time finding suitable mentors for female and minority faculty members. For example, junior women may feel most comfortable paired with senior women in their department. Such an arrangement may not be possible, however, since many colleges have few, if any, senior female faculty. Finding a suitable mentor may be even more difficult for junior minority faculty. Nevertheless, if there is a mentorship program, mentors should be provided for all junior faculty even if it means that mentors and protégés are of a different sex or race.

The mentor-protégé relationship should be encouraged even if it is apparent that the protégé will not receive a favorable promotion or tenure decision. The mentor can be useful in assisting the faculty member in his or her search for employment at another institution. A terminated faculty member who can look forward to employment elsewhere is less likely to feel rejected and file a wrongful discharge or discrimination suit against his or her former employer.

WORKING CONDITIONS

SEXUAL AND OTHER FORMS OF HARASSMENT

Several wrongful discharge and employment discrimination cases at colleges and universities have been precipitated by conditions in the working environment. One area of major concern is the treatment of women. A number of cases analyzed here raise concerns about sexual harassment. Nearly all colleges and universities have some policy that defines and deals with this widespread problem, and many restrict romantic relationships between persons in superior-subordinate relationships. In addition to requests for sexual favors, sexual harassment suits may also involve situations in which the organizational culture tolerates jokes or sexually explicit remarks that are demeaning to women. Although those who engage in such behavior may view it as a form of humor, the EEOC and courts usually regard it as a violation of Title VII.[8] Violations may also include harassment based on race, national origin, and even age.[9] Faculty members who believe that they are victims of harassment

[8]See W. Jack Duncan, Larry R. Smeltzer, and Terry L. Leap, "Humor and Work: Applications of Joking Behavior to Management," *Journal of Management* 16 (1990): 255–78.

[9]There are a number of cases of race and national origin harassment under Title VII. The EEOC has published a little-known policy against age harassment.

should have access to channels that will enable them to discuss the problem without embarrassment or fear of retaliation.

ALLOCATION OF TIME AND RESOURCES

Faculty members must be provided with the facilities and resources necessary to meet their research, teaching, and service responsibilities. Institutions that are financially strapped may find it difficult to provide all the resources that a faculty member was promised when he or she was hired. For this reason, it is wise for department heads or deans not to make specific promises to newly hired faculty unless they are absolutely certain that the resources will be available. More important, the allocation of resources should not be linked in any way to a faculty member's sex, race, or other impermissible characteristic. Allocating more resources such as travel funds, equipment, or graduate student assistant to faculty who are productive researchers is legitimate since the decision is linked to individual productivity. Similarly, giving reduced teaching loads to faculty who exhibit high levels of research productivity is permissible. The key is to give junior faculty ample and equal opportunity to meet research, teaching, and service expectations by assigning teaching loads and resources in an equitable, nondiscriminatory manner.

COLLEGIALITY AND WORK RELATIONSHIPS

Department heads and faculty members should help junior faculty establish and maintain effective working relationships with colleagues. For some academics, harmonious personal relationships come naturally, whereas for others arrogance, brashness, manipulative behaviors, or the inability to work with colleages and students pose problems. Faculty mentors can be valuable in helping junior faculty understand the organizational culture and develop good relationships. It is especially critical that female and minority candidates be given the opportunity to become part of the department and college. The previously discussed antiminority mindset can be particularly difficult for junior faculty. Senior faculty should be careful to avoid stereotyping and treating minority faculty differently because of cultural differences.

As noted earlier, a college or university may terminate faculty who are troublesome. As long as faculty are given the chance to establish productive working relationships, the institution is under no obligation to retain individuals who are abrasive to colleagues or students, who create political turmoil, or who are not productive teachers and scholars. Faculty members should first be counseled regarding their behavior, and incidents in which a faculty member has caused problems should be documented.

CAREER INTERRUPTIONS AND FAMILY RESPONSIBILITIES

Faculty members occasionally interrupt their careers to attend to personal responsibilities. Federal and state laws provide protection for employees who want to take several weeks from work for a maternity leave or other family reasons. The Pregnancy Discrimination Act of 1978 prohibits discrimination on the basis of pregnancy, childbirth, and related medical conditions. In addition, the Family and Medical Leave Act of 1993 (FMLA) requires that organizations allow employees to take up to twelve weeks of unpaid leave for the birth or adoption of a child or to care for a sick child, parent, or spouse.

Females are more likely than males to delay their careers to care for children or elderly parents. Untenured female faculty who delayed having children to finish graduate school in their late twenties and early thirties may feel compelled to take a leave of absence for childbearing and child rearing by the time they reach their early forties. In addition, women in their mid-forties and beyond are the largest group of caregivers for elderly parents. Neither the Pregnancy Discrimination Act nor the Family and Medical Leave Act appears to benefit female faculty (either tenured or untenured) who spend several years away from their jobs. In some instances, a female professor may resign from a job and either rejoin the same faculty several years later or seek employment at another institution.

Interruptions of one's academic career pose professional problems because the knowledge in most academic specialties changes rapidly. Further, interactions with colleagues, either at work or at professional meetings, are often limited or nonexistent during a career hiatus. As a result, department heads and peer review committees may believe that the research and teaching skills of a faculty member who has been on leave have eroded or become obsolete. Promotion and tenure decisions that create a double standard for women because of their marital status or perceived family burdens, however, may constitute illegal sex or age discrimination. Peer review committees, department heads, and deans should ensure that performance evaluations and personnel decisions are not tainted by stereotypes of traditional male and female domestic roles.

Cynthia Fisher, the biology professor who was denied tenure at Vassar, put her career on hold for ten years because of family obligations. The Vassar administration seemed to believe that the family demands placed on married female faculty were incompatible with the demands of a career in the "hard" sciences.[10] Thus, testimony provided during her trial indicated that Vassar was reluctant to promote or tenure married women. During the thirty years prior to Fisher's tenure review, no married woman had ever achieved tenure in the hard sciences at Vassar, even though nationwide the majority of women with Ph.D.s in these disciplines were married.[11]

The Vassar administration's bias against married women was also evidenced through remarks about Fisher's personal life and life choices before coming to Vassar. When senior biology faculty met with the college's Faculty Appointments and Salary Committee, they claimed that Fisher's scholarship was obsolete ("out of date—out of the field for ten years"). Outside experts who were knowledgeable about Fisher's research specialty, however, evaluated her published articles, *Science Citation Index* citations, and funded research grants. They concluded that Fisher's research was both current and of high quality. Anecdotal evidence was also used to bolster the expert testimony and statistical evidence.[12]

> A Dr. Karen Friedman testified that there was the Department's policy to discourage married women from advancing to tenure. Dr. Friedman personally experienced this policy when she was asked to take an unpaid leave of absence in order to qualify for tenure which she never received.[13] Another woman, Dr. Palmer, felt the prejudice against married women was so strong that she had an abortion in an attempt to protect her tenure prospects. She wrote a letter to Dr. Fisher's Appeals Committee to notify them of this prejudice, but no investigations were made into her allegations.[14]

[10]An expert witness testified that in many fields married women are more productive than single women.

[11]The hard sciences at Vassar were defined as mathematics, physics, chemistry, geology, biology, and computer science. Information on the percentage of married women with Ph.D.s in the hard sciences was compiled by the National Academy of Science and was presented during the trial.

[12]*Fisher v. Vassar College*, 64 FEP Cases 1366 (1994).

[13]After her leave, Friedman's contract was not renewed, thereby denying her the opportunity to achieve tenure.

[14]*Fisher v. Vassar College*, 64 FEP Cases 1377 (1994).

Leave of absence policies should treat similarly situated male and female faculty equitably. Faculty whose family responsibilities impair their job performance need not be given special consideration, but accommodations made to parents and caregivers can enhance a faculty member's career and life satisfaction.[15] Accommodations might include stopping the tenure clock for faculty who must take family leave, avoiding early-morning or late-night schedules for persons with caregiving responsibilities, and providing on-campus childcare facilities.[16]

PERFORMANCE EVALUATIONS

Much has been said and written about faculty evaluations.[17] The process typically entails evaluating the achievements of a faculty member over a specified period of time against a predetermined set of general criteria and standards.[18] Studies by K. L. Kasten and K. O. Magnusen indicate that the evaluation of faculty members in institutions of higher learning will (1) become more standardized and organized, (2) include a wider range of behaviors and responsibilities, (3) use criteria and procedures that are communicated to and understood by faculty members, and (4) be more flexible to accommodate different academic units and the individual talents and capabilities of faculty.[19] A survey by Peter Seldin of 616 academic deans reveals several interesting trends with regard to faculty evaluations:[20]

1. Current practices of faculty evaluation rely on one or more of the following six factors: research, teaching, academic and

[15]As noted earlier, preemployment inquiries about marriage or family situations should be avoided.

[16]See Robin Wilson, "Scheduling Motherhood," *The Chronicle of Higher Education* (March 10, 1995): A14–A15. Nancy Hensel, "Realizing Gender Equity in Higher Education: The Need to Integrate Work/Family Issues," *ERIC Digest* (Oct. 1991).

[17]See Peter Seldin, *Successful Faculty Evaluation Programs* (Crugers, N.Y.: Coventry Press, 1980); Peter Seldin, *Changing Practices in Faculty Evaluation* (San Francisco: Jossey-Bass, 1984); Jason Millman, ed., *Handbook of Teacher Evaluation* (Beverly Hills, Calif.: Sage, 1981); and John A. Centra, *Determining Faculty Effectiveness* (San Francisco: Jossey-Bass, 1979).

[18]Hani I. Mesak and Lawrence R. Jauch, "Faculty Performance Evaluation: Modeling to Improve Personnel Decisions," *Decision Sciences* 22 (1991): 1144.

[19]K. L. Kasten, "Tenure and Merit Pay as Rewards for Research, Teaching, and Service at a Research University," *Journal of Higher Education* 55 (1984): 500–13, and K. O. Magnusen, "Faculty Evaluation, Performance, and Pay: Application and Issues," *Journal of Higher Education* 58 (1987): 516–29, cited in Mesak and Jauch, "Faculty Performance Evaluation," p. 1143.

[20]Seldin, *Changing Practices in Faculty Evaluation*.

professional service, time at the institution, personal attributes, and student advising. The greatest weight is assigned to research and the least to time at the institution, student advising, and personal attributes.

2. Evaluators will display increasing concern for the quality of a faculty member's research. Greater reliability will be placed on third-party evaluators (professors at other institutions who are experts in the candidate's field) to ensure that local professional biases or political considerations do not unfairly affect promotion and tenure decisions.

3. Teaching effectiveness will be scrutinized more closely, using student evaluations as well as other course materials. With the increase in the use of microcomputers, intelligent video disks, and other computer products by students outside the classroom, faculty are likely to devote more effort to developing materials and evaluating the learning process and less effort to presenting course content.

4. Faculty will be better informed about the performance appraisal system and process, including performance measurements and standards. They will be increasingly aware of the standards for unsatisfactory, satisfactory, and exemplary performance.

5. Academic rewards such as promotion and tenure will be closely linked to faculty evaluation programs.

These trends emphasize the need for accurate and timely performance appraisals. Information gathered from such appraisals have a variety of uses, including (1) determining pay increases and promotions, (2) identifying training and development needs, and (3) gathering documentation for disciplinary actions or lawsuits by employees.

Performance appraisals should be job-relevant and valid. Ideally, the appraisal should reflect the exact nature of the job, nothing more and nothing less. Further, guidelines and forms for the appraisal should be clear and concise.

Several decisions have arisen under Title VII and other equal employment opportunity laws regarding the discriminatory effects of performance appraisals.[21] For this reason, great care should be taken

---

[21]See Gary P. Latham and Kenneth N. Wexley, *Increasing Productivity through Performance Appraisal* (Reading, Mass.: Addison-Wesley, 1981), pp. 13–35.

to design an appraisal that accounts for the tasks, duties, and responsibilities of a faculty member's job. An appraisal that considers factors that fall outside the scope of the job is said to be *contaminated*. A contaminated appraisal might consider such factors as a faculty member's lifestyle, religious practices, or other off-duty conduct. As a general rule, activities that occur away from the job should not be reflected in a performance evaluation unless these activities reflect either favorably or unfavorably on the faculty member's role as a professor or representative of the institution.[22] Information that is based on hearsay should also be excluded from performance appraisals.

A performance appraisal is *deficient* when it fails to account for certain aspects of job performance. For example, community service is included on many performance appraisals of faculty, yet it is given scant consideration in promotion and tenure decisions. To the extent that a performance appraisal system is contaminated or deficient, its validity will be diminished.

The reliability of a performance appraisal system can be diminished through a series of rating errors. For example, because of a *halo effect*, one characteristic of a faculty member's overall evaluation may dominate all other aspects of job performance. Thus, a faculty member who wins a prestigious research award but who engages in no community service might be evaluated favorably on community service because of the halo effect produced by the research award.

The *recency effect* can occur if a faculty member exhibits strong performance shortly before the evaluation or personnel decision is made but who otherwise has a lackluster record. For example, a peer review committee that is considering promoting a faculty member to the rank of full professor might be unreasonably swayed if the candidate had a recent flurry of research activity and ignore the faculty member's virtually nonexistent record of research or publications in the years before.

Past-record anchoring occurs when a faculty member's long-term reputation (either good or bad) is allowed to distort a performance evaluation. If a faculty member's strong research productivity of five

---

[22]For a general discussion of how off-duty conduct should be evaluated by employers, see Terry L. Leap, "When Can You Fire for Off-Duty Conduct?" *Harvard Business Review* 66 (Jan.–Feb. 1988): 28–36.

years ago affects his or her current ratings, then a past-record anchoring error has been committed.

Inappropriate rating patterns arise when the rater fails to make appropriate distinctions among the performance levels of various faculty. This can result in a leniency effect, which occurs when all (or nearly all) faculty receive high ratings even though their individual performance levels differ substantially.

Once the performance appraisal has been completed, a postappraisal interview should be conducted to inform the faculty member of his or her strengths and weaknesses, areas in which improvements are needed, and his or her standing with regard to promotion and tenure. These interviews should provide a detailed account of how the faculty member was rated on each dimension (research, teaching, service, and other criteria). The faculty member should then be requested to sign a document that indicates that he or she has examined and discussed the appraisal with the appropriate official and either concurs or disagrees with its contents. In the latter case, the faculty member should be given an opportunity to appeal his or her rating to a higher authority. For example, a faculty member who disagrees with the appraisal made by a department head could appeal the decision to the dean of the college. The faculty member should be allowed to explain fully and in writing the reasons for the appeal.

Performance appraisals should be based on multiple sources: student evaluations of the professor's teaching effectiveness;[23] assessments by peer review committees and department heads of the faculty member's competencies as a teacher, scholar, and faculty citizen (service and collegiality); and evaluations by deans and upper-level college administrators of his or her contributions and value to the institution. Students should be informed of the importance of teaching evaluations, and other evaluators should be trained in the use of performance appraisal instruments. The use of multiple evaluators has two advantages. First, a faculty member's job is complex and involves a multitude of roles. It is difficult for one person to assess all facets of the job. Second, the use of multiple evaluators is less likely to result in illegal disparate treatment or impact because no single individual has total control over the appraisal. The hope is

---

[23]Although formal teaching evaluations are done only once a semester (or academic quarter), student complaints about poor teaching performance should be investigated immediately, especially when multiple complaints are received.

that the sex, racial, or other prejudices of one evaluator will be diluted in an appraisal that uses multiple evaluators.

It is also important for performance evaluations to create "paper trails" that provide adequate documentation on the fairness and thoroughness of the procedure. Administrators who are held accountable for evaluating each faculty member carefully and consistently are less likely to make an unfair personnel decision that could lead to a discrimination suit. Emphasis should be placed on linking performance evaluations to specific aspects of job performance, such as journal publications and ratings of teaching effectiveness. Peer review committees, department heads, and deans should evaluate faculty in a manner that enables them to substantiate and defend each rating on both an individual and a comparative basis.

GRIEVANCE PROCEDURES

Nearly all colleges and universities have a grievance procedure available to faculty who are denied reappointment, promotion, or tenure. As discussed earlier, there may be an independent faculty committee, or a committee may be formed by a faculty senate or under the provisions of a collective bargaining agreement. In theory, faculty grievance procedures provide a safety valve against poorly conceived, unfair, or discriminatory personnel decisions. Such procedures help to ensure due process and may reduce lengthy and expensive court litigation. Grievance procedures that merely ask decision makers to reconsider their actions are of dubious value, however.

There are several hallmarks of an effective faculty grievance procedure.[24]

1. The procedure is known by and acceptable to faculty. Grievance procedures of limited accessibility are of little value to faculty who have been denied reappointment, promotion, or tenure. Likewise, grievance procedures that rubber-stamp (or are thought to rubber-stamp) the decisions of department heads, deans, or other administrators inspire little confidence in faculty with legitimate grievances. If a wrongful discharge or employment discrimination case reaches

---

[24]For an excellent discussion of the design and implementation of nonunion grievance procedures, see David W. Ewing, *Justice on the Job: Resolving Grievances in the Nonunion Workplace* (Boston: Harvard Business School Press, 1989). The hallmarks of an effective procedure discussed here were borrowed, in part, from Ewing's book.

the EEOC or courts, the weight or credibility assigned to college or university proceedings will depend on the perceived objectivity with which the grievance was handled.[25]

2. The grievance mechanism provides procedural safeguards yet is reasonably easy to use. An effective faculty grievance system need not be characterized by extensive paperwork, complex procedures, rules of order and evidence, or other pitfalls, subtleties, and traps. Such cumbersome procedures may diminish the effectiveness of the grievance mechanism.

3. The procedure allows faculty and institutional officials to present their respective cases fully. The procedure also allows ample time for fact finding, examination of the other side's evidence and arguments, and rebuttal of contentions made by the opposing party. If the procedure employs an arbitrator, ombudsman, or independent investigator, it should specify whether that individual has the power to gather the evidence or testimony to make an informed decision.

4. The procedure yields decisions that are consistent and free from external political influence. A consistent procedure is one that treats persons with similar problems in a similar fashion. At the same time, the procedure should be flexible enough to consider extenuating circumstances and institutional needs. Procedures that are influenced by the same administrators who made the original personnel decision are not likely to be effective, however.

5. In designing the procedure, a great deal of consideration is given to the final power of those who will hear and adjudicate the grievances. At one end of the spectrum are grievance committees that simply make recommendations to college and university officials about the proper course of action. These officials are then free to accept, modify, or ignore the committee's recommendations. At the other end of the spectrum are committees that have the power to grant promotions, tenure, or other compensation over the objections of university officials. University administrators want to retain as much autonomy as possible and are not likely to support the latter type of arrangement.[26]

---

[25]*Alexander v. Gardner-Denver*, 7 FEP Cases 81 (1974). In this case the U.S. Supreme Court held that a grievant claiming racial discrimination who is not satisfied with the arbitrator's decision may relitigate his or her case through the EEOC or courts under Title VII of the 1964 Civil Rights Act. *Alexander v. Gardner-Denver* applied to labor arbitration cases. The Supreme Court said that the EEOC or court would be responsible for deciding the extent to which it wants to weigh the results reached in a previous grievance or arbitration hearing.

[26]Faculty who agree to serve on internal grievance committees assume a major

6. The grievance procedure specifies whether a faculty member is required to exhaust his or her options under the internal grievance procedure before pursuing litigation in a state or federal agency or court. As noted earlier, some states have such a requirement.

---

responsibility. A single hearing can consume hours of a faculty member's time. A vivid example of the stresses imposed by grievance committee work occurred during the 1992–93 academic year at the University of Kansas. Five professors spent hundreds of hours determining whether a tenured law professor should be fired for moral turpitude and ethical violations in conjunction with an accusation of sexual harassment by a former student. The case took thirty-three days of hearings, involved forty-nine witnesses, generated an 8,000-page transcript, and culminated in a 250-page report recommending that the professor be fired. One faculty member described the hearings as "a horrendous experience." Another estimated that he spent a total of eight hundred hours on the case. Some committee members claimed that it hurt their teaching and research endeavors and thus resulted in lowering their merit pay increases. The case also generated considerable controversy on the Kansas campus about how accusations of sexual harassment should be handled. Despite the extensive internal review of his case, the law professor plans to sue. Citing his innocence and the irreparable damage to his reputation, he feels that he did not get a fair hearing because the "jurors" were employed by the university. Carolyn J. Mooney, "33 Days of Hearings, 49 Witnesses, and an 8,000-Page Transcript," *Chronicle of Higher Education*, Dec. 7, 1994, pp. A20–21.

11. Conclusion

THIS BOOK HAS ANALYZED wrongful discharge and employment discrimination litigation in faculty reappointment, promotion, and tenure decisions in U.S. institutions of higher education. It has suggested ways in which such litigation can be prevented or, at least, reduced. By now it should be clear that the resolution of disputes associated with adverse personnel decisions affecting faculty presents a host of complex legal, social, and personnel issues.

Most faculty members, including females and minorities, work their way up the academic ladder without being victimized by invidious employment discrimination. Few female and minority faculty expect to be promoted or tenured simply because of the presence of affirmative action or other programs. Furthermore, most college and university administrators bend over backward to ensure that they make the right decisions. In fact, some college officials are probably too fearful of litigation and end up granting promotion or tenure to faculty who might not deserve it.

The old adage that "an ounce of prevention is worth a pound of cure" certainly applies to the grievances and lawsuits discussed here. Wrongful discharge and discrimination suits are not created in a vacuum, and they rarely arise overnight. Rather, they are the result of months and years of neglect by faculty or college officials who fail to fulfill their professional obligations. Faculty may create problems by shunning their research, teaching, or other responsibilities to the institution. Department heads, deans, or other officials may fail to establish appropriate safeguards, resulting in inequitable decisions that are affected (at least in part) by race, sex, or other prejudices.

An examination of over two decades of court decisions reveals several important points. First, the courts have shown an almost inordinate degree of respect for the complex faculty personnel decisions that must be made by college and university administrators. Evaluating the research productivity, teaching effectiveness, service contributions, and collegiality of a faculty member is a difficult task, even for those who have spent decades in the halls of academe.

Second, the courts recognize the need to encroach on the academic freedom of colleges and universities only to the extent necessary to ensure that illegal employment discrimination has not occurred. Some legal observers may believe that the courts have been gradually softening their anti-interventionist posture. It is probably more accurate to say that the courts are forcing colleges and universities to produce peer review and other relevant documents. There is little indication that the courts are willing to challenge promotion and tenure decisions in the absence of convincing evidence of disparate treatment or impact.

Third, proving the existence of illegal employment discrimination is an uphill battle for most faculty. Although establishing a prima facie case of discrimination is not particularly difficult, the courts have granted institutions of higher learning considerable leeway in justifying adverse promotion and tenure decisions. Faculty and their legal counsel have also been thwarted in demonstrating illegal discrimination by a college or university because the federal courts have diluted the effectiveness of such tactics as faculty comparisons, statistical analyses, and arguments that institutions have unfairly changed their promotion and tenure standards over time. Even though Title VII of the 1964 Civil Rights Act was amended more than two decades ago to bring colleges and universities under its purview, the legal system has clearly not made adequate strides in eliminating discrimination in higher education. Rather than eliminating invidious discrimination against women and minorities in faculty positions, the passive stance taken by many state and federal courts appears to have exacerbated the problem.[1]

It is hoped that this book will be helpful to faculty, college and university officials, legal counsel, and others. EEOC and court decisions affecting faculty personnel decisions in U.S. institutions of

---

[1]See Joel William Friedman, "Congress, the Courts, and Sex-Based Employment Discrimination in Higher Education," *Vanderbilt Law Review* 34 (Jan. 1981): 37–69.

higher education will continue to emerge, probably at an increasing rate. The extent to which faculty members fulfill their professional obligations and colleges and universities eliminate the vestiges of employment discrimination will undoubtedly shape the course of future litigation.

Appendix
Overview of Selected Cases

Case	Law	Type of Discrimination	Initial Cause of Action	Whom Court Decision Favored	Pertinent Issues
Agarwal v. Regents of the University of Minnesota (1986, 2)	Title VII, Civil Rights Act of 1871, 14th Amendment	Religion	Termination for incompetence	Institution	Plaintiff was tenured.
Al-Khazraji v. St. Francis College (1985, 3)	Civil Rights Act of 1866	Race, National origin	Tenure denial	Institution	Distinctive physiognomy is not necessary to qualify for protection under Civil Rights Act of 1866 for race discrimination.
Anderson v. University of Northern Iowa (1985, 2)	Title VII, Equal Pay Act	Race, Sex	Promotion denial	Institution	Scholarship requirement is not a pretext for discrimination.
Arenson v. Southern University Law Center (1990, 2)	Civil Rights Act of 1866	Race	Denial of tenure-track position	Faculty	Discrimination by a predominantly black institution against a white faculty member.
Banerjee v. Board of Trustees of Smith College (1981, 2)	Civil Rights Act of 1866	Race, National origin	Tenure denial	Institution	Good discussion regarding prima facie case and standard of proof.
Behlar v. Smith (1983, 2)	Title VII	Sex	Promotion denial, Harassment	Faculty	Institution ordered to pay damages.

Note: The numbers after the case date indicate the level at which the case was heard: 0 = state court, 1 = federal district court, 2 = U.S. Court of Appeals, 3 = U.S. Supreme Court. A number of cases also involved salary and pay discrimination disputes. The applicable legislation, case outcome, and pertinent remarks surrounding a case apply *only* to promotion, tenure, or termination decisions. In addition, a few cases involved split awards in which the court favored the plaintiff on some issues and the institution on others. A number of cases that favored faculty members were either remanded to a lower court or allowed the faculty member to discover the contents of promotion and tenure documents. Cases that were nullified by subsequent court rulings are not included.

Case	Law	Type of Discrimination	Initial Cause of Action	Whom Court Decision Favored	Pertinent Issues
Bennun v. Rutgers, the State University of New Jersey (1991, 2)	Civil Rights Act of 1866 Title VII	National origin	Promotion denial	Faculty	Court favorably viewed comparison of Hispanic plaintiff's publications with those of female professor. Plaintiff was granted a promotion to full professor by the court.
Berry v. University of Texas (1977, 1)	Title VII	Sex	Promotion denial	Institution	Faculty member had failed to complete Ph.D.
Blaubergs v. Board of Regents of the University of Georgia (1980, 1) and *In Re Dinnan* (1981, 2)	Title VII	Sex	Promotion denial Termination	Faculty	The major issue was whether a peer review committee member was required to reveal his vote on a promotion decision.
Briseno v. Central Technical Community College Area (1984, 2)	Civil Rights Act of 1866	Race	Termination	Faculty	Racist remarks by college president.
Brousard-Norcross v. Augustana College Association (1991, 2)	Title VII Rehabilitation Act	Sex Handicap	Tenure denial	Institution	Female plaintiff was denied tenure primarily because of poor teaching. The court also held that she had not made out a claim under the Rehabilitation Act because she was "legally blind."
Brown v. Trustees of Boston University (1989, 2)	Title VII State Fair Employment Practices laws	Sex	Tenure denial	Faculty	Court awarded tenure.
Cap v. Lehigh University (1978, 1)	Title VII	Sex	Tenure denial	Institution	Plaintiff compared her qualifications with those of tenured male faculty member.

Case	Statute	Basis	Issue	Party favored	Remarks
Carpenter v. Board of Regents of the University of Wisconsin System (1984, 2)	Title VII	Race	Tenure denial	Institution	Plaintiff claimed that administrative duties kept him from publishing.
Carton v. Trustees of Tufts College (1981, 1)	Title VII	Sex	Tenure denial	Institution	Claim of de facto tenure by plaintiff.
Chang v. University of Rhode Island (1985, 1)	Title VII	Sex	Promotion denial Tenure denial	Institution Faculty	Multiple plaintiffs. Court found against female who was denied promotion to full professor but ruled in favor of female who used comparative qualifications to demonstrate pretext. Court discounted use of statistical evidence.
Chung v. Morehouse College (1975, 1)	Title VII	Race National origin	Termination	Institution	Asian plaintiff was terminated by predominantly black college because of poor English and speaking skills. Some evidence of racial animus.
Citron v. Jackson State University (1977, 1)	Civil Rights Act of 1866 Title VII	Race Religion National origin	Promotion denial Harassment Termination	Institution	Discussion of property interest in faculty position.
Clark v. Claremont University Center and Graduate School (1992, 0)	State law	Race	Tenure denial	Faculty	California court awarded plaintiff $1.4 million. State court upheld the verdict.

Note: The numbers after the case date indicate the level at which the case was heard: 0 = state court, 1 = federal district court, 2 = U.S. Court of Appeals, 3 = U.S. Supreme Court. A number of cases also involved salary and pay discrimination disputes. The applicable legislation, case outcome, and pertinent remarks surrounding a case apply *only* to promotion, tenure, or termination decisions. In addition, a few cases involved split awards in which the court favored the plaintiff on some issues and the institution on others. A number of cases that favored faculty members were either remanded to a lower court or allowed the faculty member to discover the contents of promotion and tenure documents. Cases that were nullified by subsequent court rulings are not included.

Case	Law	Type of Discrimination	Initial Cause of Action	Whom Court Decision Favored	Pertinent Issues
Cooper v. University of Texas at Dallas (1979, 1)	Title VII	Sex	Tenure denial	Institution	Court said that this new institution inherited its staff from a male-dominated institution and it emphasized study in male-dominated disciplines.
Coser v. Moore (1983, 1)	Title VII	Sex	Promotion denial Tenure denial	Institution	Good discussion of burden of proof issues, problems associated with using statistics, and subjectivity in promotion and tenure decisions.
Countiss v. Trenton State College (1978, 0)	New Jersey state law	Sex	Tenure denial	Institution	Plaintiff claimed excessive workload prevented her from achieving tenure. Court discussed importance of tenure decisions in institutions of higher learning.
Craig v. Alabama State University (1978, 1)	Civil Rights Act of 1866	Race	Tenure denial Promotion denial Termination	Faculty	Predominantly black institution discriminated against white faculty. Shows how use of simple statistics may help demonstrate illegal discrimination.
Craik v. The Minnesota State University Board, St. Cloud State University (1984, 2)	Title VII Civil Rights Act of 1871	Sex	Promotion denials Tenure denials	Faculty	Class-action suit. Extensive discussion of statistical evidence.

Case	Legislation	Basis	Issue	Outcome	Remarks
Davis v. Weidner (1976, 1)	Civil Rights Act of 1866	Sex	Termination	Institution	Plaintiff established prima facie case, but lost.
De Weist v. Tarleton State University (1987, 1)	Title VII	National origin	Tenure denial	Institution	Court noted that plaintiff's demeanor in court suggested that he would be a difficult colleague with whom to work.
Dixon v. Rutgers, the State University of New Jersey (1988, 0)	State law	Sex Race	Tenure denial	Faculty	The court refused to recognize a qualified privilege that protected disclosure of peer review documents if the plaintiff's charge was valid. Discovery cannot be limited by a collective bargaining agreement.
Duello v. University of Wisconsin (1993, 0)	Title VII	Sex	Tenure denial	Institution	Faculty member is not entitled to reimbursement of attorney's fees, which were incurred during optional internal grievance hearings.
Dugan v. Ball State University (1987, 2)	Title VII Civil Rights Act of 1971	Sex	Promotion denial	Institution	Plaintiff's use of statistics was not successful.
EEOC v. Board of Governors of Illinois (1992, 2)	ADEA	Age	Tenure denial Retaliation	Faculty	Colleges cannot prohibit faculty who have filed age discrimination suits from using internal grievance procedures.

Note: The numbers after the case date indicate the level at which the case was heard: 0 = state court, 1 = federal district court, 2 = U.S. Court of Appeals, 3 = U.S. Supreme Court. A number of cases also involved salary and pay discrimination disputes. The applicable legislation, case outcome, and pertinent remarks surrounding a case apply *only* to promotion, tenure, or termination decisions. In addition, a few cases involved split awards in which the court favored the plaintiff on some issues and the institution on others. A number of cases that favored faculty members were either remanded to a lower court or allowed the faculty member to discover the contents of promotion and tenure documents. Cases that were nullified by subsequent court rulings are not included.

Case	Law	Type of Discrimination	Initial Cause of Action	Whom Court Decision Favored	Pertinent Issues
EEOC v. Boston University (1984, 1)	Title VII	Sex	Tenure denial	Institution	Good example of steps used to establish a prima facie case. Evidence of sexist attitudes not sufficient to demonstrate illegal discrimination.
EEOC v. Catholic University (1994, 1)	Title VII Constitution	Sex	Tenure denial	Institution	Faculty member performed ministerial as well as academic functions. Clash between Title VII and constitutional protections.
EEOC v. Franklin and Marshall College (1985, 2)	Title VII	National origin	Tenure denial	Faculty	Court refused to recognize qualified privilege for tenure documents and held that colleges are not entitled to special treatment in Title VII actions merely because subjective criteria are used in personnel decisions.
Faculty of the City University of New York (CUNY) Law School at Queen's College v. Murphy (1989, 0)	Title VII State law	Race Sex	Tenure denial	Institution	Chancellor denied two CUNY law faculty tenure even though the candidates had passed each stage of the tenure review process.

Case	Statute	Basis	Action	Favored	Remarks
Farlow v. University of North Carolina (1985, 1)	Title VII	Sex	Promotion denial	Institution	Plaintiff tried unsuccessfully to compare her qualifications with those of two male faculty who had been promoted before the school upgraded its standards. Evidence of sexist remarks.
Faro v. New York University (1974, 2)	Title VII	Sex	Termination	Institution	This case set the tone for the "hands-off" policy of the courts in academic discrimination cases.
Fields v. Clark University (1992, 3)	Title VII	Sex	Tenure denial	Faculty	Case remanded to federal district court (where plaintiff had won earlier). Interesting discussion by court on the allocation of burden of proof.
Fisher v. Vassar College (1994, 1)	Title VII ADEA	Sex Age	Tenure denial	Faculty	Tenure denied because of discimination based on a female plaintiff's family responsibilities. Faculty member successfully used citations and comparisons of her professional accomplishments with tenured faculty to build her case.
Flanders v. William Patterson College (1976, 0)	State law	Sex Age	Tenure denial Promotion denial	Faculty	Court-ordered promotion and affirmative action remedies.

Note: The numbers after the case date indicate the level at which the case was heard: 0 = state court, 1 = federal district court, 2 = U.S. Court of Appeals, 3 = U.S. Supreme Court. A number of cases also involved salary and pay discrimination disputes. The applicable legislation, case outcome, and pertinent remarks surrounding a case apply *only* to promotion, tenure, or termination decisions. In addition, a few cases involved split awards in which the court favored the plaintiff on some issues and the institution on others. A number of cases that favored faculty members were either remanded to a lower court or allowed the faculty member to discover the contents of promotion and tenure documents. Cases that were nullified by subsequent court rulings are not included.

Case	Law	Type of Discrimination	Initial Cause of Action	Whom Court Decision Favored	Pertinent Issues
Ford v. Nicks (1984, 2)	Title VII	Sex	Tenure denial. Retaliation	Faculty	Plaintiff was awarded tenure by federal district court. His wife's case was remanded to the federal district court to reconsider burden of proof issues.
Ford v. Nicks (1988, 1)	Title VII	Sex	Termination	Faculty	Female plaintiff (spouse of plaintiff in above case) was awarded promotion, tenure, and back pay. A U.S. Circuit Court rejected the tenure award.
Frye v. Memphis State University (1991, 0)	State law	N/A	Termination	Faculty	Plaintiff reinstated after nine years. Interesting discussion regarding damages and professional reputation.
Goulianos v. Ramapo College (1986, 1)	Title VII	Sex	Tenure denial. Constructive discharge	Faculty	Atmosphere of exclusivity and belittling of women at the college led to $75,000 judgment against the institution.
Gray v. Board of Higher Education, City of New York (1982, 2)	Civil Rights Act of 1866	Race	Tenure denial	Faculty	Plaintiff allowed to discover the votes of two members of university tenure committee.
Greer v. University of Arkansas Board of Trustees (1982, 1)	Title VII	Sex	Tenure denial. Promotion denial. Harassment	Faculty Institution	Class-action suit that involved irrelevant job requirements.

Case	Legislation	Discrimination basis	Issue	Favored	Remarks
Guntur v. Union College (1992, 1)	Title VII	Race National origin	Tenure denial	Institution	Asian-Indian plaintiff made prima facie case by producing evidence that both his department and tenure committee unanimously recommended him for tenure. The college successfully rebutted the prima facie case.
Gutzwiller v. Fenik (1988, 2)	Title VII Civil Rights Act of 1871	Sex	Tenure denial	Faculty	Court said that reinstatement with tenure should be ordered only if plaintiff could not receive fair consideration of her tenure application.
Hassan v. Auburn University (1993, 1)	Title VII	National origin	Termination	Institution	Plaintiff was denied a permanent appointment because of his heavy accent and weak communication skills.
Hooker v. Tufts University (1983, 1)	Title VII	Sex	Tenure denial	Institution	Female plaintiff was denied tenure after university changed its promotion and tenure standards.
Huang v. College of the Holy Cross (1977, 1)	Title VII	Race National origin	Tenure denial	Institution	Plaintiff was denied tenure because of poor teaching and doubts concerning his service to the political science department.

Note: The numbers after the case date indicate the level at which the case was heard: 0 = state court, 1 = federal district court, 2 = U.S. Court of Appeals, 3 = U.S. Supreme Court. A number of cases also involved salary and pay discrimination disputes. The applicable legislation, case outcome, and pertinent remarks surrounding a case apply *only* to promotion, tenure, or termination decisions. In addition, a few cases involved split awards in which the court favored the plaintiff on some issues and the institution on others. A number of cases that favored faculty members were either remanded to a lower court or allowed the faculty member to discover the contents of promotion and tenure documents. Cases that were nullified by subsequent court rulings are not included.

Case	Law	Type of Discrimination	Initial Cause of Action	Whom Court Decision Favored	Pertinent Issues
Ishigami v. University of Hawaii (1979, 1)	Civil Rights Act of 1871	Race National origin	Tenure denial	Institution	University denied tenure to plaintiff because it already had enough tenured faculty with similar qualifications and the department was trying to upgrade the quality of its faculty.
Jackson v. Harvard University (1990, 2)	Title VII	Sex	Tenure denial	Institution	Court did not require the university to reveal the identity of faculty who voted to deny tenure.
Jamerson v. Board of Trustees of the University of Alabama (1981, 2)	Title VII	Race	Termination	Institution	Black plaintiff failed to establish a prima facie case.
Jawa v. Fayetteville State University (1976, 1)	Constitution Civil Rights Act of 1866 Title VII	National origin	Termination	Institution	Tenured plaintiff was terminated because of extensive interpersonal problems.
Jepsen v. Florida Board of Regents (1985, 2)	Title VII	Sex	Promotion denial	Faculty	Court recognized that pre–Title VII (1972) acts of sex discrimination could be perpetuated into the time period covered by Title VII. Plaintiff had suffered from sex discrimination since the 1950s. Her back-pay award was calculated by comparing what she earned since 1972 with average salaries of male faculty who were hired close to the time when she was hired (1946).

Case	Applicable legislation	Basis	Issues	Favored	Pertinent remarks
Jew v. University of Iowa (1990, 1)	Title VII	Sex	Promotion denial Harassment	Faculty	Plaintiff was accused of having an affair with her department head and was subjected to numerous episodes of harassment and slanderous comments by colleagues.
Johnson v. Michigan State University (1982, 1)	Title VII	Race Sex	Tenure denial Unfavorable working conditions	Institution	Black female plaintiff was denied tenure because of poor teaching, interpersonal problems, and failure to complete medical boards.
Johnson v. University of Pittsburgh (1977, 1)	Title VII Civil Rights Act of 1871	Sex	Promotion denial Tenure denial Retaliation	Institution	Good discussion of burden of proof, use of statistics, changing standards, and subjective criteria.
King v. Board of Regents of the University of Wisconsin System, University of Wisconsin–Milwaukee (1990, 2)	Civil Rights Act of 1971 Title VII Constitution	Sex	Promotion denial Tenure denial Sexual harassment	Institution	Even though the plaintiff was sexually harassed by an assistant dean, the court held that the harassment was not linked to her tenure or promotion denial because (1) the assistant dean did not participate in the personnel decisions and (2) the plaintiff did not meet the standards for promotion and tenure.

Note: The numbers after the case date indicate the level at which the case was heard: 0 = state court, 1 = federal district court, 2 = U.S. Court of Appeals, 3 = U.S. Supreme Court. A number of cases also involved salary and pay discrimination disputes. The applicable legislation, case outcome, and pertinent remarks surrounding a case apply *only* to promotion, tenure, or termination decisions. In addition, a few cases involved split awards in which the court favored the plaintiff on some issues and the institution on others. A number of cases that favored faculty members were either remanded to a lower court or allowed the faculty member to discover the contents of promotion and tenure documents. Cases that were nullified by subsequent court rulings are not included.

Case	Law	Type of Discrimination	Initial Cause of Action	Whom Court Decision Favored	Pertinent Issues
Kumar v. Board of Trustees, University of Massachusetts (1985, 2)	Title VII	Race	Tenure denial	Institution	U.S. Court of Appeals reversed lower court ruling that stated that plaintiff suffered illegal discrimination. Good discussion of university's right to make tenure decisions.
Kunda v. Muhlenberg College (1980, 2)	Title VII	Sex	Promotion denial Tenure denial	Faculty	College failed to counsel plaintiff regarding necessity of obtaining master's degree for tenure. Court awarded plaintiff retroactive promotion with tenure, granted upon the completion of a master's degree.
Kureshy v. City University of New York (1983, 1)	Civil Rights Act of 1866 Title VII	Race Religion National origin	Tenure denial	Institution	Plaintiff was denied tenure because of poor teaching and difficulties with spoken English.
Lam v. University of Hawaii (1994, 2)	Title VII	Sex National Origin	Failure to hire	Institution	Interesting discussion of how the courts view discrimination based on a combination of impermissible factors.

Case	Legislation	Basis	Issue	Outcome	Remarks
Lamphere v. Brown University (1977, 2)	Title VII	Sex	Promotion denial Tenure denial	Faculty	Class-action suit that led to a consent decree, promotion, and tenure for three plaintiffs and an overhaul of university hiring, promotion, and tenure policies. Litigation was still in progress as late as 1989.
Langland v. Vanderbilt University (1984, 1)	Title VII	Sex	Tenure denial	Institution	Female plaintiff failed to prove that Vanderbilt applied different standards to her during tenure decision.
Lieberman v. Gant (1980, 2)	Title VII Civil Rights Act of 1971	Sex	Tenure denial	Institution	Extensive use of comparisons in an attempt to demonstrate illegal discrimination.
Lynn v. Regents of the University of California (1981, 2)	Title VII	Sex	Tenure denial	Institution	Female plaintiff used university's disdain for feminist studies to help establish prima facie case. Institution successfully rebutted plaintiff's charges of discrimination. The U.S. Supreme Court denied certiorari.
Manning v. Trustees of Tufts College (1980, 2)	Title VII	Sex	Tenure denial	Institution	Plaintiff tried unsuccessfully to obtain a preliminary injunction preventing her termination.

Note: The numbers after the case date indicate the level at which the case was heard: 0 = state court, 1 = federal district court, 2 = U.S. Court of Appeals, 3 = U.S. Supreme Court. A number of cases also involved salary and pay discrimination disputes. The applicable legislation, case outcome, and pertinent remarks surrounding a case apply *only* to promotion, tenure, or termination decisions. In addition, a few cases involved split awards in which the court favored the plaintiff on some issues and the institution on others. A number of cases that favored faculty members were either remanded to a lower court or allowed the faculty member to discover the contents of promotion and tenure documents. Cases that were nullified by subsequent court rulings are not included.

Case	Law	Type of Discrimination	Initial Cause of Action	Whom Court Decision Favored	Pertinent Issues
Mecklenberg v. Montana State University (1976, 1)	Title VII	Sex	Promotion and tenure inequities	Faculty	Class-action suit that led to massive changes in personnel policies at Montana State University.
Meehan v. New England School of Law (1981, 1)	Title VII	Sex	Tenure denial	Institution	Court gave little weight to the fact that law school never had women on its tenured faculty.
Merrill v. Southern Methodist University (SMU) (1986, 2)	Title VII	Sex	Tenure denial	Institution	Court said that SMU was not required to ignore "harsh economic realities" in tenure decisions insofar as plaintiff worked in a department that was "dangerously shrinking" at the time she was denied tenure.
Mirto v. University of Maine (1986, 1)	Title VII	Sex	Termination	Institution	Plaintiff was terminated and replaced by a female.
Molthan v. Temple University (1985, 2)	Title VII Civil Rights Act of 1971	Sex	Promotion denial	Institution	Plaintiff claimed that she had been made certain promises at hiring. Issues of class action and jury trial were also raised.
Mosby v. Webster College (1977, 2)	Civil Rights Act of 1866 Title VII	Race	Termination	Institution	Plaintiff was terminated for poor teaching.

224

Case	Statute	Basis	Action	Favored	Remarks
Namenwirth v. Board of Regents of the University of Wisconsin (1985, 2)	Title VII	Sex	Tenure denial	Institution	Female plaintiff had been victimized by sex discrimination for a number of years. Nevertheless, the court did not believe that she met the minimum standards for tenure.
New York Institute of Technology v. State Division of Human Rights (1976, 0)	State law	Sex	Tenure denial	Institution	New York State court held that a state human rights commission should not grant tenure except under unusual circumstances.
O'Connor v. Peru State College (1985, 1)	Civil Rights Act of 1871 Title VII	Sex	Tenure denial	Institution	Female plaintiff's teaching, punctuality, and personal relationships created problems.
Orbovich v. Macalester College (1988, 1)	Title VII	Sex	Tenure denial	Faculty	The court allowed discovery of tenure documents.
Ottaviani v. State University of New York at New Paltz (1988, 1)	Title VII	Sex	Promotion denial Tenure denial Termination	Institution	Class-action suit that involved a host of statistical and institutional issues.
Pace College v. Commission on Human Rights of the City of New York (1975, 0)	State law	Sex	Promotion denial Termination	Faculty	Female plaintiff was terminated because she was regarded as a "troublemaker." Evidence of animosity toward female faculty by department head and male faculty.

Note: The numbers after the case date indicate the level at which the case was heard: 0 = state court, 1 = federal district court, 2 = U.S. Court of Appeals, 3 = U.S. Supreme Court. A number of cases also involved salary and pay discrimination disputes. The applicable legislation, case outcome, and pertinent remarks surrounding a case apply *only* to promotion, tenure, or termination decisions. In addition, a few cases involved split awards in which the court favored the plaintiff on some issues and the institution on others. A number of cases that favored faculty members were either remanded to a lower court or allowed the faculty member to discover the contents of promotion and tenure documents. Cases that were nullified by subsequent court rulings are not included.

Case	Law	Type of Discrimination	Initial Cause of Action	Whom Court Decision Favored	Pertinent Issues
Paul v. Leland Stanford University (1986, 1)	Title VII	Sex National origin	Tenure denial	Faculty	Stanford University was ordered to release tenure documents to female plaintiff because "it is likely that she can present evidence sufficient to create an inference . . . of bias."
Penk v. Oregon State Board of Higher Education (1984, 1)	Title VII	Sex	Promotion denial	Institution	This was a complex case that dealt with pay discrimination, class-action issues, and statistical analysis.
Perham v. Ladd (1977, 1)	Title VII	Sex	Tenure denial	Institution	Female plaintiff attempted unsuccessfully to use statistical and other comparisons to demonstrate sex discrimination by the university.
Petersen v. University of Wisconsin (1993, 1)	ADA	Disability	Termination	Faculty	Faculty at public colleges who file charges under Title II of the ADA may bypass the EEOC and file charges in federal court.
Planells v. Howard University (1983, 1)	Title VII State law	Race	Promotion denial Retaliation	Faculty	The court said that historically black institutions are not subject to a different legal standard (than historically white institutions) in determining whether their practices are discriminatory.

Case (date)	Law	Basis	Action	Court favored	Comments
Powell v. Syracuse University (1978, 2)	Title VII	Race Sex	Termination	Institution	This case provides a good discussion of burden of proof issues, congressional intent, and the use of evidence in academic discrimination cases.
Presseisen v. Swarthmore College (1977, 1)	Title VII	Sex	Promotion denial Tenure denial	Institution	Class-action suit that involved an unsuccessful use of statistics.
Pyo v. Stockton State College (1985, 1)	Title VII	Sex Race	Tenure denial	Faculty	Court may grant tenure to a plaintiff if it can be demonstrated that others with the same or very similar qualifications were granted tenure. The court may remand the tenure evaluation to the institution when there is evidence that faculty members with the same or similar evaluations were also denied tenure.
Rajender v. University of Minnesota (1978, 1)	Civil Rights Act of 1866 Title VII Federal executive orders	Sex	Promotion denial	Faculty	A class-action case that affected promotion decisions and generated $2 million in attorney's fees.
Ritter v. Mount St. Mary's College (1981, 1)	Title VII	Sex	Tenure denial	Institution	The college used a vague but increasingly rigorous set of tenure standards.

Note: The numbers after the case date indicate the level at which the case was heard: 0 = state court, 1 = federal district court, 2 = U.S. Court of Appeals, 3 = U.S. Supreme Court. A number of cases also involved salary and pay discrimination disputes. The applicable legislation, case outcome, and pertinent remarks surrounding a case apply *only* to promotion, tenure, or termination decisions. In addition, a few cases involved split awards in which the court favored the plaintiff on some issues and the institution on others. A number of cases that favored faculty members were either remanded to a lower court or allowed the faculty member to discover the contents of promotion and tenure documents. Cases that were nullified by subsequent court rulings are not included.

CASE	LAW	TYPE OF DISCRIMINATION	INITIAL CAUSE OF ACTION	WHOM COURT DECISION FAVORED	PERTINENT ISSUES
Roberts v. University of South Florida (1993, 1)	Title VII	Race	Promotion	Faculty	Court ruled that the university engaged in impermissible reverse discrimination.
Rodriguez v. Chandler (1986, 1)	Civil Rights Act of 1866 Title VII Civil Rights Act of 1871	National origin	Termination	Institution	Plaintiff claimed that he was discriminated against because of his advocacy of minority rights.
Roebuck v. Drexel University (1988, 2)	Civil Rights Act of 1866 Title VII	Race	Tenure denial	Faculty	Black plaintiff claimed that excessive service responsibilities (for which he was hired) kept him from meeting tenure standards. Other evidence of racial animus by university officials.
Rollins v. Farris (1986, 1)	Title VII	Sex Age	Tenure denial	Institution	Female plaintiff was denied tenure because of problems surrounding a department scandal, the fact that she held a split assignment, the heavily tenured nature of her department, increased standards for tenure, her lack of publications, her "inflation" of listed workshops, and her relatively weak long-term contributions to the institution.

Case	Statute	Basis	Action	Type	Remarks
Scagnelli v. Whiting (1982, 1)	Civil Rights Act of 1871 Title VII	Race	Tenure denial	Institution	Plaintiff claimed that he was entitled to de facto tenure.
Scott v. University of Delaware (1979, 2)	Civil Rights Act of 1866 Title VII	Race	Termination	Institution	Interesting analysis of class-action issues.
Smith v. University of North Carolina (1980, 2)	Age Discrimination in Employment Act Title VII	Age Sex	Tenure denial Promotion denial	Institution	An extensive discussion of establishing a prima facie case and the application of subjective promotion and tenure criteria.
Smith College v. Massachusetts Commission against Discrimination (1978, 0)	State law	Sex	Tenure denial	Institution	State commission was not clear regarding conditions for a prima facie case or standards of proof.
Soble v. University of Maryland (1985, 2)	Title VII	Sex	Promotion denial	Institution	Female plaintiff was unable to demonstrate discriminatory motive on the part of the university.
Sola v. Lafayette College (1986, 2)	State law	Sex	Tenure denial	Institution	Plaintiff claimed that the college's tenure quota violated public policy by threatening the principles of academic freedom. Therefore, the tenure decision comes within the public policy tort of wrongful discharge.

Note: The numbers after the case date indicate the level at which the case was heard: 0 = state court, 1 = federal district court, 2 = U.S. Court of Appeals, 3 = U.S. Supreme Court. A number of cases also involved salary and pay discrimination disputes. The applicable legislation, case outcome, and pertinent remarks surrounding a case apply *only* to promotion, tenure, or termination decisions. In addition, a few cases involved split awards in which the court favored the plaintiff on some issues and the institution on others. A number of cases that favored faculty members were either remanded to a lower court or allowed the faculty member to discover the contents of promotion and tenure documents. Cases that were nullified by subsequent court rulings are not included.

Case	Law	Type of Discrimination	Initial Cause of Action	Whom Court Decision Favored	Pertinent Issues
Spieldoch v. Maryville College (1975, 1)	Title VII	Sex	Tenure denial	Institution	Female plaintiff was denied tenure primarily because of differences in opinion regarding educational techniques requiring emotional and psychological disclosures by students in the classroom.
State ex. rel. James v. Ohio State University (1994, 0)	State law	None	Access to promotion and tenure files	Faculty	State court rejected the university's argument that promotion and tenure records were exempt from the state's public records act and that disclosure of such records would infringe on the university's constitutionally protected right to academic freedom.
Sweeney v. Board of Trustees of Keene State College (1978, 2)	Title VII	Sex	Promotion denial	Faculty	An early exception to the court's anti-interventionist posture. The court recognized that Keene State had applied a different promotion standard for the female plaintiff and awarded her a promotion, back pay, and attorney's fees.

Case	Applicable law	Basis	Type	Outcome	Remarks
Taylor v. Southern University (1983, 1)	Title VII	Sex	Termination	Institution	Female plaintiff was not constructively discharged, according to the court, after she resigned because of verbal harassment stemming from her questions over policy matters.
Thomasko v. University of South Carolina (1985, 1)	Title VII	Sex, National origin	Tenure denial	Institution	University rebutted prima facie case by female plaintiff who was denied tenure and terminated because of inadequate teaching and scholarship.
Timper v. Board of Regents of the University of Wisconsin System (1981, 1)	Title VII	Sex	Tenure denial	Institution	Good discussion of demonstrating pretext for discrimination.
Torres v. City University of New York, John Jay College of Criminal Justice and Lynch (1991, 1)	Civil Rights Act of 1866, Title VII, State law	National origin	Tenure denial	Faculty	Plaintiff established prima facie case by showing that his department had repeatedly recommended him for tenure.
University of Pennsylvania v. EEOC (1990, 3)	Title VII	Sex	Tenure denial	Faculty	The U.S. Supreme Court effectively eliminated the qualified privilege for tenure documents.

Note: The numbers after the case date indicate the level at which the case was heard: 0 = state court, 1 = federal district court, 2 = U.S. Court of Appeals, 3 = U.S. Supreme Court. The applicable legislation, case outcome, and pertinent remarks surrounding a case apply *only* to promotion, tenure, or termination disputes. A number of cases also involved salary and pay discrimination disputes. In addition, a few cases involved split awards in which the court favored the plaintiff on some issues and the institution on others. A number of cases that favored faculty members were either remanded to a lower court or allowed the faculty member to discover the contents of promotion and tenure documents. Cases that were nullified by subsequent court rulings are not included.

Case	Law	Type of Discrimination	Initial Cause of Action	Whom Court Decision Favored	Pertinent Issues
Villanueva v. Wellesley College (1991, 2)	Civil Rights Act of 1866 Title VII Age Discrimination in Employment Act State law	National origin Age	Tenure denial	Institution	Older male Hispanic plaintiff was denied tenure based in part on the structure of the small department in which he worked. The college expressed concerns that all faculty members would be tenured and retiring at approximately the same time. Plaintiff unsuccessfully tried to compare his credentials with those of faculty who had been tenured several years earlier.
Weismann v. Albert Einstein College of Medicine (1994, 1)	Title VII	Sex	Promotion denial Retaliation	Faculty	Former professor received $900,000 out-of-court settlement.
Welch v. University of Texas (1981, 2)	Title VII	Sex	Termination	Faculty	Female Ph.D.'s claim that she was constructively discharged and replaced with a woman who held only a bachelor's degree did not negate her charge of sex discrimination against the university.
White v. University of Massachusetts at Boston (1991, 0)	State law	Sex	Termination	Institution	Plaintiff took maternity leave and later requested part-time employment. When the institution offered her only a full-time position, she refused and was terminated.

Wilkins v. University of Houston (1981, 2)	Title VII	Sex	Promotion denial	Institution	Court held that the university is free to rely on subjective factors in rebutting a claim of sex discrimination in its promotion and tenure decisions. The U.S. Supreme Court denied certiorari.
Winston v. Maine Technical College (1993, 0)	ADA State law	Disability	Termination	Institution	Sexual addiction is not a protected disability. Plaintiff was properly terminated for sexual misconduct with female students.
Zahorik v. Cornell University (1984, 2)	Title VII	Race Sex	Tenure denial	Institution	The court provides excellent insights regarding burden of proof issues, the use of statistics, and the unique aspects of personnel decisions in colleges and universities.

Note: The numbers after the case date indicate the level at which the case was heard: 0 = state court, 1 = federal district court, 2 = U.S. Court of Appeals, 3 = U.S. Supreme Court. A number of cases also involved salary and pay discrimination disputes. The applicable legislation, case outcome, and pertinent remarks surrounding a case apply *only* to promotion, tenure, or termination decisions. In addition, a few cases involved split awards in which the court favored the plaintiff on some issues and the institution on others. A number of cases that favored faculty members were either remanded to a lower court or allowed the faculty member to discover the contents of promotion and tenure documents. Cases that were nullified by subsequent court rulings are not included.

Case Index

General Index